BATTLE FOR THE FREE MIND

BATTLE FOR
THE FREE MIND

IAN RAMAGE

FOREWORD BY H. GUNTRIP

London
GEORGE ALLEN & UNWIN LTD
RUSKIN HOUSE   MUSEUM STREET

FIRST PUBLISHED IN 1967

TO
DULCIE,
JENNIFER, ROBYN
(With apologies for some of the big
words and thanks for some of the
big thoughts)

PRINTED IN GREAT BRITAIN
in 11 point Juliana type
BY THE BLACKFRIARS PRESS LTD
LEICESTER

FOREWORD

H. GUNTRIP, B.D., Ph.D., F.B.Ps.S.

It is a pleasure to write a Foreword to the Rev Ian Ramage's *Battle for the Free Mind*, firstly because, as its title indicates, it deals unflinchingly with the major intellectual problem of our time, i.e. whether we can retain a viable faith in our own human nature as possessing the intrinsic value of 'persons', or whether we must surrender to the ideologies of mechanizers and depersonalizers who think that they alone are scientific. In starting with a penetrating, exhaustive, scrupulously fair and profoundly accurate analysis of Dr William Sargant's *Battle for the Mind*, Mr Ramage cites a typical example of a 'scientific ideology'. He shows how preconceived ideas, a loose equation of physical hypotheses with actual facts, and a mechanistic philosophy, can be combined by superficial thinking into an 'ideology' presented as 'science'. Dr. Sargant would persuade us that Wesley's conversions, cures of battle neuroses by abreactions, and communist brainwashings are all the same thing, explicable solely in terms of 'brain-mechanics'.

Mr Ramage exposes Dr Sargant's ignorance of the historical facts concerning Wesley. But of greater importance, he shows that the factual inaccuracies in Dr Sargant's treatment of 'breakdown under external stress into exhaustion' and in his treatment of 'abreaction of internal stress leading to healing' are identical: and still more important, he shows how Dr Sargant, like so many intellectuals today, ignores the differentiation of body and mind in the *unity* of human nature, which is so inescapable a fact of experience, and unscientifically assumes without proof that a 'brain-philosophy of man' which excludes the reality of personal mental experience, can be taken for granted. Pages 30-33 may well be read and re-read as a starting-point for all thinking about human problems. Mr Ramage's clear statement of Dr Sargant's naïveté in first describing brainwashing as 'an assault on the fortress of (human) integrity' and then recommending it for religious use 'to bring about some of man's noblest patterns of living', takes us beyond science to ethical and many other considerations relevant to human dignity and value.

Secondly, it is a pleasure to acknowledge the exceedingly thorough and adequate handling by Mr Ramage of his subject matter. Dr Sargant's book is only Mr Ramage's starting-point for an ever-deepening investigation of the whole problem of what man may believe about himself in this era of science. In pursuit of this aim, highly constructive use is made of the knowledge derived from modern 'depth psychology' and the 'psychotherapeutic approach'. This book is but half of a larger whole, and I hope it will whet the appetite of readers for the second volume, in which Mr Ramage explores the field of contemporary philosophy (Bertrand Russell, Logical Positivism, Existentialism), Theology (Tillich, the Cambridge School), Sociology and History. In all these fields, as in psychology and psychiatry, his reading is encyclopaedic, his scholarship

5

accurate, and his judgments eminently balanced, bringing out each thinker's contributions as well as limitations. Yet he does not make the impression of an 'intellectual' but of a real human person, concerned and grappling with the living problems of actual people; not just with arguments on the printed page, but with the practical and intellectual difficulties of our existence as human 'persons' in the scientific, technological and political world of today. Chapter 5 'Means and Ends' and Chapter 9 'Love and Liberation' can hardly be over-stressed.

CONTENTS

PREFACE

In the present ferment of theological debate it may seem sheer folly to be writing a reply to a book published ten years ago with no apparent anticipation of the coming storm. However those who will look beyond the jargon of the current 'Radical' movement to its deeper meaning, may discover in this present study, I hope, something that is relevant to the quest for 'authentic existence', the Christian critique of religion, the possibility of a genuinely worldly holiness, and the discovery of what Paul Tillich called 'a depth at the centre of life'. Indeed while they were not written with this in view at all, these pages could probably be read as a sort of critical comment on Dietrich Bonhoeffer's diatribe against existentialism and psychotherapy (which he dubbed, appropriately enough, as 'secularized methodism'); and a positive contribution in terms of theology and psychodynamics towards his theme of modern man's 'coming of age'.

Chapters dealing with these theological implications, and an appendix on the philosophical issues raised in Chapter 2, proved too bulky for inclusion in this present volume, but it is hoped that they may form the basis of a later one. In the meantime however, in view of the recent appearance within the historic Churches of what is being described as 'charismatic revival', it seems important to point out that whatever our final assessment of this movement may prove to be, it appears to have very little in common with the violent emotional reactions that concern us in this study. When these occurred under Wesley's preaching they were the birth pangs of a new life, not the means of sustaining it, nor the criterion of its value. Although he took these experiences quite seriously, Wesley knew that they were normally unrepeatable, and anything like their habitual practice he would have regarded not as a sign of spiritual maturity at all, but of something quite the reverse.

No one thinks alone, even when he lives at what many of my own countrymen still regard as the far corner of the world. The notes will give some indication of my very great indebtedness to other writers—and not the least to those with whom I have felt obliged to differ. For initial encouragement I am indebted to Mr Huia Beaumont, M.A., Dip.Ed., formerly Editor of the *New Zealand Methodist Times* who, some years ago, published the series of articles which form the nucleus of this book. Their expansion into the present form has proved a far more difficult and time consuming task that I could ever have anticipated, and I am therefore particularly grateful to many members of my congregations in the North

8

Dunedin Circuit, where most of these chapters were written, who kept on insisting that amidst all the other pressing and practical tasks of the Church, this too was important. In this connection I should like to thank especially Miss Doris Lawrence and Dr L. R. Robinson for much friendly and practical support, and Misses Betty, Edith and Lucy Hetherington who added to their understanding interest, a gift from their late father's library, of a complete set of *Wesley's Works* without which my work would have been very restricted. In my congregation at Dundas Street there were also a number of students from the Teachers' College and all faculties of the University whose friendship and open-minded questioning were a very great stimulus and help to me during those years. Finally in this group, I want to express my gratitude to the Rev and Mrs W. J. Morrison, and the people of the Te Awamutu Circuit, through whose kindness and hospitality I was able eventually to complete this writing and have the valuable experience of chaplaincy in a psychiatric hospital.

To two of my teachers in particular I am indebted: to the Rev. E. W. Hames, M.A., formerly Principal of Trinity Methodist Theological College, Auckland, who among many other good things offered his students a warm but by no means uncritical appreciation of John Wesley, and to the present Principal, the Rev D. O. Williams, M.A., Litt.D., who is also the Director of the Inter-Church Counselling Centre, and more than anyone else in our country, has drawn our attention to the Christian importance of the modern counselling movement and obliged some of us to go on asking questions about its theological significance. Thanks are also due to Dr W. P. Morrell, formerly Professor of History in the University of Otago, who read part of the manuscript some time ago and encouraged me to continue with it, and to the Rev Dr J. J. Lewis, Vice-Principal of Trinity College who read the larger manuscript and made some valuable criticisms.

I wish to thank particularly Dr Harry Guntrip of the Department of Psychiatry, Leeds University, for the stimulus of his own writings, for his help in bringing this book to publication, and finally for his kindness in contributing a Foreword. Sister Rita Snowden, F.I.A.L., has given me valuable advice in arranging publication, and I also wish to acknowledge the tolerance of the Publishers in handling a somewhat unwieldy manuscript.

It will be recognized of course that none of these many people who have helped in various ways are to be held responsible for any of the views expressed in this book.

By far my greatest indebtedness however is expressed in the dedication of this long protracted book to my wife and family, whose love and understanding over the years have helped far more than they will ever realize, to lift some of its more important themes beyond the realm of mere theory.

Auckland – New Zealand – April 1967   IAN RAMAGE

ACKNOWLEDGEMENTS

The author wishes to make acknowledgement for the use of quotations from the following works: *Battle for the Mind*, William Sargant; Heinemann, London, 1957; Pan Books, 1959. *Mental Pain and the Cure of Souls*, Dr. Harry Guntrip; Independent Press, London, 1956. *Techniques of Persuasion*, J. A. C. Brown, Penguin Books, 1963. *The Magicians*, J. B. Priestley; Heinemann, 1954; Four Square Books, 1957. *Journal of the Rev. John Wesley*, A.M.; Charles Kelly, London, 1912. *Methodism*, Rupert E. Davies; Epworth Press, London and Penguin Books 1963. *Jesus and the Future Life*, William Strawson; Epworth Press, 1959. *Psychology of Methodism*, Dr. Sidney G. Dimond; Epworth Press, London, 1932. *England in the 18th Century*, J. H. Plumb; Pelican History of England, vol. 7, 1950. *Life of John Wesley*, C. T. Winchester; Macmillan, New York, 1906. *Guilt and Grace*, Paul Tournier; Hodder & Stoughton, London, 1962. 'Some Issues Concerning the Control of Human Behaviour' by Carl Rogers; *Pastoral Psychology*, New York, vol. 13, no. 128, November 1962 and also *Science*, November 1956. 'Learning to be Free' (Part One); *Pastoral Psychology*, vol. 13, no. 128, November 1962.

CHAPTER 1

INTRODUCTION

Taking a realistic view of the world we live in we may perhaps doubt whether modern man has in fact 'come of age' as Bonhoeffer suggested. However, a good case could be made for the view that we have entered a stage in human history which could fairly be termed our adolescence — with all the mixture of turmoil, ambiguity, hopefulness and forward-thrusting vitality which that term usually implies. Modern man is on the move. He has at least glimpsed what adulthood could mean, in terms of freedom, responsibility, human dignity and the resources to do what he wills with the world. And what he has seen, he wants and sometimes fears. But he is being impelled towards it by unfolding energies within history itself that he is not able to turn back. It may be said that this has happened before, and in a sense it has, but only in a very piecemeal and relative way. Modern science and communication have changed all that, and today we are compelled to speak in these terms not of particular societies or peoples, but of modern man as such.

From time immemorial the majority of mankind have had their ways of thinking and behaving very largely moulded by others. They have had to fit into a traditional pattern of social custom and have been kept in their place occasionally by physical force, but more usually by economic pressure, political impotence and religious teaching, and most of all perhaps, by their own inertia and lack of education. This is the situation that is rapidly disappearing. The political upheavals of the last few years that have given the right to govern themselves to vast numbers of people, the surge of economic development and technological advance that are telescoping into a few decades what has previously taken centuries to achieve, the dissolution of familial and tribal patterns of life that have been undisturbed for many centuries, industrialization and the growth of cities at an astonishing speed, and the determined drive for popular

11

education and higher education among the common people—
these are by now all familiar features of life in what are still the
under-developed countries of the world.

But we are *all* involved in far reaching social change. It is not
as though the 'civilized' world has 'arrived' and can simply stand
by to help the belated revolution in the backward countries, for
we are ourselves *living* in the revolution. It may have different
features in different parts of the world, but it has a global
character that makes those who live in London or New York
dependent on events in Leopoldville or Saigon or Peking in ways
that would have been quite incredible only a few years ago. The
industrial revolution is still going on in the western world, perhaps more rapidly than ever before, and quite new features and
problems of urban living are coming to light. Many of the
traditional landmarks of morality seem to be lost in the changing
landscape. The character of home and family life has changed out
of all recognition within two generations, and the strong framework of religion that provided a philosophy of life and death for
our forbears has become strangely remote and unintelligible to
most of their children in the modern world. We are called upon
to undertake or submit to economic planning and social
organization on such a scale that old class divisions and loyalties
become obsolete, and to make difficult and complex political
decisions on which the whole future survival of mankind may
depend, but for which his past history gives us very little
guidance. It is all very unfamiliar and confusing—and very
exciting.

In such a world questions of human faith and human freedom
become probably more important and more searching than they
have ever been before. We may accept the revolutionary character of the modern world, and believe that within all this turmoil
there is undoubtedly struggling to be born, a larger and more
truly human life for the great mass of mankind. But our most
crucial problems are not about the world—but about man himself. Can man himself and *of* himself change radically enough
to meet this new situation and grasp its opportunities? Until
quite recent times most men have always lived within hierarchi-
cal and authoritarian types of social structure that have severely
limited their range of choice and change, the scope of their personal freedom, and their responsibility for their own lives and

INTRODUCTION 13

the life of the community. Even in the Western world the full
effects of political emancipation have hardly yet been felt, and
we are probably only at the beginning of man's economic and
educational emancipation and, some would add (with considerable justification, I believe), his emancipation from the dead hand
of religious conservatism and a merely traditional and legalistic
morality. Can human nature that has been so long and so well
adjusted to living within these traditional patterns endure the
kind of transformation that is needed for men and women to
become free and responsible citizens of the new world, shaping
their own destiny through social institutions that are designed
not to breed conformity, but to foster the creative development
of human personality? Can man do what he has never even
attempted before—make love and co-operation *work* as a basis
of his common life, or will he grow frightened of the enterprise,
and take refuge again in some new form of authoritarian and
restrictive discipline? Can he cease to be a child, and really come
of age?

These are the sort of questions facing mankind today which
justify our use of the term adolescence. For the adolescent is no
longer content to be a child. He has glimpsed part of the meaning of adulthood, and he both wants it and feels himself being
impelled towards it by influences largely beyond his control. For
him freedom means, quite naturally, throwing off parental control or domination, and it is perhaps only as this begins to happen that he is able to come to grips with the real issues within
himself. He learns that freedom is not only the chance to make
his own decisions, but the *ability* to make them, that adulthood
means also maturity and responsibility that are more worthwhile and more difficult to achieve than the mere cutting of
apron strings that bind him to the past.

As Erich Fromm has pointed out,[1] the fear of freedom and the
effort to escape from freedom have been part of modern man's
response to his emerging new world; we have not only the
phenomenon of mass man who endeavours to submerge his
identity and his responsibility in the anonymous life of the
crowd, but we have had also the spectacle of almost whole popu-
lations eagerly surrendering their hard-won liberties to dictators
who exercise over them a more thorough-going domination than
most of the tyrants of history. The totalitarian regimes of the

twentieth century have most pointedly asked the sort of questions that we have raised about man, and they have answered them in their systematic and far-reaching attempts to make new men for the new kind of society they are building, by means of scientific propaganda, brainwashing and indoctrination. The full extent of these activities or their long-term effectiveness we may not be sure of, but for those who value freedom as a spiritual quality and believe that human integrity would be destroyed without it, what we do know is disquieting enough.

It is against this background of the twentieth century that we can begin to assess the importance of the issues that are raised by a book like Dr William Sargant's *Battle for the Mind*.[2] We will want to know particularly what is the role of the Christian religion in relation to these issues. Is it (as most people probably believe) simply part of the traditional pattern of life from which modern man struggles to break free in his efforts to come of age? Is it (as Dr Sargant's book seems to imply) just another safe way in which man may forfeit his spiritual freedom, a sort of benign form of brainwashing that will impose on him another ready-made pattern of belief and behaviour for his own good? Or, is it fundamentally a new source of spiritual freedom and integrity, something which is completely and radically on man's side in his efforts to come of age?

Battle for the Mind (published in 1957 in both Britain and the United States, and reprinted several times that same year, with a paperback edition in 1959 which has been reprinted four times since) is an important book that raises some very serious questions for thinking people. Dr Sargant first describes the well-known experiments of the Russian physiologist I. P. Pavlov with dogs under experimental stress imposed by electrical stimulation, and the disruption of established patterns of conditioned reflex responses, and the theories of that scientist about the cortical functions of the brain under these conditions. He then goes on to draw parallels between the behaviour of Pavlov's dogs and that of human subjects suffering from battle neuroses and undergoing emotional abreaction under drugs. The explanatory hypothesis is then widened to take in the conversion techniques of various exotic cults such as the Tennessee Snake Handlers and Haitian Voodoo, the violent emotional reactions of many people of the eighteenth century under the preaching of John Wesley, and finally the more sinister and cold-blooded attempts to alter men's thoughts and beliefs that have earned in our day the titles of brainwashing and indoctrination. All these phenomena Dr Sargant purports to explain in terms of the Pavlovian hypotheses about the effects of over-stimulation on the cerebral cortex of the brain. In particular he endeavours to show that the techniques of Wesley's preaching which proved so effective in winning converts were, in effect, essentially similar to modern methods of brainwashing and indoctrination that deliberately use physiological and emotional stress in order to induce states of collapse and very high suggestibility.

Whatever we think of his particular illustrations, most Christian readers will recognize that Dr Sargant is pointing out in his own way, a fact of which we have long been aware—viz. that there *are* methods of 'evangelism' and ways of trying to bring about conversions, that are not very different either in principle or in basic technique, from brainwashing and indoctrination. In recent years we have been so concerned about this very fact, that the more thoughtful and responsible sections of the Church have seldom been in any danger of using such methods. But, on the other hand we have been so inhibited by the *fear* of using them that we have tended to do nothing wholehearted in the matter of evangelism at all, except talk about it. The failure of the Church to make use of highly emotional methods of evangelism in our day is not due, as Dr Sargant imagines, to any lack of understanding of their potency, but because, understanding their potency all too well, she has deliberately rejected such methods on moral and theological grounds. What we urgently need then is some clearer understanding of the principles at stake and the processes involved, so that we may distinguish confidently between legitimate and illegitimate methods of evangelism, and know how to use the one without fear of falling into the other.

The way in which Dr Sargant handles his material displays no awareness of this problem at all. He is obviously interested in effective techniques rather than legitimate ones; for him the matter of legitimacy is not related to the method itself, but only to the purpose for which it is used.[3] He repeatedly assures us that he intends no attack on religion, but it is very difficult to escape the impression that there is more ambiguity in his intention

The Rev William Robinson has discussed these issues in an article entitled 'Personal Persuasion'[10] in which he says very relevantly, with reference to Dr Sargant's book: ' . . . if the method is unethical, then it is wrong even if it succeeds. One grows rather tired of being told that the method must be good because it works. Methods not all that dissimilar were used with even more success in Nuremburg between 1933 and 1939.' In reply to Dr Sargant's suggestion that the Church should use brainwashing methods he says: 'The New Testament gives us a picture of God's relationships with men in which the appeal of God is always to the responsible choice of the individual. This must be our ultimate guide.'[11] And he sums the matter up thus: 'We live in an age in which man seems to have come of age. It is an age of questions. Like the adolescent, thinking man will not now accept the voice of authority; he wants to know why? A Church that tries to ride rough-shod over man's intelligence or his moral sense, will find itself, now that he has become a man, left behind among the childish things. . . . In childhood, authority is perhaps justifiable if not by itself enough. If, however, the Church today forgets that man is waking up to his own frightening moral responsibility for himself and his world, she will stand condemned by him. Methods which were unquestioned years ago exist now in a new environment, and against a new background of knowledge. The Church must unhesitatingly condemn and eschew any methods—even the successful ones—which neglect to honour the newly conscious principle of man's morally responsible personality.'

With these views I entirely agree, and would suggest also that even the concept of a successful method stands in need of further critical analysis. We are interested not only in the morality of the methods, but also in the psychological and theological validity of the results. It is true that under modern conditions and in the light of modern knowledge, to which Dr Sargant himself has contributed, there is less moral justification for the use of coercive or subversive methods in evangelism than there has ever been before. But I would add, that no matter how innocently or successfully such methods were used in the past, I find it very hard to believe that the resulting conversions were ever a valid work of saving grace. I do not believe that grace ever works that way.

Dr Sargant is a practising psychiatrist who has specialized in the development of physical methods in the treatment of mental disorders[12]—one branch of psychiatry in which it would be true to say that clinical experience in recent years has far outstripped theoretical understanding. There is a growing body of empirical knowledge of *what* works by way of treatment, but much less understanding or agreement among psychiatrists as to *why* or *how* it works. Thus there are probably many of Dr Sargant's fellow psychiatrists who would gratefully acknowledge his practical contributions in this field, without feeling any need to share all his theoretical assumptions or agree with his excursions in the more speculative aspects of psychiatry.

While psychiatry is contributing valuable insights to the pastoral practice of the Church in our day, many of the ultimate issues between psychiatry and religion have yet to be fully explored. This exploration will, I believe, in the long run prove valuable for both psychiatry and our understanding of the Christian faith, but I feel fairly certain also that it will show some current forms of psychiatry to be incompatible, not only in details of theory or technique, but in their basic assumptions, with the Christian view of man and his need. This broad discussion has begun, but it is still somewhat onesided. There is at present more evidence of Christian theologians and ministers generally, having read and tried to understand what psychiatrists are saying, than the psychiatrists on their part taking a corresponding interest in the age old wisdom of the Christian faith, about the nature of man.[13] However, the discussion must go on. I agree with Dr Sargant that someone must cross the frontiers, and even if we run all the risks of being amateur travellers (and easily mistaken for trespassers) in someone else's territory, the attempt should be made, and in each case judged on its merits.

The primary aim of this essay then, is to make a critical assessment of the interpretation which Dr Sargant has given us, of certain aspects of the Evangelical Revival, and of the nature of Christian conversion generally, with a view to arriving at an understanding of these things that is at once historically more accurate and psychologically more adequate. While the enquiry is of historical interest, its deeper concern is with the central issues of theology, and the conclusions to which we shall be led are sufficiently radical, I believe, to throw some light on the

contemporary meaning of salvation and the real mission of the
Church in the modern world.

FOOTNOTES AND REFERENCES

1. Fromm, Erich, *The Fear of Freedom* (Routledge and Kegan
   Paul Ltd., London 1942) *passim*.
2. Sargant, William, *Battle for the Mind* (William Heinemann
   Ltd., London 1957, Doubleday & Co. Inc., New York 1957,
   Pan Books 1959, reprinted 1960, 1961, 1963, 1964). References
   are given to the Heinemann Edition first, and in brackets to
   the Pan Edition afterwards.
3. *Ibid.*, pp. xi-xii (9) and 148 (141).
4. *Ibid.*, pp. 76-7 (83), top paragraph. Cf. p. 148 (141).
5. Since writing this chapter I have been informed by the Rev.
   George Carter, M.A., Dip.Ed., formerly Chairman of the
   Solomon Islands district of the Methodist Church, that a copy
   of the original edition of *Battle for the Mind* came into the
   possession of Silas Eto, a native teacher, some years ago; and
   partly on the basis of Dr Sargant's version of the work of John
   Wesley, he accused the missionaries of failing to give the
   people the 'true gospel'. Portions of the book were translated
   into Roviana and used by this teacher to assist in promoting a
   substantial pentecostalist sect that has seceded from the
   Church.
6. Quoted by Dr Martyn Lloyd-Jones (see below).
7. D. Martyn Lloyd-Jones, M.D., M.R.C.P., *Conversions Psychological and Spiritual* (*The Inter-Varsity Fellowship*, London,
   January 1959).
8. Brandon, Owen, M. A., A.L.C.D., *The Battle for the Soul—
   Aspects of Religious Conversion* (Hodder & Stoughton, 1960).
9. *Ibid.*, p. 51.
10. Robinson, William D., M.Th., 'Personal Persuasion' in *The
    London Quarterly & Holborn Review* (July 1962), pp. 212 ff.
11. *Ibid.*, p. 216.
12. As well as numerous contributions to medical journals which
    are cited in the text and bibliography, Dr Sargant in collabora-
    tion with Dr Eliot Slater has written a standard textbook,
    Physical Methods of Treatment in Psychiatry. See also his
    Watson Smith Lecture to the Royal College of Physicians,
    'Psychiatric Treatment in General Teaching Hospitals: a Plea
    for a Mechanistic Approach' reported in the *British Medical
    Journal*, July 30, 1966.
13. Cf. Outler, Albert C., *Psychotherapy and the Christian
    Message* (Harper & Brothers, New York 1954), p. 9.

CHAPTER 2

MIND AND BRAIN

The most serious cause of the confusion which runs throughout the whole of Dr Sargant's book, is his consistent failure to distinguish between the mind and the brain. It is this which leaves the discerning reader with the rather irritating feeling that he is being cheated, that something important is being left out of the argument, or at least only allowed in when it won't disturb the writer's thesis. The neglected factor is of course the mind which, in its own right really doesn't have much part in the battle once we get past the front cover of the book. There is a rather vague reference in the Foreword to 'the mind in the broadest sense'[1] which for some reason Dr Sargant thinks his book is not concerned with, and thereafter he seems for the most part to use the expression 'the brain' indiscriminately, to refer not only to the grey and white mass of nerve cells and fibres at the top of the spinal cord, but also to a whole range of processes, thoughts, feelings, desires etc. which we usually describe as 'mental'.

Now the brain itself is, of course, a physical organ, a complex piece of living electronic apparatus that is intimately interrelated with every aspect of our mental life, and with the regulation of many vital bodily functions as well. Yet despite the fact that it is somehow involved in everything we call 'mental', the brain itself remains just as much a physical organ as a liver, a lung or a big toe. On the other hand, whatever we say about the 'mind', and the activities and experiences we associate with it—thoughts, feelings, ideas and so on—one thing seems certain: they are not physical. We cannot weigh them on the scales, or measure their circumference, cut them in half, change their visible colour, measure their wave-length or even give them a location in space. This does not mean at all, that they are not real. They are just as real as brains, brawn or brickbats, but they are of a different order of reality.

This clear distinction between physical and mental is some-

21

times rather loosely criticized as *Cartesian dualism*. The philosopher Descartes (1596-1650) distinguished between 'extended substance' (matter) and 'thinking substance' (the soul) and considered that within man the two meet and interact through the 'vital spirits' in the pineal gland. 'Thinking substance' he believed is the distinguishing property of man, and all other forms of animal life are purely mechanical. The notion of 'thinking substance' we find singularly unhelpful today, nor is there any empirical evidence for the function attributed by Descartes to the pineal gland, and we are bound to admit that his rather poor estimate of the status of the non-human animal was mostly a matter of theological prejudice. Nevertheless the distinction between the physical and the mental is a quite real one, and although we see the inadequacy of Descartes' attempt to account for their relationship in man, we must own that he was at least wrestling with a real problem, and he was not willing to solve it by ignoring or writing down either one half of the facts or the other, as so much philosophy has tried to do. The distinction between the brain and the mind is quite real, and it is important for us to see what is implied by the way in which Dr Sargant neglects it.

Pure materialism has probably never been consistently held or advocated by any philosopher of top rank, but it has had its popular exponents, and there have been many approaches to scientific and philosophical questions that express a strong materialist bias. The general philosophical attitude known as Naturalism tends to assume that the whole of reality is a closed system completely enmeshed in the processes of cause and effect that govern the behaviour of matter. It thus has great difficulty in allowing any significant place at all in the total scheme of things to mind. In biology this attitude is known as mechanism (as opposed to vitalism) — the belief that living creatures are nothing more than wonderfully complex machines, and that their behaviour is to be fully explained in terms of the same type of causal processes that operate for inanimate objects. Obviously such a view can only make room for the mind in a very subordinate and dubious sense. We are reminded of the famous pronouncement of Professor Tyndall, that as the bile is a secretion of the liver, so the mind is a secretion of the brain.[2]

In psychology this approach has been most fully developed in the behaviourism of J. B. Watson and his school. The whole life and experience of man is to be understood in terms of bodily processes which are themselves a series of mechanical reactions to external stimuli. Man is thus nothing but a complex stimulus-response machine. Thinking is not simply accompanied by, but literally is, a purely physical process— a series of incipient movements of the vocal organs in sub-vocal speech.

As applied specifically to the body-mind relationship, the materialistic view has been known as Epiphenomenalism.[3] While the reality of mind is not completely denied, it is not considered to play any part whatsoever in guiding bodily behaviour. Consciousness is nothing but a series of meter readings, a passing record of certain bodily events. The function of the mind is similar to that of a speedometer in a motor car; while it records from moment to moment something of the activity of the mechanism of the car, it cannot of itself influence or alter the performance of the car in any way. According to strict Epiphenomenalism, mental events are always the mere byproducts of bodily processes that would go on just as well without any mental concomitants at all. A slight variation of this view allows that a mental event, once it is initiated by brain processes, may itself give rise to further mental events—e.g. a train of thought or deliberation, but it is still denied that this train of mental process can in any way affect bodily movement or function. Thus a person may conceivably have a certain amount of freedom in his thinking, but this would in no way affect what happens when he speaks or writes. Since these latter are physical processes, they would be simply and completely determined by physical causes just as much as an avalanche or a storm at sea.

While he does not specifically state his views on the mind-body relationship, it seems to me quite clear that for all practical purposes Dr Sargant treats his subject from an Epiphenomenalist point of view. It is true that he does not actually deny the reality of mind. Indeed he makes a gesture of excluding from his discussion certain forms of 'purely intellectual conversion',[4] but this seems little more than a convenient device to justify his assumption that intellectual factors play no significant part in the conversions he does consider. All his discussion of causative factors is restricted to a consideration of physical processes in the brain, or to use his own expressive phrase 'brain mechanics'.

That psychological factors also play a major causative role in the various experiences of neurosis, conversion or brainwashing etc. described, he does not deny; he simply ignores the possibility, and writes his book on the assumption that it can be ignored.[5]

In this respect of course, Dr Sargant is probably typical of many writers whose training and interest have been primarily in the physical sciences, and who, without necessarily making any specific declaration to this effect have, nevertheless, acquired a strong naturalistic bias which tends to emerge in everything they teach or write. So long as we are thinking within the realm of the purely physical it is legitimate to think in terms of physical causation[6]; but when it is either insisted or simply assumed in the name of science, that the sum total of any human experience or activity must be fitted into these particular categories or that what lies outside them can be safely ignored, then we are no longer dealing with science at all, but with a naturalistic philosophy that has been unconsciously taken for granted, or else accepted on quite nonscientific grounds. Since scientists, particularly outside their own specialization, are prone to be ordinary, fallible human beings like the rest of us, it is not surprising if some of them fall into this way of thinking. The physical scientist has every right to say that for the purposes of his own work he is not interested in anything other than physical causes, but when he also goes on to say, or imply, that only physical causes are worth bothering about, then this is a mere emotional carryover without any logical or experimental basis whatsover. For the purposes of concentration it may be necessary for the physical scientist to wear a particular set of blinkers, but if he ever grows so attached to them that he can't take them off, and begins to write or speak as if nothing outside his restricted range of vision is either real or important, then there is no reason why anyone else should be impressed by this curious attitude. Whatever the emotional factors that lead to this kind of confusion, it does need to be clearly recognized that there is no *logical* connection whatsoever between scientific knowledge or scientific method on the one hand, and a naturalistic philosophy on the other.

From the point of view of logic and rational thinking, all materialistic views of the body-mind relation are subject to the same quite serious objection — an objection that cannot be avoided, and so far as I know has never been satisfactorily answered. It is this: if the human mind is of such a subordinate status as the materialists claim, a mere epiphenomenon of physical processes in the brain, without any real independence of thought or expression, then it cannot possibly arrive at the *truth* about anything (including the truth about the body-mind relation)—or at least it cannot express that truth in speech or writing. If Jones the materialist and Smith who takes a different view both observe certain facts of human behaviour, and interpret them in quite different ways, it is (on the materialist assumption) quite pointless to ask which view of the matter is true. After all, if what these two men say or write is in each case the inevitable result of a sequence of physical events in their respective brains, uninfluenced by their reasoning or conscious experience, then words like true and false as applied to such statements would lose all meaning. All materialism (and indeed all determinism) carried to its logical conclusion ends in this *reductio ad absurdum* which shows that if its conclusions were true, then all its reasoning and arguments would in fact be quite irrelevant to establish its truth.

Materialism then, attempts to solve Descartes' problem by writing down the status of mind and virtually ignoring the fact of human freedom and personal autonomy, and arrives at a view of human personality that makes nonsense of its own arguments and is certainly incompatible with both commonsense and experience, and a Christian view of man. However, it should perhaps be pointed out that if we let our thinking go to the other extreme and try to solve the body-mind problem by writing down or denying the reality of matter, the result will be no more acceptable from a Christian point of view than that of the materialist's. The heart of the Christian gospel is the announcement that God who is eternal spirit, at a particular time and place in the history of this planet was literally incarnate—lived in and with a human bodily life under the material conditions of this world, for us men and our redemption. Such a gospel has no interest whatsoever then in denying the reality of matter and writing down the facts of our physical bodily existence.

If Materialism has been the favourite of the avowed opponents of Christianity, it is the philosophical tradition of Idealism that has provided the greatest threat from within. In its Greek or Oriental forms, either denying the reality of matter, or regarding our physical and bodily existence as the source of evil and human bondage from which we need salvation, this kind of thinking gave rise to the various forms of Gnosticism which threatened the very existence of the Church in the second century, the Docetic heresy that denied the real physical death of our Lord upon the cross, and the conflict with Manichaeism which persisted well into the Middle Ages. There are still Gnostic cults in existence; forms of religion so allegedly spiritual that they seek to deny the needs of the body, or else disclaim all responsibility for its actions. Manichaeism lives on in the popular misconception of sin and evil as something which arises out of instinct and bodily appetite rather than as a perversion of our total personality, while Christian Science denies the reality of both matter and evil, as the mere products of our 'wrong thinking'. This latter form of religion may be regarded as a reaction against the materialism of nineteenth century medicine on the one hand, and the Church's neglect of the ministry of healing on the other, but apart from its genuine compassion it is certainly not a Christian reaction any more than it is a scientific one.

The authentic Christian view of man is always true to the biblical tradition in which man is formed of the dust of the ground as well as being a living soul.[7] It always takes his physical bodily existence and involvement in this material world very seriously. The great events of Christianity are rooted in history, and the stuff of history is material stuff as well as spiritual stuff. We may contrast with this the Hindu form of Idealism for which the material world is maya, the realm of pure illusion, and history therefore is of no importance. Spiritual truth is not given in history, for history is a mere passing shadow. The Hindu will agree, for example, that the idea of divine redemptive suffering is a splendid one—until the Christian starts to say that it has actually happened in history.[8]

I have made this very brief excursion into philosophy to show where the two great classical attempts to avoid the body-mind problem (by denying either one side or the other) actually lead us, and I believe that every attempt either ancient or modern to avoid the distinction between body and mind turns out, in the long run, to be a variation on either one or other of these unacceptable alternatives.[9] It seems necessary to press this point because there is some tendency today to regard the whole matter as a sort of pseudo-problem created by Descartes in the seventeenth century, and no longer relevant in ours.[10] A number of factors have contributed to this modern attitude which is for many people a climate of thought even if not a clearly articulated theory.

The enormous prestige and all-pervasive influence of the physical sciences in modern life have no doubt carried with them an emotional aura of popular materialism, but there has also been on a smaller scale a certain resurgence of idealist views due to the influence of theoretical physics. Solid particles have tended to dissolve into waves of probability, or similarly abstract conceptions, and these modern views about the nature of matter have left the impression in many thoughtful minds that the distinction between mind and matter is somehow less real than was formerly supposed. Because the physicists tend increasingly to state their theories and results in terms of mathematical formulae rather than of mechanical models, it has been suggested by more than one eminent scientist that the ultimate constituent of the physical universe is 'mind-stuff'.[11] We are concerned with the interaction of the mind and the physical brain, and whether these modern theories of the structure of matter bring us any nearer to understanding this interaction is still an open question. Whatever may be the ultimate affinities between mind and matter (and personally, I am not sure whether physics *does* take us far towards discovering these), for all practical purposes, as we encounter them, mind and matter, thought and things are not the same, and nothing in modern physics really alters this fact.

Of more immediate relevance to our subject is the psychosomatic approach in modern medicine,[12] which recognizes that bodily illness can be caused or accentuated by mental conflict or strain or that, conversely, physical changes in the body may be either a contributory or major factor in some forms of mental or emotional illness. This has given rise to a renewed sense of the unity of human personality, and doctors no longer think of themselves (if they ever did) as treating sick bodies or sick minds, but try to deal with sick persons. This approach of course gives practical expression to something which most people have recognized for a long time—viz. the fact that body and mind do interact with each other in the most intimate way, and under conditions of earthly life anyway, cannot be separated. However, psychosomatic medicine in no way undermines the distinction between body and mind on which we have been insisting. On the contrary, it specifically repudiates the two classical attempts to evade the problem which we have already noted, denying that man is either all body or all mind, and treating human personality as comprising two forms of energy and activity which, though inseparable in practice must, nevertheless, be logically distinguished from each other for purposes of diagnosis and treatment, and seen in a relationship not of identity but of mutual interaction.

In modern discussion of biblical theology it is often claimed that the Bible knows nothing of the dualism of body and mind.[13] Dualism is an ambiguous word. As applied to Greek thought it usually means a practical and metaphysical *opposition* between body and mind. As applied to Cartesian philosophy it means *separation* between them, for the followers of Descartes abandoned the tenuous link he had left between body and mind through the pineal gland, and saw the two as running along parallel courses that had no direct contact with or influence on each other at all. We may safely discard both these theories as out of harmony not only with modern thought, but also with what Christianity has taught from the beginning. However, in denying that there is either opposition or separation between body and mind, we have no grounds whatsoever for denying the *distinction* between them—and that precisely is our concern in this present chapter.

If by dualism we mean the *opposition* between body and mind that characterized so much of Greek thought, then this was, of course, quite alien to the biblical way of thinking. The opposition between the flesh and the spirit for example in the writings of St Paul outlines the practical conflict between our lower nature and our higher nature.[14] In modern terms, it is concerned with a moral and psychological conflict within our being that arises ultimately out of our spiritual estrangement from God— not with any supposed opposition between the physical and the mental in the life of man. Nor is there any faintest trace of

Cartesian *separation* between body and mind in the thought of the Bible. In biblical thought man is in moral contradiction but he is a metaphysical unity. He is both made of the dust of the earth and a living soul, but the unity of his being is never called in question, because it is grounded in the creative act of God.

But if our original statement is meant to imply that the Bible knows nothing of the *distinction* between body and mind, this can be true only in the most superficial sense. True, the Bible does not speculate about this distinction after the manner of the philosophers but there is, nevertheless, throughout the Bible, a profound religious awareness of the facts of man's being which would later give rise to such speculation. 'When I consider thy heavens, the work of thy fingers, the moon and the stars which thou hast ordained; what is man that thou art mindful of him? and the son of man that thou visitest him?'[15] Although he probably didn't know much about the uniformity of nature as we understand it, or the theory of physical determinism, there is not a doubt that the Psalmist saw man as *pars naturae*, and naturalistically, a quite insignificant part of the total scheme of things, dwarfed by the immensity of the created order. Yet the wonder is, that man is more than this. 'For thou hast made him a little lower than the angels, and hast crowned him with glory and honour. Thou madest him to have dominion over the works of thy hands.'[16] Dust of the earth he most certainly is—the small dust of the universe—but he is dust that asks questions about himself, that knows his Creator is mindful of him, dust that has been given dominion and power over the works of God's hands. This dual aspect of man's being, that is part of the created order, part of nature, and yet transcends nature because of his unique relationship with his Creator—this surely is basic to the biblical view of man. Thus, there are already implicit in the Bible, the raw materials of the mind-body problem : the insights into man's nature which will inevitably raise for philosophy the question of the relationship between his physical being arising out of, and immersed in, the whole causal matrix of the material world and his spiritual freedom to transcend and use that world, without which none of his distinctively human activities would be possible.

The philosophical question itself is not raised by the Bible, but for us it has been raised, and it is idle to think that we can use the biblical point of view to avoid it. To do this would be to ignore some of the deepest insights of the Bible itself, and to repudiate in principle the intellectual fabric of our culture. Science has shown that both mind and matter are more complex, and in a sense more mysterious than our forbears imagined, and philosophers would therefore insist that traditional ways of stating the mind-body problem are no longer adequate. But however the problem is re-defined, I believe that physical and mental (mechanism and meaning) will remain as distinct though not separate factors, and their relationship with each other, like many other matters of commonplace experience, is still something of a mystery. We may not solve this mystery, but I believe we shall be nearer to a genuinely biblical point of view if we acknowledge it than if we try to ignore it. If we do try to ignore it, we shall, in all probability, not be adopting the pre-speculative thought of the Bible at all, but lapsing unconsciously into one or other of the quite unbiblical alternatives of Materialism or Idealism that were bequeathed to us by the Greeks.

The whole modern emphasis, to which both psychosomatic medicine and biblical theology have contributed in different ways, is on the unity of human personality. This is extremely important. Man is not an unstable mixture of two incompatible substances, or (to use Gilbert Ryle's figure) 'a ghost in a machine'.[17] Body and mind can no longer be thought of as two relatively self-contained systems with one definable point of contact as Descartes thought, or running along parallel lines in some sort of pre-established harmony as some of his followers believed. On the contrary, their mutual interaction and relationship are so intricate and intimate that they constitute a unity which is man. But man is not an undifferentiated unity, and even if the differentiations are so subtle and intricate that our best efforts to delineate them must always be exceedingly clumsy by comparison, I am still sure that the logical distinction between physical and mental is both valid and necessary. No matter how intimately the two interact, the brain is not the same as the mind. Both are real and both are important, and neither one can be explained or explained away as a mere emanation from, or epiphenomenon of the other.

It is important for us then to recognize that whenever we deal with human personality, whether we acknowledge it or not, we are in fact dealing with two different kinds of events, one physical and the other mental, in constant coexistence and in such intimate interaction that they form one indivisible whole. This means that anything like a complete picture of personality at any moment would be almost fantastically intricate. It is therefore inevitable that for certain practical and specialist purposes we should try to simplify the picture. Sometimes we need to be more interested in the mechanistic aspects of personality, and sometimes with its experience of meaning and freedom; and it is quite legitimate when we are working in a limited field to use, as it were, a diagram of only those things that concern us in this particular study. However, if we do this we need constant reminders that we are deliberately looking at some facts and ignoring others for the time being, and that the real picture would be much more complex than our working diagram.

For example, if our field of interest is physiology, neurology, or some branch of physical medicine, our working diagram will of necessity deal with bodily structure and function. Yet we shall have to bear in mind that while these mechanisms of personality (including the brain and nervous system) may set limits to its freedom, they are ultimately and normally the servants of its freedom and not the masters of it. On the other hand if our study is depth psychology or philosophy or theology, our working diagram of man will be concerned with a different set of facts, and we may need to be reminded that while our human freedom and apprehension of meaning are quite real, they are also closely involved in the necessities of this world — both experienced and expressed through certain bodily mechanisms which impose limits upon them, and without which they would not be at all possible under earthly conditions.

In other words, while for the sake of convenience we must work with our selective diagrams, we should often check to make sure that we are not drawing inferences from our particular diagram which a glance at the whole picture would show to be unrealistic. If we neglect to do this, and mistake one of our simplified diagrams for the whole picture, then we are in trouble; we start off with confusion and may finish up talking dangerous nonsense. This is, I believe, in effect what Dr Sargant has done. He has tried to explain the phenomena of brainwashing, religious conversion, battle neurosis etc., simply in terms of brain mechanics, and has almost completely neglected the factors of mind and meaning which are every bit as important as the others.

He tells us that after reading Pavlov's *Conditioned Reflexes and Psychiatry* he came to the conclusion that

'the part played by alterations in the function of the human brain itself had, it almost seemed, been too summarily dismissed by some in their attempts to explain the reasons not only for neurotic and criminal behaviour but for all the constant mental turns, reconsiderations and adjustments which produce so-called "normal" behaviour in any given person as he reacts to his environment.'[18]

Now this may be fair enough. It may well be that psychological explanations of behaviour both pathological and normal have been onesided, and have neglected physiological factors. If Dr Sargant's book were simply a protest or a corrective against this, we should have no cause to quarrel with it. However, he goes much further than that. He appears to complain that the explanations of conversion, neurosis, brainwashing etc., have hitherto been exclusively in terms of psychology, and wants to replace these by explanations that are just as exclusively in terms of physiology.

There is some evidence that Dr Sargant is not entirely satisfied with this swing from one extreme to the other, and in the Foreword he says

'And it must not be held against me that I do not discuss some types of purely intellectual conversion, but only those physical or psychological stimuli, rather than intellectual arguments which *seem* to *help* to produce conversion by causing alterations in the subject's brain function.'[19]

The words I have italicized in this quotation indicate a note of caution and moderation that is in marked contrast with the sweeping statements he actually makes in the main body of the book. Dr Sargant's onesided emphasis is so thoroughly interwoven with the whole fabric of his argument that it cannot possibly be corrected by a conciliatory note in the Foreword.

In the same Foreword he tells us that his

' . . . concern here is not with the immortal soul, which is the province of the theologian, nor even with the mind in the broadest sense of the word which is the province of the philosopher, but with the brain and nervous system which man shares with the dog and other animals.'[20]

Now this is dualism with a vengeance! When we are dealing with the kind of phenomena that are discussed in Battle for the Mind we cannot possibly divide man up in this way, and treat him piecemeal agreeing, as it were, to leave part of him out of the argument. Whatever Dr Sargant denotes by those terms, there seems no doubt that man's 'immortal soul' and 'the mind in the broadest sense of the word' are certainly both involved along with 'the brain and the nervous system' in all the variety of phenomena that are dealt with in his book. He cannot help dealing with these wider aspects of personality, and instead of putting them on one side as he would like to do, what he does in effect, is to subsume the whole lot under 'the brain and nervous system which man shares with the dog and other animals'.

We must also ask Dr Sargant whether he seriously believes that there is in fact such a thing as a 'purely intellectual conversion'. Surely the most rational and carefully worked through conversion must involve the brain and nervous system and the whole physiology of the person just as much as any other. I am not saying that all conversions are the same, but that whenever a person is converted it is the whole person that is involved— not merely his intellect; conversely no one is ever converted without his intellect being involved in some way. Dr Sargant's attempt to make an exception of 'some types of purely intellectual conversion' with which he is not dealing rather tends to gloss over the fact that in all religious conversion, including those with which he does deal, there are important intellectual factors involved which he passes over unnoticed so that he can treat the emotional elements merely in terms of 'alteration in brain function' as though they had nothing to do with a person's apprehension of a total pattern of meaning as well.[81]

This onesided mechanistic bias cannot of course be reconciled with a Christian view of man, and it also offends against the

C

true spirit of science, because it fails to give due weight to at least half of the relevant facts.

FOOTNOTES AND REFERENCES

1. *Battle for the Mind*, p. xi (9).

2. In his address to the British Association in Belfast. — See Sir Charles Sherrington's Introduction in *The Physical Basis of Mind*, edited by Peter Laslett, Basil Blackwell, 1952, p. 4. Probably by way of rejoinder to Tyndall, and with more than an echo of Plato, Charles Kingsley apparently made a remark to the effect that 'the soul secretes the body as a crustacean secretes its shell'. — See J. Brierley, *Studies of the Soul*, James Clarke & Co., p. 41. It is the contention of this chapter that both these statements are equally onesided; unfounded in science and incompatible with a Christian doctrine of man.

3. The word was coined by T. H. Huxley. For a brief and lucid exposition of such views see Olaf Stapledon, *Philosophy and Living*, Penguin Books, 1939, Vol. I, pp. 63-7.

4. *Op. cit.*, p. xii (10).

5. I think this is a fair assessment of Dr. Sargant's book as a whole. It is true that he also makes certain disclaimers. In the Foreword he says 'It must also be remembered that much of what is discussed here is still only a useful working hypothesis; a great deal of further research is needed before final conclusions are reached', and he repeats this caution in the Conclusions. (*Op. cit.*, pp. xii (9) and 232 (212).) Nevertheless in the body of the book, between these two cautionary notes it is hard to escape the impression that Dr Sargant is advocating explanations that he regards as proven, at least to his own satisfaction. In the Conclusion he also says 'Much also remains to be learned by the use of other approaches, including the study of the same phenomena from philosophical and spiritual bases.' (*Op. cit.*, p. 232 (212).) However, my criticism of his physiological explanations is not that they need to be supplemented by other approaches, but that they are stated in such a way as to rule out other approaches. Despite his claim that 'his discussion of psychoanalysis . . . implies no denial of its very real value in the treatment of carefully selected patients'. (*Op. cit.*, p. xiii (10-11).) Dr Sargant's opposition to depth psychology is very evident, and his explanations in Pavlovian terms are in many cases quite incompatible with a psychological approach to the same phenomena. (See below, Ch. 4.)

6. Ever since the criticism levelled against it by the philosopher David Hume, the whole concept of causation as efficient power has been extremely doubtful, of course. It may well be as Bertrand Russell suggests in *The A.B.C. of Relativity* that, in this sense, the language of cause and effect is 'merely a convenient shorthand for certain purposes'. However, I am concerned that if we are going to continue to use this 'convenient shorthand' it should also be the *appropriate* shorthand and I do not think the language of *physical* causation is the appropriate shorthand to describe the whole of human behaviour. It lacks certain essential symbols, and in trying to make do with others, it can only distort what it purports to describe.

7. Genesis 2.7 (A.V.).

8. I owe this point to a brief conversation with Dr D. T. Niles. For its importance cf. Victor White's paper on 'The Dying God' in his *God and the Unconscious*, Harvill 1952, pp. 215-33, and also C. S. Lewis in *Surprised by Joy*.

9. See, for example, A. J. Ayer's contribution to *The Physical Basis of Mind*.

10. This has been fostered by the work of Linguistic philosophers such as Gilbert Ryle, which the author hopes to discuss in a later study.

11. The phrase was Sir Arthur Eddington's who developed his idealist philosophy of nature in his Gifford Lectures *The Nature of the Physical World* (1926) and other writings. Cf. Sir James Jeans in *The Mysterious Universe* (p. 148): 'The universe begins to look more like a great thought than like a great machine.'

12. See, for example, Dr David Stafford-Clark, *Psychiatry To-day*, Penguin Books 1952, pp. 234-49.

13. Cf. H. Wheeler Robinson, with reference to the O.T.: 'The idea of human nature implies a unity, not a dualism. There is no contrast between the body and the soul such as the terms instinctively suggest to us.' (*The Religious Ideas of the Old Testament*, Duckworth, p. 83.) Similarly D. R. G. Owen, discussing the N.T. material: 'There is little trace of body-soul dualism; instead, man is regarded as a unity.' (*Body and Soul*, p. 196.) Cf. Alan Richardson: 'Unlike the Greeks, the Jews did not think of a man as being made up of a body and a soul; a man was a living body.' (*An Introduction to the Theology of the New Testament*, S.C.M. Press 1958, p. 196.)

14. Cf. Robinson, J. A. T., *The Body*, S.C.M. Press 1957, pp. 22-5.

15. Psalm 8, vv. 3-4 (A.V.).

16. Psalm 8, vv. 5-6 (A.V.).

17. *The Concept of Mind*, Hutchinson's 1949, pp. 15-16.

18. *Op. cit.*, p. xviii (15-16).

19. *Ibid.*, pp. xii-xiii (10).

20. *Ibid.*, p. xi (9).

21. It will be evident, I hope, that I am not using 'intellectual' simply to imply rational or logical thought processes, but in the broader sense to include the whole cognitive aspect of consciousness, the quest for meaning and knowledge. No doubt this is often distorted by unconscious emotional factors, but even then, the result is a *misapprehension* of *meaning*—not a mere alteration in brain function.

CHAPTER 3

DOGS AND MEN

Considering his general point of view, it is not surprising that Dr Sargant should find the theories of the Russian scientist I. P. Pavlov particularly congenial, for here was a physiologist who late in life had entered the field of psychiatry and claimed to give a purely physiological explanation of many aberrations of human behaviour that had previously been explained only in terms of psychoanalysis, or what may be designated by the general term 'depth psychology'. It seems fairly evident that Dr Sargant had already acquired his fixed aversion to depth psychology before he discovered Pavlov's alternative theories, for he tells us that as a result of reading Pavlov's book, *Conditioned Reflexes and Psychiatry*, 'It seemed more improbable than ever that many current psychological theories about the origin of human neuroses and other abnormalities of behaviour were correct.'[1] Anyway, by taking his explanations from a physiologist, rejecting psychological theories out of hand, and virtually ignoring the significance of emotional and intellectual factors, Dr Sargant arrives at a comprehensive theory which enables him to overlook the important differences between a wide variety of phenomena, and to link them together under one deceptively simple formula.

In his early experiments with dogs, Pavlov discovered that after a time a dog could be made to salivate not only in response to the natural stimulus of food, but also in response to a secondary stimulus such as the ringing of a bell that had been repeatedly associated with the food stimulus, but would now occasion the flow of saliva when it was used by itself without the presentation of food at all. Thus the original (absolute) reflex had been reconditioned to a new stimulus, and using the technique of the conditioned reflex Pavlov carried on his experiments in building up various behaviour patterns in his dogs. Reflex actions seem to have a physiological basis. Some of them are

37

effected through sensory-motor arcs in the spinal cord while others appear to work through neural paths in the cerebral cortex of the brain. Whether spinal or cortical, natural or conditioned, the common feature of reflex actions is their automatic character. Some reflexes may be partly or wholly inhibited by deliberate volitional control, but apart from this negative effect, they are involuntary and appear to work on a relatively simple pattern of physiological stimulus and response.

The importance of the conditioned reflex has, of course, been somewhat overestimated by some people who are of a behaviouristic turn of mind; they hailed Pavlov's discoveries as the scientific clue which would allow the whole of human life to be explained on a stimulus-response pattern, without the significant intervention of mind. Reflex actions are important for man's survival, and the conditioning of human behaviour patterns (reflex and otherwise) is a feature—sometimes benign and sometimes sinister—in every society; but there are no grounds for imagining that the conditioned reflex provides the basic pattern for the whole of human life. The Behaviourists claim to produce a theory which explains not only man in the laboratory but also man in the world and, as I have already argued, there are good reasons for rejecting an interpretation of man's life that would reduce his whole experience of meaning, purpose and value to a mere evanescent foam on the tide of material forces. Like all determinism, the theory has only to be taken to its logical conclusion to appear ridiculous, and I don't think we should be impressed by the suggestion that the saga of human history can, even in principle, be understood wholly in terms of Pavlov's dribbling dogs.

However, it was Pavlov's later experiments[2] in the breakdown of behaviour patterns and the production of neuroses in his dogs that provided Dr Sargant with the clue which enabled him to interpret to his own satisfaction the phenomena of battle neuroses and, later, those of brainwashing and religious conversion. Pavlov discovered that he could produce a condition of breakdown in his dogs by repeatedly increasing the stimulus to an intolerable degree; confusing the dog by a mixture of very similar stimuli, introducing a prolonged or unpredictable element of frustration, or when all these had failed, by debilitating the animal through hunger, fatigue, drugs, intestinal disorder or castration. The degree of stress that was required to produce a breakdown varied with different dogs, and Pavlov classified his dogs on this account according to the four basic temperaments enunciated by the Greek physician Hippocrates many centuries ago. At the point when stress became intolerable (the point of 'transmarginal stimulation') the dogs began to exhibit abnormal behaviour, passing through the 'equivalent phase' in which they reacted without discriminating between strong stimuli and weak, into the 'paradoxical phase' in which they reacted strongly to weak stimuli and vice versa, and finally into the 'ultraparadoxical phase' in which conditioned responses were reversed from positive to negative and from negative to positive.

The parallels which Dr Sargant discovered between the behaviour of Pavlov's dogs and some of his cases of battle neurosis,[3] and the classification of different temperamental reactions requiring different degrees of sedation are all extremely interesting, but I do not believe that they tell us more than part of the story. Even thus far, I would suggest that they are significant only under the conditions of modern warfare, with its combination of extreme fear stimulus and prolonged debilitation, or in the case of brainwashing where these factors are deliberately introduced, or in some other situation in which the particular conditions of Pavlov's experiments are most nearly simulated. But I do not think that Pavlov's experiments give us any reason to believe that we have here (as he himself apparently thought) the master clue for the understanding of neurosis in general, which would enable us to dispense with what Dr Sargant calls 'vaguer psychological theories'. Nor do I believe that Dr Sargant has succeeded in bringing the facts of religious conversion within this rather restricted category either.

After all, the stresses imposed on Pavlov's dogs, though powerful, were of necessity fairly simple and straightforward. There is no need to ask why the things that were done to them put them under stress. The answer is obvious: 'Because they are dogs, and dogs are made that way.' So, also, the stresses imposed either by battle or brainwashing are devastatingly simple, and there is no real reason to ask why these conditions constitute a stress, and the threat of breakdown to a particular man. Again, the stresses imposed are linked in some way with elemental physiological needs such as hunger, self-preservation or the avoidance of pain; and although there may be, as Pavlov suggests, constitutional factors that account for some variation in individual response, the ultimate reason why any of these situations constitutes a threat of breakdown, depends not on anything specific in the individual concerned, but on the nature of the species and the intensity and duration with which the stress is applied.[4]

But life does not often present us with these simplified situations in which stress depends merely on the intensity of the stimulus. Outside certain quite specialized circumstances such as we have outlined above, it *is* a very relevant question to ask just *why* this situation constitutes a threat of breakdown to this particular person. Why is it a stress situation for him at all?

A detonation of gelignite in a quarry is, physically and physiologically, a very powerful stimulus to the man who lives next door. Yet, one softly spoken remark made in his own drawing room may be a more powerful stimulus, impose more stress on him, occasion more changes in cortical activity and bring him nearer to actual breakdown than half a dozen blasts of gelignite. (It is still true of course that if the man were subjected to a continuous bombardment of such detonations, day and night for a considerable period, he might break down. But I repeat that these would be highly specialized circumstances relevant to a consideration of battle neuroses or brainwashing, but not to the context of ordinary life in which neuroses occur and most religious conversions take place. In the more ordinary course of life it is not simply the strength of a stimulus that counts, but its *meaning* for the individual, and that in its turn will depend on a lot of other meanings that arise out of his personal experience both past and present.)

To get back to the man in his drawing room, if we ask why this situation—this particular remark made to him by this person at this time—put him under abnormal stress, we may perhaps be led in the long run back to some of the same elemental needs that we have mentioned above. But when we ask why this particular situation is linked with such a need in the man's personality; or why, for example, in another case the death of a parent provokes not simply the normal reaction of grief but a profound psychological depression; or why a man's long sought promotion to a position of responsibility is followed by a hysterical paralysis, then the answer to any of these questions will not be in terms of human nature in general nor the intensity of any particular stimulus. It will be something quite individual in terms of a man's emotional history and experience of personal relationships, and the pattern of meaning and purpose in his present life.

In other words, when we get beyond the quite unusual circumstances that are parallel to Pavlov's experiments, the effort to understand neurosis takes us past the point where conditioned reflexes, temperamental types, simple physiological stresses and hypothetical changes in the functions of the cortex, will tell us very much that is relevant. This brings us then to the second and more radical reason why Pavlov's experiments with dogs are of limited value in interpreting human behaviour.

Both Pavlov and Dr Sargant speak so confidently of 'alteration in brain function' or 'transmarginal inhibition of the cerebral cortex' ctc. that readers of Battle for the Mind may easily overlook the fact that all these changes in brain activity are as yet matters of hypothesis, not of scientific observation. They are not empirical data drawn from actual examination of the brain, or instrumental recording of its functioning under these conditions, but are simply inferred from the behaviour exhibited by dogs or patients.[5] It is true that in the case of Pavlov's dogs, this behaviour included variations in the reflex flow of saliva that were accurately recorded, but to what extent it is safe to argue from such a specific reaction as this to a general condition of the cerebral cortex, I do not know. In any case we should still be postulating changes in brain activity that are inferred, rather than observed or directly recorded.

Now I have no quarrel with this. Science must proceed by the making and testing of hypotheses, and considering all that we know of the way in which the cerebral cortex is involved in human and animal behaviour, it seems a very reasonable hypothesis indeed, that the behaviour of Pavlov's dogs or Dr Sargant's patients under breakdown, is accompanied by certain changes in the functioning of the brain. If and when our techniques of recording brain function become sufficiently refined we may expect to confirm this hypothesis at least in general, even if not in every detail. However, my point is this: if it is reasonable (as

I think it is), on the basis of observed behaviour, to infer that there are certain changes in brain activity, it is just as reasonable to infer that there are other changes also—viz. psychological changes, emotional and cognitive changes of various kinds in the experience of the dog, that accompany the changes in his overt behaviour.

Therefore, while the picture which Pavlov gives us of his dogs, in terms of observed behaviour and hypothetical brain changes may not be at all untrue, it is never more than *part* of the total picture. There is almost certainly another half of the facts which are quite inaccessible to us. What can we know of the dog's struggle to discriminate between various stimuli; of its experience of frustration as a threat to its basic security, of its effort to cope with or to avoid overstimulation, or the changes in mood or emotional experience due to debilitation, drugs or glandular surgery? If these particular questions in relation to a dog strike some readers as being a little ridiculous, they may well be so—for all that we *know*, but unless we are prepared, with Descartes, to consider the dog as a mere machine (and I am not prepared to do this), then we are bound to postulate, along with the hypothetical brain changes, which may one day be recorded, another set of changes, a psychological aspect of the total process of which we shall, in the case of animals, never have any detailed knowledge. Of course, this limitation cannot be avoided when we are working with dogs; it implies no criticism of Pavlov's experiments. Nevertheless, a proper scientific humility will always acknowledge that even if Pavlov's hypotheses prove to be true, they will never be more than *part* of the truth about the phenomena concerned.

Dr Sargant rightly feels that people will object to having human behaviour interpreted simply in terms of canine behaviour. At the beginning of the chapter in which he makes this comparison he says: 'We have repeatedly heard it argued that comparisons between the behaviour of man and animals, such as those made in Chapter 1, are invalid; because man has a soul, or at least a far more highly developed brain and intelligence.'[6] Now there *is* of course some point in this kind of objection. It seems reasonable to infer from observed behaviour that there are quite large differences in intelligence, social and 'cultural' capacity etc. between men and dogs. However, it is

very difficult to say exactly what these differences are, and how
far they go, because we actually *know* practically nothing about
the inner life of dogs—and until dogs learn to talk, we never
shall.

However, Dr Sargant misses the real point of the objection,
I think. It is not a mere matter of human indignation but of
scientific method. It is not simply that men are not dogs, but
that even *dogs* are not dogs simply as Pavlov described them.
There must have been much more to Pavlov's dogs than his
physiological explanations encompassed, and it is this much
more—inaccessible in the case of dogs, but in the case of human
beings very largely communicable and open to investigation
that makes the comparison between the two, on the basis of
Pavlov's experiments, very hazardous indeed except in some
extremely limited situations and with very limited aims in view.
In the case of Pavlov's dogs, as we have seen, the psychological
aspects of their experience under breakdown are hidden from
us. However, in the case of human beings the situation is quite
different. Many of the psychological facts *can* be and already
have been investigated in some detail, by a variety of methods
depending on communication and personal relationship. To suggest, therefore, that our investigation of neurosis in human
beings should ever be limited to the categories which Pavlov was
obliged to use with his dogs, seems a strangely unscientific
attitude.

To sum up then, the point of the objection does not depend
on the rather abstract question of whether or not dogs have
souls, but on the quite indisputable fact that dogs can't talk and
men can.

It is true of course that in *Battle for the Mind* Dr Sargant
discusses the behaviour of human beings under certain special
conditions, which he considers in each case more or less parallel
to Pavlov's experimental situations. But even so how adequate
are his explanations along Pavlovian lines? In the cases of
battle neurosis, which of all the phenomena he describes seem
to be nearest to Pavlov's experimental conditions, although the
doctors did talk to their patients, it seems to have been only in
relation to the recent precipitating cause of their neurosis.
Investigation and treatment seem of necessity to have been confined to the alleviation of the immediately debilitating symp-

toms. Indeed, under conditions of war it is difficult to see what else could be done. While this relatively superficial treatment was probably adequate for those cases where the stress was almost entirely environmental, nevertheless, some of the other cases described did seem to involve personality factors as well. I think that most psychotherapists would feel that had it been possible to consider the long-term psychic wellbeing of the patient rather than simply the urgent need for symptomatic relief, much more than simple sedation, or the abreaction under drugs of recent traumatic experiences, would have been called for. This deeper treatment could hardly proceed very far along mechanistic lines.

The effort to account for all these cases of battle neurosis along purely Pavlovian lines seems to have led Dr Sargant into some rather forced interpretations, especially when he discusses the so-called 'focal inhibitions of the cortex'. For example he says: 'In some cases the inhibition seemed limited to small focal regions in the brain. One patient, for instance, is reported as stammering only at the mention of an officer who had called him a coward.'[7] Now since these cortical inhibitions are sup-posed to be simply the result of overstimulation, it would seem that 'focal inhibitions' imply overstimulation of the particular focal areas of the cortex concerned. It would surely be difficult to discover anything so selective as this in the battle situation, and even more difficult to correlate it with anything that we know of localization in the cerebral cortex. In the case cited above does Dr Sargant seriously mean to suggest that there is 'some small focal region of the brain' that responds specifically to the mention of a particular officer's name, and to no other stimulus? Whatever the changes in brain function that are actually involved, I would suggest that cases like this one, and cases of hysteria generally, are far more easily interpreted psychologically in terms of motivation and meaning. What par-ticular (unacknowledged) purpose does this paralysis serve? What is the emotional significance of this officer's name in terms of the patient's past experience, immediate and remote?

Many of the cases of battle neurosis cited by Dr Sargant, as well as his descriptions of brainwashing etc., do underline the importance of physiological factors in mental breakdown under certain conditions, and that is one of the lasting positive contri-

butions of his book. The evidence he adduces shows the importance not only of the brain and nervous system but also of
certain basic physiological needs which man shares in common
with dogs and other animals. I have no wish to deny that in this
respect Dr Sargant does show the relevance of Pavlov's experiments, so far as they go. I simply want to point out that nowhere
do the Pavlovian hypotheses on which he relies, by themselves
provide an *adequate* explanation of these phenomena. In all of
them there are involved psychological factors that the Pavlovian
approach cannot possibly cope with, and in many cases the neglect of these factors can only result in serious misunderstanding.

I make no attempt in this essay to discuss the phenomena of
brainwashing in any detail. Here we have again the exploitation
of fear, hunger, pain and debilitation which Pavlov's experiments help us to understand. But we also have more than this.
As Dr Sargant's chapter on 'The eliciting of confessions'[8] shows,
the exponents of this art are also experts in a sort of perverted
psychoanalysis, foraging through the victim's past to discover
and exploit deep-seated psychological anxieties and pathological
guilt feelings in order to hasten his collapse. If we are to understand these processes and evolve any defence against them, we
shall have to go far beyond the limits of Pavlovian theory.

Since my main interest in this essay is in the matter of religious conversion, I will try to show in some detail in later
chapters that in this respect, Dr Sargant's neglect of psychological factors has led him sadly astray, even to the point of
unwittingly tailoring the facts to fit his theory. His determined
attempt to interpret human behaviour along simple Pavlovian
lines to the neglect of psychological factors is, of course, bound
up with his peculiar attitude towards psychoanalysis, which we
must now consider in more detail in the next chapter.

FOOTNOTES AND REFERENCES

1. *Battle for the Mind*, p. xviii (15).
2. *Op. cit.*, Ch. 1.
3. *Ibid.*, Ch. 2.
4. Cf. Dr J. J. Conybeare: 'Fortunately most of the functional
   states that arise in war are simpler to deal with than those seen
   in civil life, determined as they are by external stress rather

than by internal conflict' — p. vi in his Foreword to *Psychological Medicine* (with an Appendix on 'Psychiatry associated with war conditions') by Desmond Curran and Eric Guttman, E. & S. Livingstone Ltd., Edinburgh 1945.

Cf. also, Suttie, Ian D., *The Origins of Love and Hate*, Kegan Paul, Trench, Trubner & Co. Ltd., London 1935, pp. 202-3.

5. Dr W. Grey Walter relates how he asked Pavlov if he saw any relation between his own work and the pioneer work of Berger in recording the patterns of electrical rhythms on the surface of the brain. 'But Pavlov showed no desire to look behind the scenes. He was not in the least interested in the mechanics of cerebral events; they just happned, and it was the happening and its consequences that interested him, not how they happened.' — W. Grey Walter, *The Living Brain*, Pelican edition Penguin Books Ltd. 1961, p. 54.

6. *Op. cit.*, p. 21 (37).

7. *Ibid.*, pp. 26-7 (41).

8. *Ibid.*, p. 177 (165).

CHAPTER 4

DRUGS AND DEPTH

It has already been pointed out that by taking Pavlov's experiments with dogs as the clue towards explaining human behaviour in a variety of situations, Dr Sargant has deliberately neglected any specific consideration of psychological factors: factors which, for the past seventy years, have been under investigation by methods that can be effectively used with human beings but not with dogs. These methods are all, essentially, ways of investigating and treating mental and emotional illness that depend on personal communication and personal relationships between the patient and the psychotherapist, and they owe their origin to the genius and work of Sigmund Freud. Freud himself always insisted that the term 'psychoanalysis' should be used only by those who continued to adhere strictly to his own views on the subject. This wish is not always respected, and the term is often applied to a variety of different forms of psychotherapy which, although owning a common ancestry, have since departed in various ways and degrees from strict Freudian orthodoxy.

To avoid confusion we could designate all these psychotherapies of Freudian origin, whether orthodox or otherwise, by the term 'depth psychology' which points to what is probably the most significant feature which they have in common—viz. the recognition in theory and practice that:

1. The mind of man includes much that is below the level of consciousness, and not ordinarily accessible to his awareness;

2. The cause of much mental illness is to be sought in dynamic conflict within this unconscious part of the mind;

3. The cure consists essentially in bringing some of these unconscious elements to light so that the patient may become aware of them and integrate them in some way with his conscious personality.[1]

The whole study of depth psychology—of psychoanalysis and

47

its derivatives—has captured the imagination of modern man
and influenced his life and his thinking in a myriad ways, some
quite superficial, and others quite profound. I don't think it will
be denied, either, that this approach has been in fact very
influential in modern psychiatry. Yet there is such a flood of
psychoanalytic literature, technical, popular and even oracular,
and some psychiatrists seem so completely and uncritically sold
on depth psychology to the exclusion of other methods that it is
not surprising if some of their colleagues react against all this
with a more or less strong aversion. Between these two extreme
positions the majority of psychiatrists probably manage a more
balanced and critical assessment of depth psychology and make
use of analytical theories and techniques along with other
methods of relieving mental illness.

Now I think that Dr Sargant makes it fairly plain in his book
that he has in fact a very strong aversion to depth psychology
and all its explanations. He does this partly by what he says and
partly by what he refrains from saying. We have seen already
how he fastened rather eagerly on Pavlov's findings as an indication that the correctness of 'many current psychological theories'
was 'more improbable than ever' and how his choice of the
Pavlovian experiments as his explanatory model has effectively
ruled these theories out of court without a hearing. Most of the
cases of battle neurosis and hysteria that he discusses are of a
type that had already been explained from the point of view of
depth psychology and if Dr Sargant was at a loss to understand
them, this could only have been because he found psychoanalytical explanations unacceptable or not worthy of serious
consideration.

At the beginning of Chapter 2 of Battle for the Mind he
speaks, with obvious reference to depth psychology, of the 'backward state' of modern psychiatry, which is allegedly due to the
fact that 'psychological theory has too often taken the place of
scientific experiment as one of the main means of accounting for
normal and abnormal patterns of human behaviour'.[2] This type
of criticism is also directed against depth psychology, somewhat
stridently, in Dr H. J. Eysenck's book Uses and Abuses of
Psychology.[3] Now I will not deny that psychoanalysts have
sometimes tended to run towards over-ingenious theories, and
even a few 'just-so stories'. But to suggest, as Sargant and

Eysenck seem to do, that depth psychology as such is unscientific because it does not resort to experiment, is quite unreasonable and displays a basic lack of understanding of the nature and purpose of this kind of psychotherapy. The academic psychologist may carry out his laboratory tests, measurements and experiments (after the classic concepts of physical science) and the data he accumulates may be important for specific purposes —but not for really understanding anyone as a living, motivated person. The fact is that when we are dealing with people in this way, we just can't experiment with them as Pavlov did with his dogs. Apart from their rights and needs as persons, the very creation of an experimental situation immediately destroys or distorts the behaviour patterns we are trying to examine. By the very nature of human behaviour and the experimental method we cannot discover experimentally how people behave outside an experimental situation. (In this regard, Dr Eysenck has been well answered by Dr J. A. C. Brown,[4] a psychiatrist who is both an orthodox Freudian and well acquainted with academic psychology.)

Yet despite this difficulty, depth psychology on the whole is a genuinely scientific attempt to explain a whole mass of empirical data that are encountered in actual clinical dealing with people, the study of biographical material and the observation of ordinary social life. From all of this there is emerging a growing body of knowledge, and what it yet lacks in precision it makes up in importance, for it has already begun to give us a clearer and more useful understanding of the intricacies of human behaviour than any other single discipline. The attitude of those who would more or less sweep all this aside, simply because it cannot be fitted into a methodological framework appropriate to the study of physics is, I suggest, more profoundly unscientific than anything we encounter in psychoanalysis.

As for the section of Chapter 4 in which Dr Sargant purports to describe the techniques of psychoanalysis,[5] readers who are acquainted with depth psychology either directly or through its literature will recognize that we have here only a rather unfortunate parody of the real thing. Here again, Dr Sargant is akin to the academic psychologist H. J. Eysenck in implying that the major contribution of the analyst is to condition the patient, and to impose his own interpretation of his symptoms by a process of

D

suggestion. It almost seems as if conditioning and suggestion are the only kinds of personal influence these two writers really understand or believe in, and they are at a loss to explain the results of psychoanalysis in any other terms. As a matter of fact, both these methods are quite foreign to psychoanalysis itself, and the results they aim at are the opposite of those sought by an analysis that goes to any depth. A good analyst is very sparing in his interpretations and rather than imposing them on the patient, spends more time tactfully declining the patient's invitation to do so. Some shortened forms of analytic treatment do make more use of interpretation, but this is usually done very carefully, with the intention not of evading the patient's critical faculties and subtly imposing the analyst's ideas on him, but of helping him to progress more quickly in his own insight into the nature of his illness. Psychoanalysts are only human, and their task is often quite difficult, and no one for one moment would suggest that they are always equally successful in carrying out their own principles. However we are not likely to arrive at an objective estimate of a movement if we decide to interpret it through its less successful or typical exponents.

For an unbiased account of the sort of thing that does go on in the course of psychoanalytic treatment, written by a psychiatrist who seems to have no axe to grind either for or against depth psychology, reference should be made to Dr David Stafford-Clark's *Psychiatry To-day*,[6] while Dr J. A. C. Brown's *Freud and the Post Freudians* gives us an account of the movement as a whole, comprehensive but by no means uncritical, and written by a Freudian.

The prerequisite of the right to criticize anything is the ability to understand what one is criticizing. It is just here, it seems to me, that both Dr Sargant and Dr Eysenck fall down; they just don't *understand* depth psychology, and their failure is not an intellectual one but a certain emotional incapacity to appreciate such things which one occasionally encounters even in psychiatrists and psychologists as well as other people. It is not suggested of course that psychoanalytic theories and techniques are beyond criticism. They do need careful critical assessment from the point of view of scientific method, provided that science is not conceived in a way so narrow as to be inappropriate to the subject matter. Theologically as well, depth psychology cannot

simply be taken at its face value, for it has not always been free
from an element of motivated woolly thinking in matters of
religion. It is still true, probably, that most psychoanalysts
following in the footsteps of Freud, tend to judge religion by the
pathological forms of it which they encounter. It would not be
surprising, then, if religious people in general tended to judge
psychoanalysis by the rather silly things some of its exponents
say about religion.

It is just here of course, that Christians need to be careful. If
there are those among us who think that 'Psychoanalysis, Freud
and all that' are inherently anti-Christian, they may even fall
into the error of imagining that someone who is anti-Freud is
naturally on the side of the angels. He may not be. There are
more formidable threats to the Christian faith than the avowed
atheism of Freud. A few years ago, in an article written rather
as a 'commendation than a criticism' of psychiatry, Professor
L. W. Grensted said

'There has been a movement away from the more personal
aspects of treatment which made the older psychotherapy as
much an art as a science, and towards the main trend of general
medical practice, with its principles firmly based in the sciences
of physiology and pathology. In short the modern psychiatrist is
much more of a scientist and much better equipped scientifically
than the pioneers of thirty or forty years ago, but his diagnosis
and his treatment are apt to be less personal, and, in the deepest
sense, less humane.'[7]

Many Christian pastors and pastoral theologians have managed
to bypass Freud's somewhat extraneous atheism, and to assimi-
late psychoanalytical ideas into a fundamentally Christian cure
of souls. But the tendency away from personal relationships
in psychiatry, which Professor Grensted notes, constitutes, I
believe, a much more real danger to Christian values. Something
of this is displayed (however unwittingly) in the attitude of Dr
Sargant, and in a slightly different way, in that of Dr Eysenck
also. Dr Sargant is a psychiatrist anxious to extend physiological
explanations and physical treatments of mental illness, while
Dr Eysenck is an academic psychologist who would like to
reduce all psychology to measurements and experimental

investigation. Both are united in their opposition to psychoanalysis; the alternatives they suggest definitely move away from
the enlargement and liberation of conscious personality which
psychoanalysis tries to achieve, and which is also, I would suggest, one of the aims of the Christian cure of souls.

In this regard Dr Eysenck's views and, in particular, the
alternative methods he suggests for the treatment of neurosis,
have been fairly summarized and effectively criticized by Dr H.
Guntrip, a psychotherapist on the staff of the Leeds University
Department of Psychiatry, in the following passage:

'Psychotherapy is a field in which scientific investigation and
testing, and the personal therapeutic approach must learn to
work together, with mutual respect, and not with the one-
sidedness and antagonism that Eysenck manifests.

'Instead of treating patients as persons whose troubles and
conflicts lie in the region of motives and purposes, he treats them
as bundles of habits which must be corrected by scientific devices
based on what he calls a new psychology of learning. These
methods of scientific therapy, however, turn out not to be so
new after all. They boil down to three: the reconditioning of
conditioned reflexes, habit substitution, and suggestion. For the
first he cites an electrical device for waking up the nocturnal
enuretic when he wants to pass water, for the second the substitution of chewing gum for cigarettes, and for the third, post-
hypnotic suggestion and curing children of nail-biting by playing gramophone records giving appropriate suggestions while
they sleep. Why the patient passes water in his sleep, or smokes
compulsively, or bites his nails does not apparently matter. So
long as you scientifically put a stop to these tension-relieving
symptomatic activities, the nature of the tensions seems to be
irrelevant. That might perhaps be relegated to psychotherapy as
an adjunct to these 'more fundamental methods'.

This really would be comic if it were not tragic. It is a mere
'symptom therapy', a collection of natty little tricks to cure
nasty little tics . . .

'Dr Eysenck has depersonalized the human person and
excluded motives. The need to love and be loved, the fact of love
embittered to a choking, stifling hate by frustration of all really
human needs, hopes and goals, these are facts that are far more

important and momentous than the annoying symptomatic
habits that Eysenck's therapy cures.'[8]

It is not without significance that the ingenious conditioning
device advocated by Dr Eysenck for waking the nocturnal bed-
wetter[9] was developed in the United States by Dr O. Hobart
Mowrer, a psychologist who has also made a vigorous attack on
psychoanalysis on allegedly religious grounds.[10] I have known a
child who was 'cured' of bed-wetting by this device, to the
delight and relief of her mother, whose main interest was of
course to save washing and disgrace. Fortunately the child's real
need was subsequently detected, and she received more adequate
psychotherapy, during which the source of her emotional disturbance was traced to a quite serious lack of maternal affection
at a deep level. When the real issues were thus laid bare the
mother, of course, had to face a much more serious demand than
her child's bed-wetting ever imposed on her; but the child had
the chance of at least a partial recovery, instead of having her
rejection-anxiety buried decently out of sight, to continue warping and debilitating her personality all her life, and the personalities of her children after her.[11]

The same trend in British psychiatry which was noted by
Professor Grensted in the passage quoted above was assessed
somewhat differently by Dr Sargant in these words: 'Psychiatric
research in Great Britain has, however, become far more realistic
since World War II. Drugs and other physical methods of treatment gave such undeniable results, in the treatment of acute
civilian and military war neuroses, that physiological aids to
psychiatry were given a high research priority, and this policy
has persisted.'[12]

I have already suggested that war neuroses, because they
depend on quite abnormal environmental stresses rather than
individual personality factors, are hardly typical, and I cannot
see that reliance on methods of treatment which gave undeniable
results for such specialized cases is necessarily very realistic for
psychiatry in general. No doubt there are forms of mental illness
for which only some kind of physical treatment as yet avails,
although, according to Dr Stafford-Clark, some of these should
also be accompanied by a more personal psychotherapy 'before,
during and after treatment'.[13] Without this precaution, there is

not a doubt that all physical methods lend themselves much more readily to treating the patient, simply as a case rather than treating him as a person.

On the other hand psychoanalytic theories and techniques have shown a marked tendency to develop from the purely biological form in which they originated to one which stresses the importance of personal relationships and personal values in both the understanding and treatment of neuroses. Christianity should always have a stake in anything that involves a genuine respect for personality and seeks to promote the integrity of persons through costly involvement in personal relationships. When the use of purely physical methods of treating mental illness are advocated then (as they seem to be by Dr Sargant) not simply as a necessity in some cases, but as a welcome substitute for the other more personal forms of treatment that are available, we should be mindful of what this kind of realism could imply. For those who still feel that the greatest threat to Christian values from within modern psychiatry comes from psycho-analysis, this comment from the Freudian, Dr J. A. C. Brown, is worth quoting:

'The very real danger today is that neuroses may cease to be dealt with by psychological methods based on understanding at all, and that with new pharmacological and medical or surgical methods we shall be "cured" by being made insensible to con-flicts rather than facing up to them and trying to understand what is wrong with our way of life. Instead of realizing that there are circumstances which justify attitudes of guilt, remorse, shame, anxiety or injustice, we shall treat them as inconvenient "symptoms" to be dispelled by a tranquilizer or thymoleptic drug.'[14]

While the wider significance of these different trends in psychiatry should not be overlooked, my main concern in this chapter is to show how Dr Sargant's neglect of depth psychology affects his interpretation of the phenomena of emotional abreaction in general, and those of religious conversion in particular.

Dr Sargant discovered that if many of his patients suffering from battle neurosis could be induced to abreact the fearful experiences which they had endured—i.e. to recall or act them out with a sufficiently powerful discharge of the appropriate emotion, their symptoms would disappear. In this process, emotional discharge rather than mere intellectual recall, is the all important thing. These facts had of course been known for some time previously and it is important to realize that Dr Sargant and his colleagues, following out the pioneer work of depth psychologists, were making use of these abreactive treatments before they became acquainted with I. P. Pavlov's work. However, he does claim that in certain respects Pavlov's work helped them to improve the technique.

The significance of emotional abreaction was one of the early discoveries of Freud and his collaborators which led them to develop the characteristic concepts of depth psychology — the theories of the unconscious, dynamic conflict and emotional repression. Emotion that becomes too painful for the conscious personality to tolerate, or too dangerous to its security to express may often be repressed—i.e. driven completely out of consciousness into the unconscious part of the mind. This process of repression is itself an unconscious one—not something which a person does consciously or deliberately. Emotion thus repressed does not go out of existence but continues to be active in the unconscious, setting up a dynamic conflict there, striving to get past the repression, and often managing to express itself in a disguised form in dreams, symptoms of bodily illness, anxiety, obsessional or compulsive behaviour, or some other disturbance of the personality either mild or serious.

Freud thus accounted for the various symptoms of neurotic illness in terms of dynamic conflict in the unconscious, between repressed emotion and a repressing force to which at one stage he gave the graphic name 'the Censor'. I think that most psychoanalysts would still admit that the process of repression is itself something of an unexplained mystery. It is doubtful, for example, if there is any well defined and organized entity in the personality corresponding to the name 'the Censor', which was only a convenient sort of way of referring to something which we frankly do not understand. Nevertheless, the fact of dynamic conflict between repressed emotions and something, some force that prevents their reappearance in consciousness and direct expression, is not seriously in doubt among those who have tested out this hypothesis in therapeutic practice with patients suffering from neurosis. Nor is the sense of such conflict entirely absent from our ordinary personal dealing with ourselves and others. It must be emphasized, then, that this is no mere arm-chair philosophy of human nature, but is based on a mass of clinical evidence and careful investigation that may be examined in the voluminous literature of depth psychology, either technical or popular and which helps, as well, to make more intelligible a wider area of more normal human experience and behaviour.

The healing techniques of depth psychology, therefore, seek in a variety of ways to reduce or overcome repression; thus bringing back into consciousness, or rather enabling the patient to accept back into his own conscious awareness again, material that has been previously (and unwittingly) driven out and kept out of consciousness because it was experienced as too painful, or too dangerous to tolerate. As Dr Gilbert Russell says: 'To become conscious; that is the task, in a sense the only task; and an entirely new technique, which owes more to the genius of Freud than to anything else, has been evolved to meet it.'[15] He points out that in this type of treatment, the therapist's 'main interest throughout . . . is that the patient shall be *more conscious* — that his consciousness of himself shall expand and deepen.'[16] Dr Stafford-Clark writes of all these forms of treatment that have developed from the outstanding and pioneer contribution of Freud, as sharing 'this aim of increasing awareness and thereby liberating the patient from the bondage of unconscious conflict and emotion'.[17]

The release of pent-up emotion, stimulated to an intolerable level by the terrors of modern warfare is, of course, one example of this process of bringing something that has become unconscious back into the field of consciousness again. In the presence of mortal danger the natural expression of emotion is in flight; but under the circumstances of battle this is usually physically impossible, or morally unacceptable, to other powerful demands of the personality. Fear may therefore mount to a pitch at which it can no longer be tolerated by the conscious personality, and repression will take place. For all that we know this process of emotional repression may well be accompanied by some sort of cortical inhibition, such as that which Pavlov postulated. Indeed, the fact that emotional abreaction can be brought about by the use of drugs, as well as by purely psychological methods, does seem to suggest pretty clearly that as with emotion generally, the whole process of repression and its reduction has both a physiological and a psychological aspect.

But the wider interest of depth psychology in this process of increasing awareness and bringing unconscious material to light, in order to free the patient from its domination, has to go well beyond the type of emotional abreaction that may suffice to disperse the immediate symptoms of a battle neurosis. In more general practice it is found that the most significant, extensive and damaging repressions are associated not simply with some specific traumatic experience or experiences, but arise out of the patient's history of personal relationships, and especially the parent-child relationships of the early years. Powerful emotions arising naturally in the course of these relationships (but for some reason or other too dangerous or unacceptable to be given direct expression at the time) may be driven underground, to become the source of neurosis or personality distortion in later life. These are the emotions long since forgotten which often need to be brought to light, and acted out during psychotherapy. As Dr Guntrip says: ' . . . psychotherapy of the psychoanalytic type is giving the patient an opportunity (which he may use, misuse, or refuse to use) to work over with another person all his difficulties in personal relationships so that he may have a chance of solving them in an atmosphere of patient understanding, and so grow more mature.'[18]

Particularly in the deeper seated and longer established neuroses, as distinct from those produced by recent trauma, it is important to bring repressed material back to consciousness; and to do this in such a way and at such a rate that it can be assimilated by the patient, and integrated in some way, into his conscious personality. The use of hypnosis or drugs to lower the degree of repression and facilitate the recall of repressed material, had been tried by psychoanalysts as far back as 1936, largely in an effort to shorten the long process of analysis, but according to Dr Nigel Walker

'Many psychoanalysts, however, and especially the more orthodox British ones, are opposed to them. They argue that while hypnosis or drugs temporarily break down the barrier that separates the patient's conscious from her unconscious mind, this is done too quickly, so that the patient must either forget or in some other way dissociate herself from what she has said under the influence of the facilitant, since otherwise she would be intolerably distressed by it.'[19]

To sum up then, the phenomena of emotional abreaction which Dr Sargant and his colleagues encountered had long been known, used therapeutically, interpreted dynamically, and placed within a wider setting of both theory and practice by depth psychology. Dr Sargant must have been fully aware of all this but in accord with his general bias he chooses to ignore it. He tries, instead, to interpret emotional abreaction along purely Pavlovian lines as simply another example of the imposition of strain, leading to terminal exhaustion or collapse.

In the traumatic experiences which lead to battle neurosis and the terrors deliberately imposed in brainwashing, we may well have processes roughly parallel to the experimental stress situations imposed on Pavlov's dogs, resulting in various stages of abnormal behaviour and culminating in terminal exhaustion and collapse. However, it must be pointed out that nowhere in these experiments with dogs, as described either by Dr Sargant or by Pavlov himself, do we see anything that even looks like emotional abreaction. The abnormal behaviour or collapse of Pavlov's dogs was always the direct result of imposed stresses—not of the release or acting out of pent-up emotion. To restore them after breakdown, Pavlov's dogs were never treated abreactively, but were given simple sedation. The fact is that emotional abreaction simply will not fit at all into the Pavlovian formula of breakdown under stress because it is psychologically and dynamically the exact opposite of such a process—it is the *recovery* from breakdown.

Describing the emotional abreactions of his patients under barbiturates and ether, Dr Sargant tells how it occurred to him and his colleagues that 'this collapse phenomenon, which we were now repeatedly observing, might correspond to Pavlov's "transmarginal inhibition", which occurs when the cortex has become momentarily incapable of further activity'.[20] Apparently, then, Dr Sargant concluded at this point that the breakdown under stress and the subsequent emotional abreaction which brought about the recovery of his patients, were not at all the opposite of each other but both examples of essentially the *same* process of 'cortical inhibition'. This is strange reasoning indeed, and certainly flies in the face of common sense; to reach such a conclusion Dr Sargant completely ignores the psychodynamics of both breakdown and recovery, and overlooks some rather obvious differences in their outward manifestations as well.

When we enquire what are the common features of both breakdown and recovery which lead Dr Sargant to see both processes as amenable to similar explanations, we find that both involve something which can be described as 'collapse', and both involve striking changes in behaviour. However, an examination of Dr Sargant's own evidence will show very clearly that the changes in behaviour involved in the two processes are exactly opposite; that in the respective contexts of breakdown and abreactive recovery, the word 'collapse' means two entirely different things. In Chapter 2, the collapse that supervenes as a result of intolerable strain is a condition that endures for some time, and is manifest in breakdown, restriction of personality, debilitating symptoms and patterns of abnormal behaviour. In Chapter 3, the collapse that supervenes at the end of emotional abreaction is a comparatively short-lived physical exhaustion resulting from violent emotional discharge. It soon passes quite spontaneously to be followed at once by healing, liberation of personality, and the disappearance of neurotic symptoms and abnormal behaviour patterns.

Thus to labour the obvious is almost an embarrassment but, nevertheless, necessary because Dr Sargant seems to have obscured it even from himself. Several times throughout *Battle for the Mind* he treats the phenomena of emotional abreaction as though they were simply a matter of breakdown under imposed stress. Indeed much of the subsequent argument of his book depends on this assumption. The manifest differences between breakdown and abreactive recovery cannot of course be accounted for within a Pavlovian formula at all; they require some sort of dynamic explanation. The Pavlovian experiments, the battle situation and the brainwashing ordeal all involve the imposition of intolerable stress; the process of emotional abreaction, on the other hand, involves just the opposite—the *release* of intolerable stress. Abreaction does not *impose* stress, but releases a flood of emotion pent up (repressed) as a result of previous stress.

In his effort to interpret emotional abreaction according to a Pavlovian formula, Dr Sargant, for some reason which he does not make entirely clear, attached special importance to the behaviour of Pavlov's dogs during and immediately after the Leningrad flood of 1924.[21] During this flood the dogs were nearly drowned, and manifested every sign of terror as the water rose higher in their cages. They were dragged down through the water to safety in the nick of time but some of them were in a state of breakdown and collapse, and on testing them again, Pavlov discovered that all their conditioned reflexes which he had carefully built up through months of work, were completely erased. Pavlov interpreted this as a further stage of 'protective inhibition' beyond the equivalent, paradoxical and ultra-paradoxical phases already observed.

In using this incident to illustrate the effects of emotional abreaction, Dr Sargant's line of reasoning seems to be that just as the violent emotional experience of the dogs wiped out their conditioned reflexes, so the emotional discharge of abreaction wipes out neurotic symptoms. It will be noted first of all that this argument assumes that neurotic symptoms are of essentially the same nature as conditioned reflexes—which is, to say the least, a rather large and dubious assumption for which no evidence at all is adduced. Furthermore, it implies that emotional abreaction is simply a further stage of the process which leads to breakdown whereas, as I have already shown, the two processes are in fact the opposite of each other. It will be noticed that the collapse of Pavlov's dogs after their terrifying experience was the collapse of breakdown and inhibition: not the transitory collapse followed by healing and release, which is typical of the abreactive experience. Indeed, as both Dr Sargant's and Pavlov's descriptions make abundantly clear, the whole incident was an extreme example of breakdown under stress, very similar to some of the worst battle experiences of Dr Sargant's patients. It was not in any sense an example of emotional abreaction at all.

So far in this discussion, for the sake of clarity, I have deliberately dealt only with those types of simple abreaction that were brought about by the use of drugs. It is important to notice that many of Dr Sargant's patients *were* able to abreact sufficiently for their recovery, by this means alone. However there were other patients who could not be induced to abreact with drugs alone. For these, Dr Sargant and his colleagues used a supplementary technique of suggesting to the patient that he was again in some terrifying situation, calculated to arouse the same sort of emotions of fear and anger that had caused his original breakdown.[22] It was while they were developing this technique of suggestion, Dr Sargant tells us, that he first became acquainted with Pavlov's work, and it was undoubtedly this kind of abreactive technique which made use of fear stimulation as well as drugs, that helped him to confuse the whole process of abreaction with the sort of breakdown under stress that was typified in Pavlov's experiments.

This calls for several comments. Firstly, Dr Sargant's reliance on the simple Pavlovian formula of Stress-Cortical Inhibition-Breakdown, which ignores psychodynamics and can therefore give no account of the difference between breakdown and recovery, is bound to lead to this kind of confusion. For, despite the deliberate stimulation of fear employed, what happened as a result were certainly not instances of breakdown; they were genuine abreactions, essentially the same as those induced by the use of drugs, without suggestion. Whatever part the fear stimuli played in the process, the flood of emotion poured out was not simply aroused by these immediate stimuli (as in the case of a breakdown under stress) but was the release of *repressed* emotion originally stimulated by the battle trauma but denied adequate expression at the time. As in the case of the simple drug abreactions, the patient's collapse was the short-lived physical exhaustion followed by the disappearance of his symptoms, not the crippling collapse of breakdown under stress.

Secondly, if we take some account of the psychodynamics of breakdown and recovery, the part played by the stimulation of fear in Dr Sargant's abreactive techniques is not difficult to understand. The whole point about repression and abreaction is the dynamic conflict between powerful repressed emotion on the one hand, and the repressing force on the other. The situation may be usefully likened to that of a river accidentally dammed up by some obstruction. If the obstruction is not removed, the waters may back up till the river bursts its banks, and carves out new channels for itself (symptom formation or abnormal behaviour patterns). Or, builds up to such a pressure that it will suddenly burst the dam and rush through with a force that sweeps all before it, and may for a time flood the surrounding countryside (a more violent type of breakdown, with sudden, quite out of character anti-social behaviour, or possibly psychosis). The problem, then, for psychotherapy, is somehow to break down the dam before these things happen, or if they have already begun to happen, to finish breaking down the damn and get the waters out of their off course channels, to control their destructive turbulence, and get them flowing naturally again.

In the more usual techniques of psychotherapy, the dam is, as it were, dismantled gradually, so that the waters (i.e. the pent up emotion) can come through at a rate and in a way that can be controlled and assimilated without undue damage or disturbance. When drugs are used, the dam is, as it were, broken down much more suddenly and the rush of waters (i.e. the emotional discharge) is much more sensational. However, in some of Dr Sargant's patients, drugs alone would not suffice. The 'dam' was too strong to be sufficiently weakened by drugs. He and his colleagues therefore hit on a way to increase the pressure behind the dam, by fear stimuli applied through suggestion. In terms of our analogy of the dammed up river it was as though they had, for example, diverted an adjacent stream into the river behind the dam. It was this combination of deliberately increased emotional pressure *behind* the repression, along with the weakening of the repression itself by the use of drugs, which in these cases enabled the breakthrough of emotional abreaction.

It will be seen then, that although Dr Sargant and his colleagues developed the additional technique of suggestion to be used along with drugs in some cases, the whole process was not essentially different from what happened with the use of drugs alone. In both cases the situation to be dealt with was a dynamic conflict between repressed emotion on the one hand, and a repressing force on the other. The possibilities of a healing abreaction depended finally on changing the strength of these two factors in the personality *relative* to each other.

Thirdly, it will be seen that while the powerful stimulation of fear played a part in the original breakdown, and in the abreactive recovery as well when Dr Sargant's new technique was used, in these two instances fear was aroused in two very different situations and applied in two different ways, with opposite results. In the original battle situation which had caused the breakdown, fear was aroused in circumstances which prevented its being given any adequate expression (i.e. in escape or shelter). Denied the normal discharge it rose, therefore, to an intolerable level and finally had to be repressed. It is important to note that fear alone would not cause breakdown. It is the combination of fear and circumstances in which fear cannot be fully expressed and discharged in appropriate behaviour that may induce repression and breakdown. As Dr Sargant points out, the soldier who runs away terrified at the first shot, will not break down.[23]

On the other hand, during the abreactive treatments, fear was stimulated in circumstances where every encouragement was being given for its fullest possible expression, and the forces which had originally brought about its repression had been considerably weakened by the use of drugs. In these very different circumstances, fear could therefore be an aid towards healing abreaction, instead of a source of crippling repression. If Dr Sargant's patients had simply been sent back into the terrors of battle — i.e. into a situation where fear could not be appropriately expressed, then no amount of fear stimulation would have produced an abreaction.

It is also worth noting that in the battle situation fear was aroused consciously, and with the full awareness of the person, but in the abreactive treatments fear was stimulated in the *unconscious* part of the patient's mind. Suggestion is a technique of by-passing the rational, conscious function of the mind, and implanting ideas or beliefs in the unconscious. Under the influence of drugs, the patient was in a highly suggestible condition—i.e. his conscious rational functions were temporarily suspended or inhibited and the unconscious level of his mind was therefore much more directly accessible to suggestion. Obviously, if the patient had been fully conscious and aware of his surroundings, it would have been quite impossible to arouse him to terror by suggesting that he was in a battle situation again. To be effective in the abreactive technique, fear had to be aroused not in the conscious part of the mind as it had been in battle, but in the unconscious; the emotional pressure had to be built up *behind* the repression.

Suggestive techniques such as these can quite accurately be spoken of as a form of stimulation, since they help to raise the intensity of repressed emotion to a pitch at which it can 'break through'; but the action of the drugs used is exactly the opposite. They do not stimulate anything, on the contrary, they *depress* or lower the strength of repression. Popular usage, of course, refers to alcohol as a stimulant but popular usage is concerned mainly with appearances, not with medical accuracy. Medically, it is fully recognized that the action of alcohol on the brain and central nervous system is not to stimulate, but to depress certain of its functions. Psychologically this depression or inhibition of certain brain functions means the temporary lowering of repressions; and the consequent release and expression of emotions, hitherto held in check, give rise to the false impression that alcohol itself is a stimulant. It is significant then that Dr Sargant is content to lapse into this rather loose and inaccurate way of speaking when he refers a number of times to the 'stimulation' of emotion by barbiturates, ether and alcohol.[24] Medically these drugs are not stimulants at all but depressants, but in terms of Dr Sargant's discussion of the subject this distinction is of no importance. The simple reason being he really takes us no further in understanding the true nature of emotional abreaction than popular misconceptions about alcohol would take us in understanding the nature of intoxication.

Coupled with his strong bias against depth psychology, Dr Sargant's use of fear stimulation in his abreactive techniques has led him to the quite erroneous view that abreaction can be understood as a form of breakdown under strain—i.e. in terms of Pavlov's hypothesis of inhibitions of the activity of the cerebral cortex due to transmarginal stimulation. I hope that the above explanations make it quite clear that this is not the case, that the apparently common element of fear in both breakdown and recovery does not really make them amenable to the same kind of explanation at all, and that the process of emotional abreaction cannot be understood in terms of Pavlovian experiments but requires explanation in terms of dynamic psychology.

There are of course other methods of lowering repression and facilitating the healing release of pent up emotion, without reliance either on drugs or powerful emotional stimulation. These other methods will be discussed later, because they are of much more significance in understanding religious conversion than anything which Dr Sargant takes into account.

At the price of some repetition it will be of value to sum up the argument of this chapter, because it has direct bearing on most of what follows. I have tried to show then that if we are to understand, rather than misunderstand, the whole range of phenomena that Dr Sargant discusses it will be necessary for us to distinguish, in a way in which he fails to do, between three different types of psychological process:

1. The direct imposition of extreme emotional stress and strain leading to abnormal behaviour and finally to what Pavlov termed 'terminal exhaustion', with possible inhibition of brain function, emotional repression and breakdown. (To this category belong the Pavlovian experiments with dogs, the traumatic experiences leading to battle neuroses, the experiences of Pavlov's dogs during the Leningrad flood, and the use of debilitation, terror and fatigue in brainwashing.)

2. The release of repressed emotion, a process known in its more spectacular forms by the term 'emotional abreaction'. Provided that the repressed material brought to light can be acceptably assimilated, this is an essentially healing process. It may involve temporary collapse and exhaustion, but this soon passes, to be followed by the disappearance of debilitating symptoms and the enlargement and liberation of conscious personality. The release of repressed emotion is therefore not a process of breakdown, but one of recovery. We may distinguish in general, two ways in which it may occur:

(a) By means of weakening or lowering the degree of repression. (To this category belong the simple drug abreactions used by Dr Sargant and his colleagues, without the additional use of suggestion, and, in a less spectacular though more significant way, the working out of emotional and inter-personal conflicts through the transference situations of psychoanalysis.)

(b) By means of weakening the repression on the one hand, and building up the force of the repressed emotion trying to get past it, on the other. (This was the new technique developed by Dr Sargant and his fellow psychiatrists in 1944.)

I think that a detailed and informed examination of the rather bewildering variety of religious phenomena with which Dr Sargant confronts us, would probably show that they include

E

some which would belong to each of the above three categories. From the point of view of Christian ethics and theology it is a matter of considerable importance, I believe, to know to which category an alleged conversion belongs, or what type of conversion an alleged process of evangelism seeks to promote. It is one of the odd things about Dr Sargant's book that he seems quite unaware of this issue. Before we go ahead then, to examine his treatment of the work of John Wesley, it will be as well to turn aside and look at this important matter of principle.

FOOTNOTES AND REFERENCES

1. Cf. the Editorial Introduction by Professor C. A. Mace to Mrs Frieda Fordham's book An Introduction to Jung's Psychology, Penguin Books, 1959, p. 7.

2. Battle for the Mind, p. 21 (37).

3. Eysenck, H. J., Uses and Abuses of Psychology, Penguin Books 1953, see especially Ch. 12.

4. Brown, J. A. C., Freud and the Post-Freudians, Penguin Books 1961, pp. 190-6.

5. Op. cit., pp. 65-8.

6. Stafford-Clark, David, Psychiatry To-day, Penguin Books 1952, Ch. 7 and especially pp. 173-7.

7. Quoted from his article in the Church of England Newspaper, in his Foreword to Mental Pain and the Cure of Souls by H. Guntrip, Independent Press, London 1956, p. 7.

8. Guntrip, op. cit., pp. 169-70. For a fuller discussion of this important issue see Dr Guntrip's later works Personality Structure and Human Interaction, The Hogarth Press, and The Institute of Psycho-analysis, London 1961, Ch. III, and especially Healing the Sick Mind, George Allen and Unwin Ltd., London 1964, Ch. 11. (This latter book I regard as by far the best introduction to the meaning and purpose of psycho-analysis that I have read.)

9. Eysenck, op. cit., pp. 210-11.

10. Mowrer, O. Hobart, The Crisis in Psychiatry and Religion, D. Van Nostrand Company Ltd., New Jersey 1961.

11. Cf. an almost parallel case quoted by Guntrip, Healing the Sick Mind, pp. 149-50.

12. Sargant, op. cit., p. xix (16). Cf. Dr Sargant's Watson Smith Lecture (see note 12, Ch. I). In the section dealing with psychotherapy in this lecture, the subject is treated almost entirely in terms of drug abreaction, and we find the same failure to understand the significance of abreaction, and mistaken stress on suggestibility that are characteristic of Dr Sargant's earlier writings.

13. Stafford-Clark, op. cit., p. 196.

14. Brown, op. cit., p. 215.

15. In his essay on 'Individual Treatment in Psychiatry' included in Christian Essays in Psychiatry edited by Philip Mairet, S.C.M. Press, London 1956, p. 128.

16. Op. cit., pp. 130-1.

17. Stafford-Clark, op .cit., p. 173.

18. Mental Pain and the Cure of Souls, p. 171.

19. Walker, Nigel, A. Short History of Psychotherapy, Routledge & Kegan Paul, London 1957, p. 114.

20. Battle for the Mind, p. 44 (56).

21. Ibid., pp. 14-16 (32-3). Frolov, Y. P., Pavlov and his School, pp. 214-16.

22. Sargant, op. cit., pp. 47-51 (58-61).

23. Ibid., p. 38 (50-1).

24. Ibid., pp. 45 and 52 (56 and 62).

CHAPTER 5

MEANS AND ENDS

Most Christian readers of *Battle for the Mind* will probably feel
as I do, that if Dr Sargant's account of Wesley's work were true,
then it would seriously discredit the eighteenth century Evangelical Revival and, indeed, give us some grave misgivings about the
whole practice of evangelism. It is rather significant then that
Dr Sargant himself does not see the matter this way. Although
he is quite convinced that the methods used by Wesley to win
converts were essentially similar to modern brainwashing techniques, he is also at great pains to assure his readers that he
intends no attack on religion. In the Foreword he says: 'Having
beliefs of my own, and owing much to a religious upbringing, I
am particularly anxious to give as little offence as possible to
readers who may hold similar or quite different religious tenets.'[1]
   The Foreword opens with these words:

'It must be emphasized as strongly as possible that this book is
not concerned with the truth or falsity of any particular religious or political belief. Its purpose is to examine some of the
mechanisms involved in the fixing or destroying of such beliefs
in the human brain. Some critics will perhaps doubt whether it
is possible to separate two parts of a whole in this way. But if a
greater understanding of the problem is ever to be achieved,
continued attempts must be made to do so.'[1]

Now, I doubt whether it *is* possible to separate two parts of a
whole in the exact way in which Dr Sargant tries to do it, and I
believe that his attempt to do so has unwittingly contributed to
a greater *mis*understanding of the problem. However, he further
stresses the same point by saying that his study ' . . . is concerned
with brain mechanics, not with the ethical and philosophical
aspects of a problem which others are very much more com-
petent to discuss'.[1]

At the level of conscious thought and intention, we must of course accept the sincerity of these assurances. No doubt, Dr Sargant sincerely intends to imply nothing with regard to the 'truth or falsity of any particular religious or political belief', and to avoid offending 'the religious or ethical susceptibility of any reader'.[2] However, in neither of these intentions does he succeed, and I cannot escape the impression that despite his scientific training, his thinking is unfortunately subject to a certain emotional blind-spot which prevents him from seeing the plain logical consequences of his own views, and probably also accounts for his peculiar attitude towards depth psychology on the one hand, and the faith of his fathers on the other.

Many Christian readers may not have any clear idea of the psychology of conversion, but most of them, I think, would consider that whatever actually goes on, the changes that take place in the personality of the Christian convert are not only different from those involved in brainwashing and indoctrination, but diametrically opposed to them; they are changes in the other direction. When we are told then, that the mass conversions of the Evangelical Revival were examples of brainwashing, the initial reaction is one of disillusionment. However, Dr Sargant does not intend any attack on the Evangelical Revival. Indeed no; he seems to be almost an admirer of 'Wesley the master brain-washer'. In fact the reader soon realizes that he is not discrediting Wesley's conversions at all, but commending them. He is saying in effect that apart from some vague exceptions, this is what Christian conversion is — a form of brainwashing for benign purposes — and see how well Wesley did it! This assertion is of course far more serious than any deliberate attack on the Evangelical Revival would have been. It strikes right at the heart of the whole Christian belief about conversion.

In Christian conversion the whole movement is not towards enslavement, but towards liberation of personality. Jesus said that he had come ' . . . to preach deliverance to the captives . . . to set at liberty them that are bruised'.[3] To those who would be his 'disciples indeed' he promised 'Ye shall know the truth, and the truth shall make you free',[4] and when some of the bystanders objected that they were 'Abraham's seed and were never in bondage to any man', he pointed to their spiritual bondage from which he had come to liberate them: 'Verily, verily, I say

unto you, Whosoever committeth sin is the servant of sin. And
the servant abideth not in the house for ever; but the Son abideth
forever. If the Son therefore shall make you free, ye shall be free
indeed.'[4] In the words of William Robinson already quoted, 'The
New Testament gives us a picture of God's relationship with
men in which the appeal of God is always to the responsible
choice of the individual.'[5]

The call of Jesus to men was a call to autonomy and responsibility: 'Henceforth I call you not servants . . . but I have called
you friends.'[6] And John Wesley struck the authentic note of
Christian experience when he described his own conversion in
terms of a transition from 'the faith of a servant to the faith of
a son'.[7]

There is a similar emphasis on the importance of freedom as a
mark of the new life in Christ, in the writings of St Paul. 'Where
the Spirit of the Lord is, there is liberty.'[8]

'For as many as are led by the Spirit of God, they are the sons
of God. For ye have not received the spirit of bondage again to
fear.'[9]

Paul's great struggle to disentangle the religion of grace from
the religion of law, was really his effort, while preserving the
positive values of the law, to set men free from the compulsive
(super-ego) morality it had come to represent, into the spontaneous morality of love, and the 'glorious liberty of the children
of God'.[10] While the Church may sometimes have neglected this
New Testament idea of conversion, and all too often denied it in
practice, I think that Dr Erik Routley is right in maintaining
that one of the distinctive results of Christian conversion is that
the person now does good out of a genuine love of goodness
rather than out of a mere sense of duty.[11] Psychologists will
recognize such a change as a significant gain in real freedom.

As opposed to all this, what revolts us about the whole business of brainwashing and indoctrination is that it is a deliberate
attempt to enslave another's personality, to impose one person's
will on another, to infringe his personal liberty and integrity;
by stress, fear and the use of suggestion to get past his critical
judgment and make him accept as 'his own' patterns of belief
and behaviour which are in fact predetermined and stamped on
his mind by someone else. Brainwashing and indoctrination,
then, are essentially an assault on personality, a process of

undermining genuine spontaneity and restricting psychological or spiritual freedom.

In terms of the psychological distinctions made at the end of the last chapter,[12] brainwashing belongs to the first category, of a process of breakdown under strain, restriction of freedom through repression and the substituting of compulsive behaviour patterns for normal conduct. On the other hand what Christians mean by conversion belongs to the second category of healing processes, with the breaking of repressions and the consequent enlargement of conscious personality and the appearance of spontaneous behaviour in the place of compulsions. It is Dr Sargant's failure to make the all important distinction between these two quite different types of psychological process which enables him, somewhat blandly, to tell us that conversion is a form of brainwashing; and at the same time to imagine that he is not saying anything to which a Christian should take exception.

In the light of these facts we must assess the use which Dr Sargant makes of the familiar doctrine, that the end justifies the means. In discussing any application of this doctrine it is always important to distinguish between the end that is intended and the end that is actually achieved. We may easily change the means, without changing the end that we *intend* to achieve, but I doubt whether we can very often change the means without a corresponding change in the end result that we actually *do* achieve.

In the Foreword of *Battle for the Mind* we are told that ' . . . the ultimate test of both political and religious values is not definable in terms of *how it happens*, but of *what is achieved*'.[13] Now the gist of my argument so far is that what is achieved in any process akin to brainwashing is something quite different from what is achieved in genuine conversion, and it is different because of how it happens.

It must not be thought that this distinction is based on purely theoretical considerations. Most Christian ministers and indeed most Church people who have moved around at all have met the products of religious brainwashing, and are well acquainted with their characteristics. The difference between such people and one who is genuinely converted may not be easy to define or even to describe with any precision, but they are certainly recognizable to the careful observer, and they are of great practical importance. It is not simply a matter of *what* a person believes, but *how* he believes. We may have two people who give assent to the same creed and the same principles of conduct but may, nevertheless, be in two quite different spiritual and psychological states. It is true that the person who has been religiously brainwashed rather than genuinely converted usually does tend to have certain typical emphases or distortions of both belief and conduct, but these are only secondary and derivative. The real differences between such people and the genuine convert are not so much in the intellectual content of their beliefs nor in the formal standards of their behaviour, as in the depth and freedom of their personality that are expressed, or not expressed, through these things.

Dr Sargant's effort to avoid dealing with the ethical implications of the problem does not of course succeed. In fact the whole idea of the scientist *qua* scientist being a sort of amoral being whose work is removed from the realm of ethical judgments and responsibility has shown up somewhat badly in our day as a dangerous piece of wishful thinking. Readers of *Battle for the Mind* are left in no doubt that in the view of the author, brainwashing, indoctrination and kindred processes because they are simply means to an end, are in themselves morally neutral. What makes them either good or bad is simply the purpose for which they are used. Now this is actually an ethical judgment of far reaching importance. There is no sensationalism in *Battle for the Mind*, no anti-Communist hysteria, but Dr Sargant regards brainwashing (as practised by the Communists) as an 'assault made on the fortress of integrity',[14] which must be resisted in every way possible. The evil of this sort of thing is so self-evident that it can be taken for granted. However, it is just as quietly taken for granted that, used for the right purposes, to implant the right beliefs or behaviour patterns, these very methods are quite acceptable. Having decided to his own satisfaction that John Wesley's methods were essentially the same as those of the brainwashers or those which Pavlov used to produce breakdown in his dogs, Dr Sargant says

' . . . so here John Wesley's methods and results will be selected as typical of those seen in an effective and socially valuable religious setting. Nobody can doubt their religious efficacy or social value; for his preaching converted people by the thousands, and he also built up an efficient system for perpetuating these beliefs.'[15]

Discussing 'Brainwashing in Religion and Politics', he says 'All such methods can be used to bring about some of man's noblest patterns of living. But we must also realize how they can be used to destroy them'.[16] The same point, regarding the possibility of using brainwashing and indoctrination for either good or bad ends is made again in the final chapter: 'If we are to promote true religion, preserve our democratic ways of life and our hard-won civil liberties we must learn to recognize that these same methods are being used for trivial or evil purposes instead of noble ones.'[17]

All this, as I have already pointed out, rests on the implicit ethical judgment that brainwashing and similar methods of changing people's beliefs and behaviour are in themselves morally neutral and become either good or bad only in terms of the purpose for which they are used. With this judgment I profoundly disagree. I am absolutely convinced that such methods are not evil because the Communists use them — they are intrinsically evil no matter who uses them, or for what purpose. To my mind they represent a flat denial not only of the spiritual values of the Gospel, but of anything recognizable as morality, and no amount of good intentions or noble purpose will alter this in any fundamental way. No matter what social changes may be brought about in this way or how 'happy' the victims may be made to feel as a result, I cannot believe that there are any genuine human values that can be promoted by the use of methods which undermine spiritual freedom and destroy personal integrity. I cannot argue this at any length here, but simply state it with the fullest possible conviction. Indeed it seems to me personally that this may prove to be one of the most important watersheds of human conviction in our modern world.

A few more pages of mechanistic psychology may not be much help to genuine human understanding, a debunking of the Evangelical Revival, whether intended or not, is naturally rather disturbing to Methodists, and a garbled account of the work of

John Wesley may leave them justly annoyed, but none of these things is of first rank importance. However, when Dr Sargant develops his line of thought to its logical conclusion, and suggests in all seriousness that the Church should understand and deliberately make use of the brainwashing type of method to propagate the faith, I believe that his book ceases to be merely mistaken or confused, and in spite of the author's intention, becomes in the most radical sense anti-Christian.

We are told that

'All evidence goes to show that there can be no new Protestant Revival while the policy continues of appealing mainly to adult intelligence and reason, and until Church leaders consent to take more advantage of the normal person's emotional mechanism for disrupting old behaviour patterns and implanting new.'[18]

Dr Sargant agrees with what he considers was Dr Johnson's view, that in order to convert the common (uneducated) people 'one has to try to overwhelm them emotionally',[19] and in his final summing up he says:

'Must a new concentration on brain psychology and brain mechanics weaken religious faith and beliefs? On the contrary a better understanding of the means of creating and consolidating faith will enable religious bodies to expand much more rapidly. The preacher can rest assured that the less mysteriously "God works his wonders to perform", the easier it should be to provide people with an essential knowledge and love of God.'[20]

To anyone at all sensitive to the mission, frustrations and temptations of the Church in our day, this last quotation will open up a whole vista of distasteful possibilities, I think.

In the long and varied history of the Church there is so much in which we should glory, and be deeply grateful to God for, but there are other things too—things that should make us burn with shame. I think it has to be admitted that at times the Church has resorted to tactics which were in principle not very different from modern methods of brainwashing and indoctrination, and has usually thought that she served God thereby. Nor have these things been the exclusive responsibility of any one tradition or branch of the Church either; we all have elements of well meaning devilry that stain our heritage of grace. There are a variety of ways of doing this sort of thing, of course; it is not necessary to subject the victim to torture or the fear of burning, to take him through harrowing meditations on the horrors of hell, or work on him through highly emotional preaching or crowd suggestion. There are much more subtle, respectable and friendly ways of engineering consent in our day; and unfortunately there are still well meaning people within the organization of the Church who are so insensitive to the real meaning of the Gospel that they would be eager to use them. With regard to the Church's failings in the past in this way, I doubt whether any pleas of either ignorance or good intentions will really exonerate us. But with the modern methods that are available, and in the light of what we now know of both the ethical principles and the psychological processes involved, any well-meaning suggestion that we should deliberately make use of such methods as a 'means of creating and consolidating faith' or 'to provide people with an essential knowledge and love of God', I find completely obnoxious, and I believe that if the Church were ever carried away by it, we should be guilty of a more gross betrayal of the Gospel than we have ever made before.

I cannot conceive of any more important or far reaching ethical issue facing the human race in our day than this one: to what extent (if at all) and in what circumstances, is it ever right to use methods of persuasion and changing men's beliefs or behaviour, that deliberately infringe their personal integrity and restrict their genuine initiative and spontaneity by imposing our will on theirs? Is it ever right to exploit states of emotional excitement or heightened suggestibility in such a way that a person's normal exercise of critical judgment is inhibited? And he will, on our suggestion, accept as his own beliefs or practices which he would in ordinary circumstances repudiate? Of course, if we happen to live West of the Iron Curtain, most of us would agree that the use of the sort of methods described by Dr Sargant, in order to make people toe the Communist line, is thoroughly bad. But we do not see the matter clearly if we simply leave it here, for the real ethical issue to be faced has no essential connection with either Communism or cruelty. What if the persuader is acting from the highest motives, for the good of the other person? What if the belief he is trying to implant by such methods is obviously true, and the behaviour pattern he is trying to impose would make the other person much happier and more socially acceptable? What if the methods used were not at all crude, violent or painful, but quite the reverse? . . . Would it still be wrong to indoctrinate in this way? That is the crucial question, and it is not at all a fanciful or hypothetical one.

The point in stating the question like this, is that the ways and means of manipulating human personality are many and varied, and the immense growth in recent years of what the Americans call the behavioural sciences is opening up new possibilities in this field. Furthermore, provided that there are available methods of manipulation that are neither crude nor cruel, there seem to be plenty of well-educated and well-intentioned people who are ready to use them for commercial purposes, and some who advocate their much wider use for the social betterment of mankind. Brainwashing of the more violent kind is always something of a special expedient. The rape of the mind is never likely to be respectable, but it will seldom be necessary either. Systematic seduction — betrayal without violence — is likely to become the greater threat. Demagogues and dictators have always known intuitively how to exploit frustrated idealism, the emotional contagion of the crowd, the compulsive desire to conform, and so on, and how to combine this with the judicious use of threat and terror. Adolf Hitler knew a great deal about this, but in the light of post-war developments in both the media of mass communication and the psychology of thought control, even his amazingly effective propaganda machine would probably appear, by modern standards, crude and obsolete.

Dr Robert Oppenheimer told the American Psychological Association in 1955 that 'the problems that psychologists will pose for society by their growing ability to control behaviour will be much more grave than the problems posed by the ability of physicists to control the reactions of matter'.[21]

Vance Packard in his well-known book *The Hidden Persuaders*[22] has given us a glimpse of the large-scale attempt at the psychological manipulation of human personality in the field of advertising and salesmanship. Motivational Research is undertaken in a quite ambitious way, in order to discover the unconscious motivations of a potential buying public, that can be deliberately exploited without their knowledge or consent, to create or stimulate a demand for a particular product or a quite irrational preference for a particular brand. Those who are sceptical or uncomprehending about depth psychology may doubt the effectiveness of this sort of thing. However it is notable that out of the one hundred largest advertising agencies in the United States over sixty of them, at the time when Packard wrote, were using this depth approach.[23] Both the basic research and the sales promotion programmes based on its results were heavily financed by large business concerns whose directors are not prone to throw away thousands of dollars on mere whimsical ideas. The underlying principle of this 'merchandizing in depth' or the 'engineering of consent', as it is termed when applied to public relations, can be understood by means of the well-known phenomenon of post-hypnotic suggestion. A person under hypnosis may be told by the hypnotist, for example, that in half an hour's time he will get up and open the window. When he comes out of the trance he will remember nothing of what transpired but exactly half an hour later he will rise and open the window. Asked why he does this, he will probably explain that he thinks the room is getting stuffy, or that 'It's time we had some fresh air'. These rationalizations, supplied by his own mind, he will take at their face value and be quite unaware of the fact that he is actually opening the window because the hypnotist told him he would. In a somewhat similar manner, the 'depth approach' in advertising seeks to implant in the minds of potential consumers, certain suggestions which will influence them powerfully without either their knowledge or consent, because in this case they are geared to some strong unconscious motivation in their personalities. The customer can thus be influenced to adopt a brand preference which has nothing to do with any objective qualities of that particular brand as distinct from others. Of course he will firmly believe that he buys this particular brand of cigarette because he prefers the taste of the tobacco, or is convinced on quite rational grounds that it is less likely to give him lung cancer, and be happily unaware of the fact that he has been manipulated to do this through a careful study and exploitation of unconscious processes in his own mind.

The extent to which human behaviour can be influenced by such methods may still be a matter of dispute, but surely one of the most significant things which Vance Packard's book does show us is that large numbers of trained psychologists in the United States who believe such methods *do* work, some of them university teachers, are quite prepared to sell their knowledge and skill to the advertising business in order to dupe the general public or exploit them for commercial gain. Is this not another melancholy example of the modern prostitution of science? No doubt the usual arguments in defence will be urged—that the scientist is simply a researcher and technician, concerned with gaining and applying knowledge, and cannot be held morally responsible for the use that others make of his work. Or the usual rationalizations, about competitive big business being in the public interest, may be used, and in spite of the fact that the consuming public has to pay the cost of this colossal fraud, some would suggest that advertising of this kind is, all things considered, more or less legitimate even if not particularly commendable or high minded. But what happens when these same methods come to be employed for political purposes? Do the Behavioural Scientists still maintain their fiction of moral neutrality? In this regard Carl Rogers has this to say:

'To hope that the power which is being made available by the behavioral sciences will be exercised by the scientists, or by a benevolent group, seems to me a hope little supported by either recent or distant history. It seems far more likely that behavioral scientists, holding their present attitudes, will be in the position of the German rocket scientists specializing in guided missiles. First they worked devotedly for Hitler to destroy the USSR and the United States. Now, depending on who captured them, they work devotedly for the USSR in the interest of destroying the United States, or devotedly for the United States in the interest of destroying the USSR. If behavioral scientists are concerned solely with advancing their science, it seems most probable that they will serve the purposes of whatever individual or group has the power.'[24]

Vance Packard tells how the psychological manipulators began to turn their attention to politics in the United States in the nineteen fifties and he quotes from the *New York World-Telegram* describing preparations for the 1950 Congressional Campaign: '... the politicians are beginning to apply all the smart advertising techniques used by mass production America to merchandize autos, bath salts and lawn mowers'.[25]

The 'persuaders' began to work on political campaigning as a form of merchandizing, and according to Packard

'... in a few short years, climaxing in the Presidential campaign of 1956, they made spectacular strides in changing the traditional characteristics of American political life. They were able to do this by drawing upon the insights of Pavlov and his conditioned reflexes, Freud and his father images, Reisman and his concept of modern American voters as spectator-consumers of politics, and Batten, Barton, Durstine and Osborn and their mass merchandizing lore.'[26]

In the opening chapter of his book *Techniques of Persuasion* Dr. J. A. C. Brown describes some of the features of modern mass society that press in upon men the feeling that they are '... being subjected, openly or by hidden means, to psychological pressures applied by those who hold the real power in mass society.'[27]

Contrasting the 'eighteenth century view of a society with that of the new mass society' he says:

'In mass society, on the other hand, many more people receive opinions than are able effectively to express them; for the public has become a conglomeration of individuals who have to accept their beliefs and ideas through the new mass media. Communications are such that effective answering back is almost impossible, and there is consequently reduced hope that opinion can be realized in action, since the channels of action are controlled by the authorities. Finally, there is no autonomy from government recognized institutions; for these reach down into the masses ...'[28]

Commenting on the influence of the media of mass communication he says:

'... for even in the democracies the radio and television are controlled either directly or indirectly by the government or, worse still, by commercial companies paid by advertisers who "give the public what it wants"—that is, according to this view, the rubbish it has been conditioned to want. In non-totalitarian countries there still exists the theoretical possibility of playing one medium off against another, but this becomes less and less realistic, firstly because most people tend to get all their information from the same newspapers, radio stations and periodicals and are rarely seeking counter-opinions to their own; secondly, because genuine competition between media is often more apparent than real.'[29]

Finally, commenting on the lot of the person living under a totalitarian regime, he says:

'Yet (paradoxically, because the authoritarian's use of power is open and naked like that in the Middle Ages) it may be that the citizen living under these circumstances feels less manipulated than the American or Englishman whose real fear is of the "hidden persuaders" who attempt to manipulate him unawares.'[30]

The general effect of Dr Brown's book seems to be to reassure us that there are very real limits to the extent of the changes that can be effected in human behaviour and belief by these hidden persuaders. I hope we can rely on this reassurance, but I should think that the well-documented accounts of the changes they *can* make are disturbing enough. The sense of a coming mass society which will be a 'world of unseen dictatorship . . . still using the forms of democratic government'[31] is something of a nightmare in a good deal of modern writing. In one of J. B. Priestley's novels, Lord Mervil, a cynical and successful man, says:

'Now we're rapidly arriving at a time when a few men, who know their own minds, can dominate and use millions of people who have to have their minds made up for them. It's as simple as that. Don't think the trend can be reversed; it's gone too far and it's moving too fast. Mass communications become stronger in their effects every year. This is inevitable. People in the mass are not only losing their independence but are losing any desire to be independent and active-minded, sharply differentiated individuals. They prefer a mass existence, mass standards with which they feel more comfortable in their circles.'[32]

Brushing aside the misgivings of his companion who says 'I agree, but I don't know that I like it', Mervil continues:

'There's no need to shake our head over it, even if we're feeling benevolent and noble. At last people in the mass are getting what they want. They want reasonable security, food and clothes and shelter and medical attention, some education, but not too much, easy work, no trouble, no worry, no loneliness and fear, mass emotions, mass entertainment, a smooth road from the cradle to the grave. They've known for some time now that life is essentially meaningless, so they want to get through their share of it as painlessly as possible. Now here is something I've proved over and over again, risking my fortune, my career. Move in that direction, along that smooth road, and at once you succeed. Go the other way and you're up against a wall. Just try selling the mob some real freedom and not just empty talk about it, some hard work, responsibility, solitude and thought, any prospect of suffering—and see how many buyers you have. Very well, we can give them what they want, are giving them what they want.'[32]

The theme is not very new. After all, I don't suppose Mervil's kind of world would be very different in principle from Plato's Republic, except that Plato's kings were to be philosophers instead of business tycoons, with all the technical resources of the twentieth century at their command. Hobbes' Leviathan in the seventeenth century advocated in the most thoroughgoing way the need for the complete control of the masses, with provision for the appropriate indoctrination to keep them submissive and avoid anarchy. With the same essentially benevolent intention Dostoievsky's Grand Inquisitor gives classic expression to the doctrine that the masses should be duped with 'mystery, miracle and magic' to keep them satisfied and submissive to authority for their own good. However, the development of the modern state, the pressures of mass society and the growing knowledge of psychological means of manipulating human personality and 'engineering consent', all combine to bring these theories of despotic control, benevolent or otherwise, within the

F

range of possibility. George Orwell's 1984 gives us a frightening picture of such a society ruthlessly controlled for selfish ends, while Aldous Huxley's *Brave New World* is a brilliant and disturbing satire on the idea of a utopia carefully and completely engineered to provide the maximum of 'happiness' at the expense of any real freedom.

Both these books deserve the epithet of horrifying, but not everyone is horrified. H. J. Eysenck, for example, after describing the various conditioning techniques which he proposes in place of deep psychotherapy, has the insight to add 'Thus does reality catch up with the wild extravagant fantasies of Huxley's *Brave New World!*'[33] Eysenck seems to regard this fact as a matter of commendation rather than a serious indictment of his whole point of view. An attitude very similar to that of Eysenck is adopted by B. F. Skinner, Professor of Psychology in Harvard University, in a remarkable discussion with Dr Carl Rogers on 'Some Issues Concerning the Control of Human Behaviour'.

Skinner is the author of a utopian novel *Walden Two* which he describes as ' . . . essentially a proposal to apply a behavioral technology to the construction of a workable, effective and productive pattern of government.'[34] According to Skinner, 'It was greeted with wrathful violence'. One of the adverse comments he quotes is from *The Quest for Utopia* by Negley and Patrick, who say:

'Halfway through this contemporary utopia, the reader may feel sure, as we did, that this is a beautifully ironic satire on what has been called "behavioral engineering". The longer one stays in this better world of the psychologist, however, the plainer it becomes that the interest is not satiric, but messianic. This is indeed the behaviorally engineered society . . . yet not even the effective satire of Huxley is adequate preparation for the shocking horror of the idea when positively presented. Of all the dictatorships espoused by utopists, this is the most profound, and incipient dictators might well find in this utopia a guidebook of political practice.'[35]

Skinner's own reaction to this is interesting. He writes:
'One would scarcely guess that the authors are talking about a

world in which there is food, clothing, and shelter for all, where everyone chooses his own work and works on the average only four hours a day, where music and the arts flourish, where personal relationships develop under the most favourable circumstances, where education prepares every child for the social and intellectual life which lies before him, where—in short, people are truly happy, secure, productive, creative and forward-looking. What is wrong with it? Only one thing; someone "planned it that way".'[36]

How far people could be 'truly creative and forward-looking' in such an engineered society may be a matter of dispute, but it is significant anyway that Skinner does not deny the charge of dictatorship, but is content to point out that people would be happy to be dictated to. He would probably agree with Rogers' assessment of his position:

'As Skinner has indicated in his writings, we would then look back upon the concepts of human freedom, the capacity for choice, the responsibility for choice, and the worth of the human individual as historical curiosities which once existed by cultural accident as values in a prescientific civilization.'[37]

In contrast to all this Rogers himself wants to move in the direction of a truly open society as distinct from the closed society which *Walden Two* would represent. He therefore believes that

'It is possible for us to choose to value man as a self-actualizing process of becoming; to value creativity, and the process by which knowledge becomes self-transcending, . . . to discover the conditions which necessarily precede these processes . . . to set these conditions . . . (and) establish certain qualities of interpersonal relationship . . . (which will help) individuals to become more self-responsible, make progress in self-actualization, become more flexible, and . . . more creatively adaptive.'[38]

Rogers is, of course, the pioneer of that extremely significant form of psychotherapy known as 'Client-centred' or 'Non-directive' counselling, in which all the stress is on a sincere and unconditional acceptance of the client as a person in his own right. There is a determined effort to avoid, on the one hand, even the most subtle or benign forms of manipulation, and to foster, on the other, the client's own freedom and powers of self-realization. The values which Rogers wants to see promoted in his open society are, then, not a mere matter of theory but concern processes of personal development which he claims to have observed during psychotherapy. It is doubtful whether any other school of psychotherapists have documented and criticized their own work more thoroughly than Rogers and his associates have done.[39] Rogers' own description of the kind of freedom he is interested in is worth quoting:

'The freedom which I have been trying to describe is essentially an inner thing, something which exists in the living person, quite aside from any of the outward choice of alternatives which we so often think of as constituting freedom. I am speaking of the kind of freedom which Frankl vividly describes in his experience of the concentration camp, when everything—possessions, identity, choice—was taken from the prisoners. But even months and years in such an environment showed only "that everything can be taken from a man but one thing: the last of the human freedoms—to choose one's own attitude in any given set of circumstances, to choose one's own way". It is this inner, subjective, existential freedom which I have observed. It is the realization that "I can live myself, here and now, by my own choice". It is the quality of courage which enables a person to step into the uncertainty of the unknown as he chooses himself. It is the discovery of meaning from within oneself, meaning which comes from listening sensitively and openly to the complexities of what one is experiencing. It is the burden of being responsible for the self one chooses to be. It is the recognition by the person that he is an emerging process, not a static end product. The individual who is thus deeply and courageously thinking his own thoughts, becoming his own uniqueness, responsibly choosing himself, may be fortunate in having hundreds of objective outer alternatives from which to choose, or he may be unfortunate in having none, but this freedom exists regardless.'[40]

In the light of this conception of freedom the full seriousness of all forms of psychological manipulation should be evident, for while all other kinds of domination may restrict his outward freedom, it is the propagandist, the brainwasher, the 'hidden persuader' that seeks deliberately to take from man what Frankl calls 'the last of the human freedoms' and to enslave him in the inner citadel of his being. What Skinner doesn't seem to realize is that no amount of happiness, security or material bounty could possibly justify this. As Jesus said, 'What shall it profit a man if he shall gain the whole world and lose his own soul?'[41] The biggest threat to our spiritual well-being and freedom then, will come not from the obviously malign brainwasher or the political tyrant, but from those who, like Skinner himself, have nothing but the good intention of making us happy—so damned happy, we'll be happy to be damned!

There is then, I would suggest, scarcely any more important choice before us than that between the diametrically opposed views represented respectively by Skinner and Rogers. Which one we align ourselves with, will ultimately depend on our view of human nature—and here we return to Dr Sargant's book and the deeper implications of his general viewpoint. I have already argued in Chapter 2 that a purely mechanistic view of human personality should be rejected because it is untrue. But what is involved in its untruth? Far more than a mere error in reasoning, or ignorance of the facts. Basically a mechanistic view of human nature rests on an *evaluation* of certain facts. It is a value judgment.

It must be admitted that man is to a very great extent involved in determinism. Physically he is subject to all the necessary causal processes of organic chemistry and physiology, as well as the more obvious laws of motion and mechanics. Psychologically he is subject to various compulsions that influence his thought and his behaviour from below the level of consciousness, and while they remain thus, are therefore beyond his knowledge or control. Socially he is born into a ready-made world of custom, convention and public opinion that exerts its pressures upon him throughout his entire lifetime, in ways both subtle and powerful; and his practical freedom of movement and enterprise is limited by his own physical needs and the material resources of the world, linked together by a maze of economic process which he seldom understands and can usually do little to alter. But tell it all out at length, and still the whole is not told about man; there is much more to him than all this, and the crucial question is how we evaluate this 'much more'.

There is so much truly human enterprise and experience that simply cannot be accounted for in terms of determinism and the network of forces that bear on man's conscious personality from outside. There is his experience and exercise of freedom without which so much human undertaking would lack all the meaning and purpose which man is convinced it bears — a freedom, incidentally, which in the face of external threat he always insists on treating as real and important; even when, like Pavlov, he solemnly uses it to propound deterministic theories of human behaviour. There is man's acknowledgement of moral obligation —the 'ought' that always implies the 'can', and the inescapable sense of moral responsibility which springs from the profound conviction that his choices are real choices in which he participates as agent, and not simply as the spectator of some inevitable process that goes on in the mind. Now if we are prepared to treat all this human experience of freedom, morality and responsibility as a mere illusion to be explained away, a trivial detail that can be safely ignored, or a temporary anomaly that will sooner or later be reduced to scientific (i.e. deterministic) terms, then we can take a mechanistic view of human personality. On the other hand, we may evaluate this side of human nature quite differently and see man's freedom, though as yet limited in scope, as the most typically *human* thing about him, to be increased in every way possible so that he becomes less at the mercy of the causal processes that flow through his being, and more able to use them for his own purposes and self-chosen goals. This view of human nature I will call the personalistic one; it is, I am sure, the only estimate of man that is consistent with Christianity, but it is of course accepted also by many humanists like Dr Carl Rogers.

If we take the mechanistic view of human personality, then the *most* we can hope to do for man is to make him happy; if we take the personalistic view, the *least* we can try to do is to set him free. Now these are two quite different programmes. We can in some sense *make* a person happy, but we can never *make* him free. We can refuse to enslave him or dominate him, we can try to break through other things that are enslaving him, and encourage him to break free. We can try to help him towards a personal relationship with God who will both enable and encourage his freedom at deeper levels of his being than any human person can . . . but finally neither God nor man can force him to be free. As a matter of faith and on the basis of some experience we may believe that man's growth in freedom will eventually increase his happiness, but in the meantime, before this becomes clear, the process of liberation is often going to be more disturbing than enjoyable. Modern totalitarian movements and tendencies towards conformism, the resurgence of authoritarian religion, and elements of our own experience show us that when it comes to a point, there is much in all of us that would rather draw back and avoid the responsibility of freedom.[42]

If we then decide to regard our fellow man as basically an automaton, a complex stimulus-response machine, and particularly if we do this with the benign intention of making him happy, this is not a mere matter of theory; we are *doing* something to him. We are encouraging him to sink back into this essentially subhuman level of being, or perhaps never to emerge from it—to remain a happy puppet rather than endure the growing pains of becoming a responsible person. By our very attitude towards him we have taken a major step towards actually reducing him to the condition of a mere machine. What I am trying to say is that the theoretical devaluation of human nature, wholeheartedly accepted for any purpose at all, will sooner or later result in the practical degradation of man. I cannot agree then that Pavlov's 'limited mechanistic approach' is simply a methodological device; more fundamentally it is an *attitude towards man* which will either permit or promote social and political movements that bring about his spiritual enslavement and degradation. It should be noted that this fact has little or nothing to do with the actual ethical or political intentions of the person who expounds such views, but is a logical outworking of the hidden value judgment that underlies them.

As Dr Sargant is careful to point out, Pavlov was not a typical scientist of the Soviet regime. He did much of his best work before the Revolution, and for most of his life remained a somewhat irascible and outspoken critic of the new order. We may agree that

' . . . it is extremely doubtful whether he ever foresaw that his work could be used as an instrument of Soviet policy. Since he always demanded and obtained freedom of thought for himself, it is unlikely that he would have wished to curtail freedom of thought for others.'[43]

Yet at a deeper level than his political intentions, the Communists must have found Pavlov's fundamental attitude towards human nature completely congenial. Indeed both movements grew up together in the same soil, for, as shown by Pavlov's biographer, there was already in pre-Revolutionary Russia a strong movement towards a completely mechanistic interpretation of human nature, under the influence of the physiologist Sechenov.[44] While the determinism postulated by the Marxists was basically economic rather than physiological, both movements could find common cause in rejecting any personalistic doctrine of human nature, ignoring the possibility of spiritual freedom, and regarding man as completely dominated by various forces that could be manipulated either for his happiness or his misery.

Before we leave this discussion of the ethical issues, we should perhaps enquire how far science is committed to the sort of mechanistic interpretation of human nature which Pavlov and Dr Sargant adopt. Many scientists would probably claim that this is the scientific view of man, but if this were the case, then in the light of our discussion we should have to conclude that the scientific account of human nature is profoundly inimical to human welfare and human values. But I cannot believe this to be the case. Quite apart from the immense practical benefits which it bestows upon us, the pursuit of science requires in some respects at least, qualities of character of the highest moral order; qualities which are quite incompatible with a mechanistic view of man. After all, if we leave aside for a moment the secondary questions of method and technique, surely the essentially scientific attitude has never been better described than in the famous words of T. H. Huxley: 'The willingness to sit down humbly before the facts.' Now it is precisely this which the mechanistic view of man does not do, because as we have already seen, it decides beforehand to ignore certain facts, or to explain them away as unimportant or illusory. Thus no matter how much scientific jargon it may employ in argument, the mechanistic view of human nature is essentially *unscientific* in the primary and most important sense. It was undoubtedly a good thing when psychology broke free from philosophy, so that it could look for its own facts instead of being merely the subject of *a priori* theories; but it would be rather ironical if it were now to be tied down to the procrustean bed of a science that dictated beforehand how much of its subject matter could be treated and how much ignored.

Most of the common elements of the scientific method—the disinterested pursuit of truth, reliance on observation, correlation of data and inductive reasoning, the making, testing and modification of hypotheses—are compatible with a personalistic view of human nature, although some of them will call for a more difficult discipline on the part of the scientist dealing with persons rather than with things. However so long as we deal with man as a person, we shall be able to make only a very limited use of either experiment or quantitative measurement. It is this fact which will cause misunderstanding between the academic psychologist like H. J. Eysenck who is primarily interested in such methods, and the depth psychologist who must try to understand his patient as a person.

Underlying this particular tension there is a rather more profound issue which science must face. We do not know or observe *persons* in the same way as we know or observe *things*. In terms of Martin Buber's famous distinction we may say that in most branches of science the appropriate attitude of the scientist towards his subject is an 'I-It' attitude, but when we are dealing with persons as persons, the only appropriate attitude is an 'I-Thou' attitude. These are two quite different attitudes and should not be confused. Because man is partly immersed in the determinisms of nature and society, as well as transcending them, some aspects of his being can be investigated by the typical 'I-It' methods of physical science—experiment and measurement. However we must not imagine that once having tested and measured a particular individual in a variety of ways, we can assemble the results to make a sort of composite picture of him as a person. That would be like trying to take a number of sections of a flat map—say a Mercator's projection, and assemble them together into a globe. As a *person* man can only be known in some form of genuine 'I-Thou' encounter.

It is the tendency of scientists to carry over the 'I-It' attitudes that are typical of most branches of science and to apply them quite inappropriately to the study of man that underlies the mechanistic view of human nature which is always a potential threat to man's integrity as a person. Now I am not trying to lay the whole blame for this on science or the scientists. After all, the inability or unwillingness to adopt genuine 'I-Thou' attitudes is a very common human failing, and the tendency to devaluate man and treat him as a thing rather than as a person, is much older than science and had been operating to distort every other aspect of human life, including religion, centuries before science came on the scene. In fact this tendency is surely one of the most persistent expressions of that radical distortion of our nature which the theologians call original sin. But when this perversion becomes linked with the technical competence of science and its well-deserved prestige in the modern world, we may well have another instance of the worst being the corruption of the best.

I would suggest then that science is in no way committed to a mechanistic view of human nature. Whether there can be such a thing as a scientific view of human nature at all will depend, in the long run, on the ability of science to admit genuinely 'I-Thou' attitudes into its study of man. If this does not happen, then the psychology of personality will be under constant stress of distortion in the direction of the 'I-It', and in order to preserve its authentic character may have to break away again, and while maintaining most of the features of a science, declare itself to be a study *sui generis*, just as its subject, man as a person, is *sui generis*.[45]

FOOTNOTES AND REFERENCES

1. *Battle for the Mind*, p. xi (9).

2. *Ibid.*, p. 235 (214-15).

3. Luke 4.18. William Manson comments on the whole of this verse: 'The term *the poor* is to be taken in its inward spiritual sense ... and similarly the expressions *captive, blind, oppressed* indicate not primarily the down-trodden victims of material

force, such as Rome's, but the victims of inward repressions, neuroses and other spiritual ills due to misdirection and failure of life's energies and purposes.' Manson, William, D.D., *The Gospel of Luke*, The Moffatt New Testament Commentary, H. & S., London 1930, pp. 41-2.

4. John 8.31-6.
5. Robinson, William D., M.Th., 'Personal Persuasion' in *The London Quarterly & Holborn Review*, July 1962, p. 216 (above, Ch. 1, p. 18).
6. John 15.15.
7. Wesley's *Journal* (Standard edition edited by Nehemiah Curnock), Vol. I, footnotes on pp. 422-3.
8. II Corinthians 3.17.
9. Romans 8.15.
10. Romans 8.21.
11. Routley, Erik, *The Gift of Conversion*.
12. Above, Ch. 4, p. 65.
13. Sargant, *op. cit.*, p. xi (9).
14. *Ibid.*, p. 226 (206).
15. *Ibid.*, p. 76 (82).
16. *Ibid.*, p. 148 (141).
17. *Ibid.*, p. 235 (215). Dr Sargant has apparently continued to believe that such methods can be used for either good or bad purposes. In a lecture on 'Brainwashing, conversion and mass hysteria' arranged for young people by the Royal Society of Medicine fairly recently, he is reported as saying that 'such methods can be dangerous and used for good and evil'. (Quoted from a press report in *The Evening Star*, Dunedin, N.Z., January 2, 1965.)
18. *Ibid.*, p. 77 (83).
19. *Ibid.*, p. 235 (214).
20. *Ibid.*, pp. 234 (213-14).
21. Quoted in the discussion between B. F. Skinner and Carl Rogers on 'Some Issues Concerning the Control of Human Behavior' reported in *Pastoral Psychology* (New York), Vol. 13 No. 128 (November 1962), p. 20.
22. Packard, Vance, *The Hidden Persuaders*, David McKay, 1957. References are to the Pelican edition 1962.
23. *Ibid.*, p. 11.
24. Rogers, *op. cit.*, p. 22.

25. Quoted by Packard, *op. cit.*, p. 150.
26. *Ibid.*, pp. 149-50.
27. Brown, J. A. C., *Techniques of Persuasion*, Penguin Books 1963, pp. 34-5.
28. *Ibid.*, p. 32.
29. *Ibid.*, pp. 33-4.
30. *Ibid.*, pp. 35-6.
31. Kenneth Boulding, University of Michigan. Quoted as part of the heading to Ch. 17 in Packard, *op. cit.*, p. 149.
32. Priestley, J. B., *The Magicians*, William Heinemann 1954; Four Square Books 1957, pp. 37-9 (Four Square edition).
33. *Uses and Abuses of Psychology*, p. 216.
34. Skinner, in Skinner and Rogers, *op. cit.*, p. 17.
35. Quoted by Skinner, in Skinner and Rogers, *op. cit.*, p. 18.
36. Skinner, in Skinner and Rogers, *op. cit.*, p. 18.
37. Rogers, in Skinner and Rogers, *op. cit.*, p. 25.
38. Rogers, in Skinner and Rogers, *op. cit.*, p. 27.
39. See, for example, Carl Rogers' *Client-Centered Therapy*, Houghton Mifflin Company, Boston 1951, *passim*.
40. 'Learning to be Free' (Part one) in *Pastoral Psychology* Vol. 13 No. 128, November 1962, p. 51.

Christian readers will probably be uneasy about the Pelagianism implied in this quotation, and indeed in all the work of Carl Rogers and his associates. 'Client-centred counselling' arose of course within humanism, and does appear to share the essentially Pelagian assumptions of that tradition. However, if we do encounter God in the depths of our being and in the depths of our meeting with others (and here I believe Paul Tillich and J. A. T. Robinson are right) then the Pelagianism in Rogers' work may be more apparent than real. (See my article 'Some Theological Reflections on Pastoral Counselling' II, *London Quarterly & Holborn Review*, October 1962, p. 304.)

The quotation from V. E. Frankl is from his book *From Death-Camp to Existentialism*, translated by I. Lasch, Beacon Press, Boston 1959, p. 65.
41. Mark 8.36.
42. See Fromm, Erich, *The Fear of Freedom*, Routledge & Kegan Paul Ltd., London 1942, *passim*.
43. Sargant, *op. cit.*, p. 2 (22).
44. Frolov., Y. P., *Pavlov and his School*.

45. There would still be a place of course for academic psychology with its experimental procedures, tests and statistical methods, but we should need to realize its strict limitations in the understanding of personality. It is interesting to find H. J. Eysenck maintaining that this kind of psychology has nothing to do with 'understanding human nature'. Since he is one who seems to believe that science is committed to 'I-It' attitudes, it is not surprising that he regards psychoanalysis as 'unscientific'. He says that this is in no way to deny its truth-value, but such is the power of prejudice that he cannot maintain this point of view for long. Science is unfortunately a rather emotive word today, and scientific is a prestige term not only for selling soap but even for serious writers. The description unscientific thus carries for most people the suggestion of untrue, inaccurate or just plain woolly. Thus in his chapter headed 'What is wrong with Psychoanalysis?' he gives the answer 'It is unscientific'.—Eysenck, op. cit., Ch. 12.

PART II

HISTORY

CHAPTER 6

FACT AND FICTION

John Wesley was an amazing man, and any reader whose only acquaintance with him is through William Sargant's book should read one of the numerous biographies.[1] After enumerating some of the greatest men of the eighteenth century, the *Cambridge Modern History* adds: 'But more important than any of these in universality of influence and range of achievement, were John Wesley and the religious revival to which he gave his name and his life.'[2]
Again, Augustine Birrell, K.C. wrote:

'No man lived nearer to the centre than John Wesley, neither Pitt nor Clive, neither Mansfield nor Johnson. You cannot cut him out of the national life. No single figure influenced so many minds, no single voice touched so many hearts. No other man did such a life's work for England.'[3]

Even biographers who were partly or wholly unsympathetic to Wesley, such as Southey,[4] Marjorie Bowen[5] and Ronald Knox[6] pay willing or unwilling tribute to his greatness. Nevertheless he was not beyond criticism. Even if Knox's *Profile of John Wesley*[7] is rather biased, it says some shrewd things as well as some unfair ones. Despite his nobility of character and complete freedom from personal ambition, many of Wesley's contemporaries must have felt with considerable justification that he was sometimes a most exasperating person to deal with. Even though he was so often right, some of us lesser men could perhaps love him more if he had not always appeared so quietly and utterly sure about his own rightness. By modern standards of church government and group method he was often distressingly autocratic, and as happens with even the greatest of men, there were occasions when he said or did things that were just plain stupid. But tally

G

it all up against him and he still remains a very great man, and a very human man, and there is certainly no need for one of his modern followers to rise up in hot indignation to defend him against his critics. That is not my motive in examining Dr Sargant's account of his work.

But I shall not pretend to be disinterested in this enquiry, because there are much more important issues at stake than the reputation of John Wesley—issues that have a direct bearing on the theology and practice of the modern church. It has been pointed out, for example, that Wesley was a child of his age, that he lived long before the insights of modern psychology, and that even if he did engage in brainwashing, it was all innocently done and with the best of intentions. Now this may clear Wesley's character, but it does not establish the validity of his methods, and that is the real issue in which we are interested. What we want to know is whether the very numerous conversions of the Evangelical Revival were in fact what history has supposed them to be : a genuine work of divine grace in which men and women were set free for spontoneous Christian living; or whether they were simply due to a process of psychological manipulation, in which Wesley and his preachers imposed their beliefs on people whose capacity for genuinely independent thought and action had been broken down by the ordeals of evangelism. The answer to that question is of far more than historical interest, because it not only affects our estimate of the Evangelical Revival as such, but to a large extent it will affect our whole belief in the validity of evangelical doctrine.

The gist of what Dr Sargant says[8] is that Wesley, by the powerful and effective use of hellfire preaching, so terrorized his hearers that many of them collapsed under the strain; they broke out in violent emotional reactions, and when they had finally reached a state of exhaustion and abnormal suggestibility, were persuaded to accept Wesley's brand of salvation and handed over to the Methodist societies for systematic indoctrination. The whole of this alleged process has its parallels in the other phenomena that Dr Sargant describes. The terrors of hellfire preaching correspond to the ordeals of certain primitive religions, and those employed in Communist brainwashing, and the experimental stressed imposed on Pavlov's dogs. The bizarre emotional reactions are supposed to be essentially the same as those observed in voodoo cults, in the irrational conduct of the victims of battle neurosis, and the 'ultra-paradoxical' behaviour noted by Pavlov when his dogs broke down. The final collapse is that state of 'terminal exhaustion' which supervenes in many different circumstances when the cortex of the brain, strained beyond endurance by 'transmarginal stimulation', responds with a state of 'protective inhibition'.

In support of this ingenious theory Dr Sargant quotes from Wesley's *Journal* a few accounts of the strange things that often occurred under his preaching—the hysterical outbreaks, swooning, roaring, screaming, violent paroxysms, convulsions and states of collapse among some of the people. These could hardly be said to have been characteristic of the Evangelical Revival as a whole, but they naturally have attracted much attention due to their spectacular nature. They were mostly confined to the earlier years and a large number of them occurred at Bristol. They brought much scandal and disrepute on the movement, especially amongst the large hostile section of the population who were content to form their verdict on the basis of hearsay evidence alone. The mere recital of these things may seem an embarrassment to the modern mind, but they are all set out in a quite matter of fact way in Wesley's *Journal*, and have been treated fairly and sometimes at considerable length in the standard biographies and histories of early Methodism. We shall return to some of the accounts of these strange phenomena in the next chapter.

In the meantime, the question that concerns us is What evidence does Dr Sargant bring for his repeated assertion that these violent outbursts were the result of Wesley's hellfire preaching? The answer, I'm afraid, is devastatingly simple: None; none whatsoever—because there is no evidence to bring. In his Foreword Dr Sargant tells us that 'John Wesley and his methods demand particular study at the present time from politician and priest alike, even if the hellfire doctrine he preached may seem outmoded'.[9] It seems a pity that our writer had not taken the trouble to make such a particular study himself before making sweeping statements about Wesley's methods with which he is so obviously unacquainted. The general apology which follows for 'any inaccuracies' that arise in his book due to the fact that the author has had to go outside his own field, is noted, but it will hardly excuse the sort of bold assertions that Dr Sargant makes about Wesley's preaching, in the face of contrary evidence that is readily available to anyone who cares to look it up. Anyone who is acquainted with the literature of early Methodism or who will take the trouble to read any of the standard lives of John Wesley, some of which are by non-Methodist authors, will realize, I think, that Dr Sargant's picture of him as a hellfire preacher who achieved his 'great success' by making a 'tremendous assault on the emotions'[10] is completely misleading. In his Introduction Dr Sargant tells us how he first stumbled upon the idea that 'many of the results that were being achieved by abreaction under drugs were essentially the same as those obtained, not only by Wesley and other religious leaders, but by modern "brain-washers" ',[11] and that Pavlov's experiments with animals would provide evidence to explain them. Dr Sargant's moment of insight seems to have been not entirely unlike a sudden conversion, and his description is worth quoting in full. After describing the techniques which he and his colleagues developed in 1944,[12] to promote abreactions by the use of fear-provoking suggestion, he goes on:

'One afternoon when this technique was being applied to the more normal victims of severe bombing stress—it was less helpful in the treatment of chronic neurotics—I happened to visit my father's house, and picked up one of his books at random. It was John Wesley's Journal of 1739-40. My eye was caught by Wesley's detailed reports of the occurrence, two hundred years before, of almost identical states of emotional excitement, often leading to temporary emotional collapse, which he induced by a particular sort of preaching. These phenomena often appeared when he had persuaded his hearers that they must make an immediate choice between certain damnation and the acceptance of his own soul-saving religious views. The fear of burning in hell induced by his graphic preaching could be compared to the suggestion we might force on a returned soldier, during treatment, that he was in danger of being burned alive in his tank and must fight his way out. The two techniques seemed startlingly similar.'[13]

Now I have carefully examined all the examples of emotional

excitement which Dr Sargant cites from Wesley's *Journal*,[14] and I can find nothing either in the quotations or their context to give any grounds for his suggestion that they were brought on by 'a particular sort of preaching' such as he describes. The suggestion that Wesley ever persuaded anyone that they had to make a choice, immediate or otherwise, 'between certain damnation and the acceptance of his own soul-saving religious views' is quite out of harmony with either his beliefs or his methods. The reader will comb the record of his preaching in vain to discover any of the 'graphic' descriptions of 'burning in hell' that were sometimes used by other evangelists. Dr Sargant's moment of insight seems to have misled him. He has argued from an apparent similarity of effect to an imaginary similarity of technique. Fruitful hypotheses may sometimes be born like that, but they need to be tested by the evidence and modified or abandoned if they do not fit the facts.

In the chapter on 'Techniques of Religious Conversion' we are told that shortly after his conversion Wesley 'hit upon an extremely effective technique of conversion' which Dr Sargant describes as follows:

'First of all Wesley would create high emotional tension in his potential converts. He found it easy to convince large audiences of that period that a failure to achieve salvation would necessarily condemn them to hellfire for ever and ever. The immediate acceptance of an escape from such a ghastly fate was then very strongly urged on the ground that anybody who left the meeting 'unchanged' and met with a sudden fatal accident before he had accepted this salvation, would pass straight into the fiery furnace. This sense of urgency increased the prevailing anxiety which, as suggestibility increased, could infect the whole group.'[15]

Now as comment on the work of John Wesley, this is ingenious, fanciful and perverse, and has so little relation to the facts that one is tempted to think of Hitler's advice on propaganda, that if we are to tell a lie we should tell a big one. As we shall see shortly, Wesley did believe in hell, and even in hellfire, but we have no grounds whatsoever for believing that he used this as a technique for arousing emotional tension, or a big stick to terrorize his hearers into submission. As a matter of well attested fact,[16] the fear of hell played a remarkably small part in his preaching. As before, these bold assertions of Dr Sargant are quite undocumented, and the very language of people leaving a meeting 'unchanged' and having a 'fatal accident' is surely reminiscent of later and lesser evangelists much nearer to our own day than Wesley.

After telling us in the same rather bland way that 'Fear of everlasting hell . . . affected the nervous system of (Wesley's) hearers very much as fear of death by drowning did Pavlov's dogs in the Leningrad flood',[15] Dr Sargant goes on to quote (apparently by way of illustration) the autobiographical account of the conversion of John Nelson, who later became one of Wesley's preachers. This is taken from Ronald Knox's book Enthusiasm, and tells how Wesley's 'countenance struck such an awful dread' on Nelson that his 'heart beat like a pendulum'. However, if Dr Sargant had had that quotation from its original source in Nelson's Journal, he might not have been so eager to quote it in this connection. Nelson describes his own years of spiritual discontent and fruitless searching, in which the fear of hell had played a comparatively minor part, and his chief concern seems to have been a sense of personal estrangement from God, moral failure and real guilt. He continues:

'In all this time I did not open my mind to any person either by word or letter; but I was just like a wandering bird cast out of the nest, till Mr John Wesley came to preach his first sermon in Moorfields. Oh that was a blessed morning to my soul! As soon as he got upon the stand, he stroked back his hair, and turned his face towards where I stood, and I thought fixed his eyes upon me. His countenance struck such an awful dread upon me, before I heard him speak that it made my heart beat like the pendulum of a clock; and when he did speak, I thought his whole discourse was aimed at me. When he had done, I said, "This man can tell the secrets of my heart; He hath not left me there; for he hath showed me the remedy, even the blood of Jesus." Then was my soul filled with consolation, through hope that God for Christ's sake would save me; neither did I doubt in such a manner any more, till within twenty-four hours of the time when the Lord wrote a pardon on my heart.'[17]

When the two sentences quoted by Dr Sargant are reset in their context, the description of Nelson's 'awful dread' and pounding heart looks rather different. There is a certain numinous feeling that trembles on the brink of joy and liberation, but there is not much sign of the terrors of hellfire. The 'discourse' which Nelson felt as though it were aimed at him personally on that occasion, was based on Isaiah 55, 'Ho! every one that thirsteth, come ye to the waters.'[18] It was in fact rather characteristic of the preacher to be more concerned about the waters of life than the fires of hell.

Southey had some very sour remarks to make about the more violent emotional responses to Wesley's preaching;[19] Knox treats them at great length, with an avowedly critical intention of putting Wesley in his 'rogues gallery',[20] and it would be hard to find a more supercilious and jaundiced account of Wesley's work than Marjorie Bowen's *Wrestling Jacob*[21] which dwells with obvious relish on the more embarrassing incidents. Yet not even any of these three writers attributes them to Wesley's hellfire preaching. Dr Sydney G. Dimond, in a work which includes a detailed psychological examination of the abnormal emotional phenomena that occurred in the Evangelical Revival, has this to say about Wesley:

'On the voyage out to Georgia, having observed how soon the awe inspired by the storm disappeared, he writes "For the future I will never believe them to obey from fear who are dead to the motives of love". In his preaching Wesley was always sparing in his use of fear as a motive. The four volumes of his sermons which form part of the doctrinal standards of the Methodist Church contain no sermon on hell nor indeed on heaven. The only sermon of Wesley's on hell is an elaborate argument, illustrated by many quotations and classical allusions which stamp it as an early academic exercise.'[22]

After discussing these abnormal phenomena at some length in his *Life* of Wesley, Professor C. T. Winchester had this to say:

'It is singular that no such results attended the preaching of Whitefield, though far more impassioned than Wesley's. Whitefield wrote, in fact, to expostulate with Wesley for encouraging such physical manifestations. But Wesley never did encourage them. Nor was his preaching drastic and minatory; he did not terrify people with lurid pictures of future punishment; on the contrary, it is evident from the *Journal* that his preaching was concerned almost entirely with the invitations and promises of the Gospel.'[23]

Since Dr Sargant has said so much about Wesley's preaching and given us several extracts from his *Journal* that really say so little about it, readers who are unfamiliar with the *Journal* may be interested in the following extracts which are rather more typical. They are taken from the *Journal* of 1742:

'Friday—May 28th: ... We came to Newcastle about six, and after a short refreshment, walked into the town. I was surprised: so much drunkenness, cursing and swearing (even from the mouths of little children) do I never remember to have seen and heard before, in so small a compass of time. Surely this place is ripe for Him who "came not to call the righteous, but sinners to repentance".'[24]

He began his preaching campaign on the Sunday, and the *Journal* records:

'At seven I walked down to Sandgate, the poorest and most contemptible part of the town, and, standing at the end of the street with John Taylor, began to sing the hundredth Psalm. Three or four people came out to see what was the matter, who soon increased to four or five hundred. I suppose there might be twelve to fifteen hundred before I had done preaching; to whom I applied these solemn words: "He was wounded for our transgressions, He was bruised for our iniquities, the chastisement of our peace was upon Him; and by His stripes we are healed."

'Observing the people when I had done, to stand gaping and staring upon me with the most profound astonishment, I told them, "If you desire to know who I am, my name is John Wesley. At five in the evening, with God's help, I design to preach here again."

'At five, the hill on which I designed to preach was covered from the top to the bottom. I never saw so large a number of

people together, either in Moorfields or in Kennington Common.
I knew it was not possible for the one half to hear, although my
voice was then strong and clear; and I stood so as to have them
all in view, as they ranged on the side of the hill. The word of
God which I set before them was "I will heal their backsliding,
I will love them freely". After preaching the poor people were
ready to tread me under-foot out of pure love and kindness.'[25]

II

During the early years of the Revival it was inevitable that
violent emotional reactions under Wesley's preaching should
bring much scathing criticism, particularly from people who had
never heard him preach, or had any dealings with the Methodist
movement. Indeed there have been very few men who have been
subject to so much torrent of abuse, slander and misrepresentation
from so many different directions; and over such a long period
as John Wesley was; and then he lived long enough to vindicate
himself and his movement and be acclaimed as something of a
public hero and national patriarch. For the most part, Wesley's
only defence was to appeal to the facts. In his famous encounter
with Beau Nash, the socialite king of Bath, when the dandy told
him 'Your preaching frightens people out of their wits' he had
only to reply 'Sir, did you ever hear me preach?'[26] and the argument was completely in his hands. One of the reasons why
Wesley published so much, and particularly his sermons, was to
defend himself and his movement against such misrepresentation
and misunderstanding. Unfortunately the precaution seems to
have been lost on Dr Sargant, for in this book of his, so copiously
furnished with quotations, footnotes and references, and in
which his main argument hinges on his estimate of Wesley's
preaching, there is not one single reference to, or quotation from
any of Wesley's published sermons, nor does anything he has
written show any evidence of his having read them.

Wesley published one hundred and forty-one sermons. These
are all still readily available in libraries today,[27] and the famous
Forty-Four that are part of the doctrinal standards of Methodism
are still being reprinted from time to time.[28] There seems no good
reason why such relevant material should be ignored by anyone
who writes about the preaching of John Wesley. In the case of

other evangelists who have been unashamedly renowned for
their advocacy and practice of hellfire preaching, Dr Sargant has
no difficulty in establishing their technique from their own
writings.[29] But in the case of Wesley, who is after all his chief
character, undocumented assertion has to serve in the place of
evidence.

In the published sermons there are few references to hell,[30] and
none of the long harrowing descriptions of the torments of the
damned that other revivalists used with such effect. It is a matter
of perennial debate of course whether Wesley's printed sermons
are in the form in which they were preached. It is usually suggested that as we have them they would be such heavy going
that they would hardly win any response at all. They would
certainly have been little use to a more emotional preacher like
Charles Wesley, or a dramatic orator like Whitefield, but for
John—the man in whom moral earnestness and loving concern
seemed so naturally wedded to orderly thinking and lucid expression—who can say how these rather pedestrian sentences
could have come alive for his hearers? At any rate, whatever
differences in form and style there may have been between the
written and the spoken sermon, there is not likely to have been
any significant change in theological emphasis. We need to
remember that John Wesley published his sermons in a day
when a robust belief in hell was not considered at all theologically embarrassing, except among some of the intellectuals—the
Deists and Latitudinarians with whom he was always more or
less at loggerheads anyway and never at all careful to placate. If
the fear of hell had played such an effective part in his preaching,
as Dr Sargant asserts that it did, there seems no reason in the
world why Wesley should have played down this element in his
published sermons.

Rupert Davies in his book *Methodism*, published a few years
ago, reminds us that

'The popular image of an evangelist, and still more a revivalist,
is of a man with a crude, ill thought-out hell-fire theology, who
alternatively wheedles or terrifies his hearers into accepting his
message; the theology he is thought to have taken over
ready-made from some literalist interpreter of the Bible; his
emotionalism is believed to spring from a defect in his own

personality. There have indeed been revivalists and evangelists of whom these criticisms have been perfectly just. . . . But, so far at least as Great Britain is concerned, they all came after the time of the Wesleys, and it would be unhistorical in the extreme to have the modern evangelist-image in one's mind when studying the Methodist Revival.'[31]

This is a salutary warning, the kind of image which Dr Sargant has of Wesley is very plausible to the modern mind, and has a tendency to persist in spite of overwhelming evidence to the contrary.

For most of us there are a number of things that are emotionally associated on at least one level of our minds as essentially restrictive and morbid. They do not cohere in any logical or well thought out way, but (according to the individual's past experience) form part of that choking cloud of piety from which he must keep free, or a system of unintelligent nonsense which he must ridicule. The sort of things associated in this complex are suggested by such expressions as sin, judgment, everlasting punishment, salvation, hellfire preaching, biblical literalism, moralism, emotionalism, evangelism etc. There are, no doubt, a variety of historical reasons why these particular things should be thus emotionally charged for the educated mind of modern Western man. A careful critical examination of these will often (though not always) show that what is being rejected is not the theological reality with which the Church is vitally concerned, but some perversion of it which should be just as unsavoury to the Christian mind as it is to the secular.

Now when we move into the world of early Methodism, unless we exercise considerable historical discipline in our thinking, this whole reaction system is activated in our minds immediately. All the emotive words like sin and law, judgment and salvation are used with great freedom and we very easily read into the whole story some quite misleading and inaccurate interpretations. To read Wesley's sermons, for example, is to move right back into a form of exegesis that is quite unashamedly and unselfconsciously fundamentalist; but before we dismiss the whole lot with an impatient shrug, we need to be reminded how different was Wesley's fundamentalism from its modern counterpart. Again we are indebted to Rupert Davies who says of Wesley in this regard:

'But in all these matters he was in complete accord with the other theologians of his time. It was not that, like the modern fundamentalist, he had heard of the critical theories of the Bible and rejected them; he had never heard of them because they had never been put forward. . . . On the basis of his study of the Bible he produced a coherent body of doctrine on the subject nearest to his heart, the salvation of mankind, and the significant fact is that the Scriptural exegesis in which it is grounded is ruled out by modern scholarship at very few points. . . . His literalism did not prevent him from penetrating to the core of the Biblical message, whereas modern literalism tends to do exactly that.'[32]

Most eighteenth century Christians believed in a literal and spatial heaven and a literal hell with literal hellfire, and that those who finally neglected God's offer of salvation would go to hell. Let it be frankly admitted that thus far, John Wesley was no exception. It is of course ridiculous to suggest that he discovered hellfire preaching and so 'hit upon an extremely effective technique of conversion'.[33] He was certainly no innovator of hell. The preaching of hell and its torments went back many centuries before Wesley's day, and the only remarkable or distinctive features about his handling of these themes were (i) the way in which he modified and softened the traditional teaching as it came to him in the eighteenth century, and (ii) the fact that it was never a dominant theme in his preaching, and he made so little effective use of hell as a means of frightening people into heaven.

We shall look at the ways in which Wesley softened the traditional doctrine shortly, but as regards (ii), in addition to what has already been said, it is worth noting that his more sombre and forbidding sermons were usually preached to the complacent and well-to-do,[34] among whom he won practically no response at all. On one occasion after he had preached to a genteel audience on the text 'Ye serpents, ye generation of vipers, how can ye escape the damnation of hell?' somebody said to him 'Sir, such a sermon would have been suitable for Billingsgate; but it was highly improper here', to which Wesley replied 'If I had been in Billingsgate, my text should have been "Behold the Lamb of God which taketh away the sin of the world".'[35] His rather sonorous and apocalyptic utterance on 'The Great Assize'[36] was preached not to a vicious Bristol mob whom one might well suppose to be in danger of the judgment, but before a travelling High Court judge and all his majestic retinue. Nor were these isolated examples; as Sydney Dimond says,

'Wesley's general practice was to speak strong and stern words in Churches where he had wealthy and critical congregations, and to choose scripture passages of the most tender and affectionate type for exposition to the ignorant and debased crowds in the colliery and industrial areas.'[37] It is important to note however, that it was among these latter audiences 'the ignorant and debased crowds in the colliery and industrial areas' that nearly all the more violent reactions to Wesley's preaching occurred.

III

From the vantage point of the twentieth century it may be easy to criticize Wesley's somewhat materialistic conceptions of heaven and hell, but they were not entirely crude by any means. Despite his literalism he had seen that the essential point was the possibility of a continuing fellowship with God[38] or an absolute loss of that fellowship. Most modern Christians have succeeded in sublimating their conception of heaven completely in these terms, and leaving aside the unanswerable question of the precise conditions under which our fellowship with God will be continued beyond the limits of this world. However, we have not succeeded anywhere near so well in translating the reality of hell into such terms, and at least one modern writer who will not be suspected of obscurantism has suggested that this failing has somewhat impoverished our religion.[39]

There is probably no more difficult theological question for the modern thinking Christian than that of the final destiny of the unsaved. Of the two words in the New Testament that are translated in the Authorized Version as 'hell', William Strawson points out that 'Hades' is 'closely associated with death rather than with hell',[40] and that the other term 'Gehenna' is mentioned twelve times, and with one exception it belongs to the utterances of Jesus himself as recorded in the Synoptic Gospels.[41] This latter term which was also in use in contemporary Jewish literature derives, of course, from a reference to the valley of

Hinnom to the west of Jerusalem, which was used as the city rubbish dump, and Jesus' hearers would understand the allusion to the more or less continually smouldering fires of destruction. Nevertheless, as Mr Strawson says, while Jesus was 'using the thought-form of his day, he was not, however, tied to it',[42] and he points out certain significant differences in Jesus' use of the term 'Gehenna' as compared with its use in current Judaism. For example, 'In the sayings of Jesus there is no suggestion that the righteous will gloat over the wicked when they see them in Gehenna. Nor is there the idea that the delights of heaven are increased by contrast with the torments of hell.'[43] Against the background of cruel suffering endured by the Jews, and the apocalyptic thirst for vengeance on their oppressors, which so often coloured their ideas of Gehenna, 'The teaching of Jesus about hell must be regarded as mild, without emphasis on details, and restricted in application'.[44] Mr Strawson adds:

'The terminology is undoubtedly influenced by our Lord's obligation to use language which his contemporaries could understand. It is no exaggeration to say that if he were to use the idea of Gehenna at all, he could scarcely have used it with less controversial or objectionable meaning. To say that he need not have employed the idea at all is to forget that Jesus had to use the ways into human understanding which contemporary thought made possible. Most of all we must not assume that Jesus did not really believe in hell, for there is abundant evidence that he did.'[45]

And he closes his summary of Jesus' teaching about Gehenna thus: 'His words leave us with a firm impression of his belief in hell, and a constant reminder that his chief concern was not to tell people they were going there, but to warn of its dangers so that they might escape them.'[46]

Now this does not solve the problem for the modern Christian of course, but simply makes it more acute. Did Jesus really mean that the unsaved will suffer the torments of the damned for ever and ever? Not only our modern mind, but our *Christian conscience* finds this suggestion utterly revolting. Pre-Christian or unchristian conceptions of God may have been compatible with the suggestion that a lifetime of sin would be punished by an eternity of excruciating pain, either physical or spiritual, but surely it is Jesus himself that has so changed our understanding of the nature of God, that from a Christian point of view such a suggestion *should* be both revolting and ridiculous. We must acknowledge, I think, that pre-Christian and unchristian conceptions of God have in fact played a very large part in historical Christianity, and that the modern protest against the idea of everlasting punishment is in the profoundest sense a *moral* protest and a Christian protest.

At the same time it must also be admitted that there are, sometimes, other motives at work in our modern reluctance to come to terms with Christ's teaching about hell. There is a very understandable desire to avoid even the contemplation of ultimate loss, or the necessity for painful decision, and without any real concern for Jesus' revelation of the Living God, we may find it all too easy to drift into a 'heads I win, tails I can't lose' attitude towards the life and death issues he sets before us. Existentialism, with all its stress on the importance of choice, decision, commitment, is in many ways a struggle to escape from the sort of spiritual torpor into which this attitude has led so many of our generation, and even to get back, in a form that is not repugnant to reason or morality, something that was formerly supplied by traditional Christianity, but in a form which we can no longer accept. There must be *decision* — an all important decision on which man's whole destiny hangs, a real and momentous choice between God and the void, being and non-being, meaning and meaninglessness.

One form of Existentialist answer to this demand is, of course, to assert that reality, life, the universe, or whatever we like to start from is essentially meaningless, and the only meaning we shall ever find there is the meaning we choose to put into it. The choice before man is simply then to choose out of his own mind, and unsupported by any objective reality, the meaning and values he will live by; to affirm these with his whole being, and thus rescue his life from meaninglessness while he is living it— always acknowledging, however, that he has no destiny and that the things he has lived by will die with him forever. To this, the Christian must retort that man does not create his own meaning at all. The meaning of his existence is *given*—given in the continuing activity of God's grace in creation and redemption, and man chooses himself, affirms his own true being, in free response to this grace. But the prevenient activity of grace does not mean for the Christian (unless he is the strictest kind of Calvinist) that his essence is prior to his existence—that he is free only to choose between meaninglessness on the one hand and some foreordained pattern or blueprint of his life, on the other. If man's life under God is always responsive, it is also meant to become fully *responsible* and the Christian, just as much as the Existentialist, must grow towards the maturity of the autonomous self-creating personality. All along the way, a man chooses not only *whether* he shall respond to God, but also *how* he shall respond, and in every case it is God's will that his response should be genuinely his own act and should add to his own being. But his very freedom to choose, to respond or not to respond, is itself the gift of God's grace, and if he does choose to respond, and howsoever he chooses to make that response, he will be responding to grace. The man who is being saved is the man whose autonomy grows out of his experience of being accepted by God, and who chooses to use his freedom to go on accepting this acceptance. Thus his freedom grows as he uses it to acknowledge his ultimate dependence on God, a dependence which does not destroy his responsibility but enables him genuinely to claim his own personal existence. A Christian is God's self-creating creature.

For the Christian the existential choice is between responding or not responding to the given grace of God. But what happens to the person who chooses not to respond to God's grace? Need we suppose that there is some objective alternative in which he becomes involved in spite of himself, or does he simply encounter the void in his own soul, enter a world of not-being within, and become overwhelmed by the meaninglessness of his own existence? Taken to its full depth surely this would be terrible enough to give to the choice which faces man, all the ultimate significance that anyone could require. We still do not know, of course, what this other alternative of saying 'No' to God finally means. Does it mean that we literally have the power of self-destruction, and that the end of this state is that we simply cease to be? Or does it mean that we would linger on endlessly with a kind of negative 'being' in the void we have created? Or in this condition would we in any sense retain the ability to reverse our choosing and begin to respond to God, and so recover our true being? These are of course familiar questions—the ones which Christian people have long asked about the destiny of those who depart this life without having accepted the offer of salvation, and a positive answer to each of these three questions in turn, would correspond respectively to the three alternatives of Conditional Immortality, Eternal Punishment and Universalism.

My point in stating the whole problem in these existential terms is that it loses nothing of its essential meaning when we altogether leave out what has become, for most people, the traditional Christian belief that hell (whatever its nature and duration) is an objective condition; and that it ultimately depends on the punitive purposes of God towards the unrepentant sinner. All the problems for the Christian conscience arise out of this idea that hell is initiated by God, and that it represents not an inevitable consequence of sin, but a deliberately inflicted punishment.[47] Neither of these ideas is at all easy to reconcile with the revelation of God which we have in Jesus Christ—unless we regard the punishment of hell not as the torment of endless retribution, but as a means of the sinner's reformation which will allow him a second chance.

Of course this doctrine of the second chance, while it does remove the frightful suggestion of divine savagery and retributive vengeance, still has its own peculiar difficulties. The Universalist answer to these—that all men will eventually turn to God and be saved, raises problems about human freedom, but it is also a sublime act of faith in the endlessness of God's patience and the infinity of his grace. If we are bound to the traditional view of hell as a divine punishment for sin, this would seem to be the most acceptable form of doctrine, but it must be admitted that there is usually in such teaching, a certain loss of existential urgency. We may recall the words of John Baillie :

'But if we decide for universalism, it must be for a form of it which does nothing to decrease the urgency of immediate repentance and which makes no promises to the procrastinating sinner. It is doubtful whether such a form of the doctrine has yet been found.'[48]

But *are* we bound to the traditional view of hell as punishment, rather than simply as dire consequence? Has the

H

traditional view any sound basis? Is it not possible, as I have
suggested, to retain the existential truth in the doctrine of hell
and reject the punitive element altogether? Whatever may be
thought of this suggestion, I think a fair case could be made out
to show that in the use which Jesus made of the concept of
Gehenna it was always the existential aspect, rather than the
punitive, that was to the fore. As William Strawson says,

'While later Christian literature painted the torments of hell in
glowing colours, we note that all we can justifiably say of the
teaching of Jesus in this regard is that he used the conception
without giving details or emphasizing minute aspects of the
matter.'[49]

Jesus did not threaten men with punishment, but called them to
a life and death decision.

Modern biblical scholarship also makes other suggestions
about the teaching of Jesus in the Synoptic Gospels, which were
inevitably beyond the range of Christian thinking in John
Wesley's day. With our modern understanding of the Bible, very
few Christians today for example, would feel any necessity whatsoever to think of hellfire as literal fire. Pointing out the natural
association of destructive fire with the valley of Hinnom, and
hence with the word Gehenna William Strawson says 'Although
fire gives rise to the thought of torture in contemporary Jewish
thought, the more prominent notions connected with fire are of
the sovereignty of God and the possibility of destruction'.[50]
This writer feels on the whole, that in the combined notions of
Gehenna and fire 'the emphasis still rests more upon the idea of
destruction than upon the idea of punishment',[51] and he therefore inclines towards an interpretation of the teaching of Jesus
in line with the doctrine of Conditional Immortality. Furthermore, New Testament scholars now generally agree that the
Greek word *aionios* translated in the Authorized Version as
'eternal' or 'everlasting' does not in fact mean everlasting at all;
it refers not so much to duration as to a new quality or dimension of experience. Thus, commenting on the phrase *kolasis
aionios* in Matthew 25.46, Alan Richardson says

'but if we reflect that *aionios* in this context probably does not
mean "everlasting", we shall be spared the moral anxieties raised

by the translations "eternal punishment" (RV) or "everlasting punishment" (AV). The real issue concerns the character of the punishment as that of the order of the Age to Come as contrasted with any earthly penalties.'[52]

It will be noted then, that in both these instances there is a clear movement away in biblical interpretation from the idea of everlasting torment or punishment for the unsaved,[53] which in Wesley's day seemed to any conscientious student of the Bible the only possible meaning of our Lord's words. William Strawson points out that of 'punishment which leads to eventual restoration . . . there appears to be no sign in the words of our Lord',[54] but this does not, of course, preclude us from building such a hope on the foundation of our whole faith in God as revealed by Jesus, as a God of infinite love and saving purpose. Nor should such a hope be considered less truly biblical for being built on such a broad foundation rather than on any particular recorded sayings of our Lord. Bearing in mind both this larger hope, and the existential quality of the New Testament writings, J. A. T. Robinson has written:

'The New Testament continually stresses the need for decision for Christ here and now and without delay, but it does not give to the moment of death the overriding significance which it later acquires. On the one hand it asserts that a man must make up his mind "now", "while it is called today"; it does not say "any time before death". The moment, the opportunity for decision, may in fact be lost before death. And, on the other hand, it never dogmatizes to the extent of saying that after death there is no further chance. Indeed it could not do this without limiting quite intolerably the inexhaustible love of God.'[55]

IV

But in marked contrast to the teaching of Jesus himself, popular Christianity fairly soon reverted to the interpretation of 'Gehenna' that it had received in Jewish Apocalyptic literature; and laid the stress heavily on the punitive side of the doctrine, often developing it to the most repulsive and extravagant lengths. While it was Augustine who fastened the dogma of everlasting punishment on Western Christendom, it probably came into prominence in the first place, as John Baillie suggested, during the Church's experience of cruel persecution in earlier centuries. Thus Tertullian, contemplating the spectacle he will behold at 'that fast-approaching advent of our Lord', writes:

'Which sight gives me joy? which rouses me to exultation?—as I see so many illustrious monarchs . . . groaning now in the lowest darkness . . . ; governors of provinces too, who persecuted the Christian name, in fires more fierce than those with which in the days of their pride they raged against the followers of Christ.'[56]

In the fires of persecution, such an attitude is at least understandably human, although it is certainly not Christian. But unfortunately this vindictive, gloating overemphasis on the punitive aspect of eschatology was destined to hold sway over both the popular imagination and the minds of theologians for a long time. 'Throughout many ages', says Dr J. H. Leckie, 'the minds of theologians were in a state of chronic eschatological intoxication. Their imaginations rejoiced in pictures of torment and woe.'[57] This 'insane licence', as Leckie calls it, was dominant throughout the Middle Ages and is given typical expression in the minute descriptions and varied torments of Dante's *Inferno*. But the same writer goes on to remind us that 'the tone of Protestant discourse during many generations' was not 'very different in temper from that of the Roman'. He continues:

'Preachers of great repute for sanctity and zeal painted their pictures of Gehenna in colours of a crude vulgarity. . . . They depicted the future state of the masses of men as one of a torture like that of the rack or the vivisection table, protracted to all eternity. It was a state of every nameless outrage, of every agony and shame, of every unendurable wrong. And over all this scene of sordid cruelty the saints of heaven watched and were glad. Any one who desires to have full and copious illustration of this kind of frenzied assertion need only consult the sermons of many popular teachers, from the time of Tertullian on to the present day.'[58]

As Leckie points out, the Church 'in its official statements regarding perdition . . . has been very guarded and reserved'. It did not endorse the excesses of popular preachers, but on the other hand it did tolerate them, and Leckie suggests that 'This aspect of popular teaching has done more, perhaps, than anything else to provoke a revolt against the whole Christian view of the world'.[59] In the near half century since Leckie wrote those words there has no doubt been a sharp swing away from this kind of popular preaching, but some of the harmful effect still lingers.

It is not difficult to see the conception—or misconception of God, which underlay such terrible teaching. To our modern mind, no matter how great the sin of man, a God who could deliberately plan and inflict such torment upon him would be a hateful tyrant and a hideous monster, and it amazes us that former generations of Christians did not realize this. Yet the history of human thought — both Christian and otherwise — abounds with instances of beliefs for long calmly accepted, that become so morally repugnant to the people of a later and more enlightened generation that they have the greatest difficulty in understanding how anyone but moral blackguards could ever have believed them. This is, of course, one of the most cheering evidences that the Holy Spirit is at work in the world from generation to generation.

During many centuries of the Christian era—and, of course, for a very long time before—the only experience which most men had of human sovereignty was that of a more or less absolute despotism or tyranny. Rulers might be good or bad, but nobody seriously questioned their right to do what they liked with their subjects. Might was right, and the only way of challenging the right of the ruler was to assassinate him or in some other way forcibly depose him. In that case a new despotism would be substituted for the old, but no one thought of challenging the whole idea of despotic sovereignty as such. It is at least understandable then, how the Christian Church, despite some very clear indications to the contrary in the teaching of Jesus, began carrying over these ideas of despotic and tyrannical sovereignty into her thinking about God—especially when she found it necessary to affirm the sovereignty of God over the despotic rulers of the earth. It is doubtful whether the Church has even yet rid herself entirely of this paganism.

For a long time the right of the sovereign even included the right to torture, punish or destroy his subjects, as he saw fit. There was no one to whom he was answerable—unless to God himself, and therefore if he chose to ignore God, as most rulers did, he had no particular need to provide any moral pretext for such behaviour. It must have been infinitely easier then, and in a sense more natural for people who lived and died under such a regime, and regarded it as normal, to think of God, the very King of Kings, as punishing his disobedient subjects with ever-lasting torture. The logical outcome of such thinking was the suggestion put forward in embryo by Augustine, and which haunted the Church for centuries before it was formulated with awful clarity by John Calvin—that men and women would be consigned to the abode of endless suffering, not because they had freely refused the offer of salvation, but because God by his own arbitrary choice or sovereign decree had elected them for such a fate before they were born. As Dr W. R. Matthews says, 'The terrible doctrine of predestination to endless torment lies like a scar over the face of much traditional Christian theology'.[60]

This then, was the more or less traditional background of Christian thinking about hell, that was still very real to most people in the eighteenth century; and when we assess the teaching of John Wesley against it we find that what he had to say on this theme was, by contrast, much more strictly scriptural both in content and proportion. This led to two general characteristics:

1. He either omits or specifically repudiates on scriptural grounds, some of the worst features of what had become the traditional popular teaching about hell; thereby restoring the original balance that it had in the teaching of Jesus himself, for whom the existential element clearly outweighed the punitive.

2. By comparison with our approach to the doctrines of hell in the light of modern biblical scholarship, his exposition is still limited by the literalist interpretation of scripture which seemed the only one possible in the eighteenth century.

With regard to 1. we must first of all note that Wesley rejected quite uncompromisingly the Calvinist teaching that men are predestined to hell by the arbitrary decree of a just God, and here at least, he was prepared, if necessary, to imperil his biblical literalism by asserting quite dogmatically 'No scripture can mean that God is not love'.[61] Whatever else he thought about hell, Wesley made it abundantly clear that no one ever went there simply by the intention of God. Hell was only for 'those who in spite of all the warnings of God, *resolve* to have their portion with the devil and his angels'.[62] Throughout his long ministry he was loved or hated very largely for his impassioned proclamation that Christ was offered as Saviour for *all* men. Wesley rejected the Calvinist teaching that—irrespective of anything they may freely do or refrain from doing—God had irrevocably decreed that some men should be eternally saved and the rest eternally damned. He thought this was not only untrue, but blasphemous nonsense. We will need to discuss this more fully when we come to consider his central teaching about the love of God (in Chapter 8). In the meantime, we note that of all the controversies in which he became embroiled, none was so important to him as this rejection of the predestinarian element in the current teaching about hell. Also, although he did not understand the full implications of his own action, he was in fact (as some of his opponents realized) striking a serious blow at the most fully developed form of the concept of the 'tyrant God' which actually underlay all that is most repugnant to the Christian conscience in the traditional doctrine of hell.

Apart from references to hell in some of his general sermons, where they never form a dominant theme, the only writings of Wesley's which we have on the subject are one sermon and a few brief comments on his *Notes on the New Testament*. The idea of hell and future torment when it appears at all in the general sermons is used most sparingly—perhaps at first sight surprisingly so. Considering that Wesley believed that those who 'neglect so great a salvation' would in fact go to a hell of everlasting fire, it is mortifying to think of the use he *might* have made of such a doctrine—even if he had acted only from the entirely commendable motive of trying to save his fellows from such a fate. The history of Christian preaching abounds with examples of those who from these very good motives have made the most terrifying use of this doctrine and others, of course, whose very motives have been corrupted by it and degenerated into an almost hideous savagery. However we cannot be content with what Wesley might have done, because we have ample evidence of what he *did*—and it was something entirely different from what Dr Sargant imagines him to have done. Wesley was vitally concerned with presenting God's offer of salvation to men as something which required their responsible decision and acceptance. It was, therefore, always the existential aspect of the doctrine of hell, rather than its punitive and terrifying aspect which was uppermost in his mind when he did make use of it in his preaching. He might in all seriousness warn his hearers to 'flee from the wrath to come', but he never belaboured them with graphic and terrifying descriptions of the pains of hell in order to press them towards a decision. He has himself explained his reasons for this attitude—so diametrically opposed to the technique with which Dr Sargant credits him. Firstly, he was interested in much bigger and more immediate issues. His preaching seldom left the dimension of existential choice for very long, but it was a choice that concerned the here and now, rather than the hereafter. Of the issues of life and death which he set before his hearers, certainly hell was one aspect of the negative alternative, just as heaven was one aspect of the positive one, but in neither case was this *post mortem* possibility anything like the major consideration. Thus in his 'Farther Appeal to Men of Reason and Religion' he writes:

'By salvation I mean, not barely, according to the vulgar notion, deliverance from hell, or going to heaven; but a present deliverance from sin, a restoration of the soul to its primitive health, its original purity; a recovery of the divine nature; the renewal of our souls after the image of God, in righteousness and true holiness, in justice, mercy, and truth.'[63]

The whole content of his preaching and ministry was consistent with this. Secondly, although he faced men and women with this existential choice, and did it with an effectiveness that has seldom been equalled in the history of the Church, he was much too profoundly aware of its nature to imagine that men could be terrified into making a saving response to the offer of God's grace. We have already noted how, very early in his career, he had resolved 'never to believe them to obey from fear who are dead to the motive of love', and he never went back on that resolve. Thus, we find him in his sermon on 'The Nature of Enthusiasm', which was one of his doctrinal standards, advising his people: 'Beware you are not a fiery, persecuting enthusiast. ... Never dream of forcing men into the ways of God. ... Even those who are farthest out of the way never compel to come in by any other means than reason, truth and love.'[64] We begin to see then, why this man who, in common with nearly all the serious-minded Christians of his day, held such a potentially terrifying doctrine of hell, yet felt obliged to use it with such considerable restraint in his preaching.

V

Wesley's one sermon on 'Hell'[65] is not included in the Standard Sermons which he regarded as the summary of his essential teaching. It was originally printed in the *Arminian Magazine* and belonged to a group of his sermons which he tells us he had never intended to publish in permanent form.[66] However, he heard that someone else was about to do so, and having suffered before at the hands of eighteenth century editors, well-meaning and otherwise, he finally decided to publish them himself. This was done in 1788, only three years before his death. This is not a pleasant sermon; the heavy shadow of the tyrant God hangs over it more than it usually does in the writings of Wesley. Nor is it improved for the modern reader by its biblical literalism and its rather naïve use of the latest scientific marvel by way of illustration.

It commences with a solemn warning, based on the sayings of Jesus in the Synoptic Gospels, which, as we have seen, Wesley could only interpret as implying that hell would be a matter of endless duration. He points out, however, quoting Matthew 25.41, that all this was 'originally prepared not for the children of men but "for the devil and his angels"', and he reiterates this in his New Testament Notes on this verse, adding the wry comment (with a sidelong glance at the Calvinists?) that human beings would be regarded as intruders. The sufferings of hell are divided into those of loss and those of positive pain. The former include loss of sensory pleasure ('There is no grandeur in the infernal regions'), the loss of personal relations with others, and finally, and most tragically of all, the loss of fellowship with God: 'Banishment from the presence of the Lord is the very essence of destruction to a spirit that was made for God'. The positive sufferings are, first of all, those of a highly personalized remorse and guilty conscience, and then literal hellfire. The whole passage dealing with hellfire takes up two pages out of the total of ten, but even those two pages are largely taken up first by an argument based on Wesley's literalist exegesis, that the fire must be material and not figurative, and then with a similarly pedestrian argument that the idea of everlasting fire is not intrinsically ridiculous, because of the recently discovered properties of asbestos![67] (Augustine solved the same problem by suggesting that those in hell would have bodies like a salamander which he believed suitably fire-resistant). Then follows a paragraph in which we see both the positive and negative sides of Wesley's biblicism, and his sharp rejection of the worst features of the traditional popular teaching about hell:

'Many writers have spoken of other bodily torments, added to the being cast into the lake of fire. One of these, even pious Kempis, supposes that misers, for instance, have melted gold poured down their throats; and he supposes many other particular torments to be suited to men's particular sins. Nay, our great poet himself supposes the inhabitants of hell to undergo a variety of tortures; not to continue always in the lake of fire, but to be frequently "By harpy-footed furies haled" into regions of ice; and then back again through "Extremes by change more fierce". But I find no word, no tittle of this, not the least hint of it in all the Bible. And surely this is too awful a subject to admit of such play of imagination. Let us keep to the written word. It is torment enough to dwell with everlasting burnings.'[68]

We may also note at this point that there is no hint in this sermon or anywhere else in Wesley's writings of the saints in glory gloating over the tortures of the damned, such as we have noted in the traditional teaching. Then finally, there follows the actual description of hellfire, which occupies about half a page—about five per cent of this sermon which is entirely devoted to the subject of hell. The sermon ends with a reminder of the extremely vicious, cruel and uncongenial company we should have to keep in hell, and a rather long-drawn-out reiteration of the endlessness of all these sufferings—which is easily the worst part of the whole thing.

Now there is, of course, a fair bit of positive spiritual insight in this sermon, but it is heavily overshadowed for us by the sheer repulsiveness of physical pain deliberately inflicted, and the senseless immoral horror of endless endurance, both of course arising largely out of the limitations of eighteenth century exegesis. Indeed, we get the impression that Wesley too found all this extremely unpleasant; and the eagerness with which he rejects as unscriptural the suggestions of other tortures indicates that he is not enamoured of the idea of physical pain as such, but feels forced to accept it and even justify it, because, and only because, it is thus far in the scriptures. Indeed it is difficult to see what other course was open to Wesley and his contemporaries so long as fidelity to God meant also fidelity to the letter of scripture.[69] However it must also be admitted that these views simply did not create for Wesley and most of his generation, the acute moral problem that they do for us. Even apart from our greater freedom of interpretation, many modern Christians would surely want to take up Wesley's great cry 'No scripture can mean that God is not love', and apply it against his own views about hell, just as he applied it against the Calvinist teaching about the double decree. All of which reminds us with something of a jolt of the vast revolutions of thought that the human race has passed through in the last two centuries, so that in some ways the thinking of the eighteenth century was nearer to that of mediaeval and ancient times than what it is to ours. As we have seen already, the concept of sovereignty, human and divine, was one element that was thus affected, and while Wesley's own more central teaching did so much in the long run to change this, some of his beliefs about hell give us another indication that he was still very much of an eighteenth century man, and had not worked this out with complete consistency, but in some aspects of his teaching was still influenced by the concept of the tyrant God. On the whole then, we are profoundly glad that Wesley made so little use of some of his beliefs about hell, but we are still rather sorry (though not altogether surprised) that he even held them.

His sermon on 'Hell' was apparently not one of Wesley's favourites. For example, between the years 1747 and 1761 he kept (or one of his friends kept for him) a very full Sermon Register[70] with details of all his preaching, covering about seven thousand different occasions; but there is no mention whatsoever in it of the sermon on hell. No doubt he did preach it on other occasions, but the only reference to it I have been able to trace in the *Journal* is an entry for April 26, 1769 when, preaching at Brickkilns, near Derry in Ireland, Wesley records: 'Finding the bulk of the hearers quite senseless, I spoke as strongly as I could on "Where their worm dieth not, and the fire is not quenched'. But I did not perceive they were at all affected. God only can raise the dead.'[71] I think it will be beyond dispute that there were many others in the eighteenth century who were much more at home in proclaiming hellfire. Compared, for example, with the lurid and enthusiastic efforts of his great contemporary Jonathan Edwards, even Wesley's one sermon on hell looks a very mild and ineffective affair, and I suggest that we have good reason, both theological and historical, to agree with W. L. Doughty 'that Wesley was not at his best nor wholly happy' in expounding 'The Terrors of the Lord'.[72]

VI

Before leaving this present subject we must look briefly at some of the other features of Wesley's teaching which make it hard for most moderns to enter sympathetically into his thought, and sometimes give emotional support to the quite misleading image of the hellfire preacher.[73] To start with, Wesley's estimate of the sinfulness and hopelessness of natural man, while it simply reflected the most serious theology of his day, does strike us as quite unreasonably sombre—although perhaps less extravagant when we know something of the widespread degradation, triviality and corruption of the society he lived in.[74] Yet his theology at this point was probably influenced also by a certain moralistic bias in his own upbringing, and his doctrine of man would certainly need to be modified in the light of a great deal of more recent thought about human nature.

However, before we dismiss Wesley as a narrow-minded prude, snooping around to spoil people's fun, all loaded up with pathological guilt feelings and projecting them onto others, let us get this side of his teaching into proper focus. After discussing what he calls Wesley's 'relentless teaching about man and sin' Rupert Davies goes on to say:

'But all this so far is a mere preamble to Wesley's real message. He has no delight in speaking of the Fall and doom of man, or of the small remnant of God's gifts still left with him. He referred to these matters only because otherwise the announcement of God's grace would be made *in vacuo*; he had to remind his hearers of the situation which elicited the divine mercy. But it is with the divine mercy and grace that he is really concerned. . . . The grace of God is the centrepiece of the whole Wesleyan theology.'[75]

It seems fairly plain that in Wesley's thought and experience the fear of the Lord was quite different from the fear of hell or punishment. It was something quite consistent with rejoicing, an essentially moral and religious fear far more akin to reverence than to terror, that his preaching and sometimes his mere presence,[76] inspired in people and this no doubt did contribute to his greater success in winning converts. For his message was no more fear provoking, in the ordinary sense, than that of the other great men of the revival, and as a preacher he was less emotional than his brother Charles, and decidedly less eloquent than George Whitefield. But as Dr Fitchett pointed out,

'Wesley saw with Dante-like vision, and had the power to make others see, the supreme fact of the spiritual world, the close relation in which the human soul stands to God; how near God is to man; in what relation man's sin stands to God's purity, man's need to God's pity, and all man's acts to God's judgment. So from the dim, remote far-off spaces of the heavens, God appeared to Wesley's hearers, a Figure loving and awful, and above all at the very touch.'[77]

This kind of reverential awe is a new dimension of experience, a greater depth of all feeling, rather than a greater intensity of any one particular feeling. It is an elemental response of one's whole being to the immediate presence of the Numinous or the Holy, which is not merely a daunting presence, but also one that is supremely evocative of love, joy and liberty in a far more radical sense of those words than they can bear in any other context. In Rudolf Otto's phrase, the *'Mysterium'* is not only *'Tremendum'* but also *'Fascinans'*[78] and any logical polarity of these two aspects is, as any true worshipper knows, transcended in the experience of adoration, and what Wesley called, in a favourite phrase of his, 'rejoicing unto God in reverence'. It was in this setting then, before such a God immediately present to him and his hearers, that Wesley was able to present his message existentially, as a life and death issue in the here and now, and to evoke a response that was immensely more rich and more Christian than any mere fear of a hellfire that awaited in the future.

VII

While Wesley's preaching of the law undoubtedly contributed to this sense of the Numinous, this was more in terms of a sort of Kantian reverence for the moral law and thus for God the law-giver, rather than in terms of the fear of punishment as such. His application of the law was usually a detailed invitation to his hearers to examine their outward conduct and inward motives, which uncovered in their minds not so much a fear of hell as a moral fear—fear and dismay at their moral failure.[79] It was a firm principle of Wesley that men should 'abhor sin far more than death or hell; abhor sin itself far more than the punishment of it'.[80] The strong element of guilt in these reactions was not the sort of chronic guilt colouration that can be imposed by powerful suggestion, but rather, an acute experience that soon gave way to a sense of forgiveness and release, and thus indicates a healing abreaction of buried guilt by the lowering of emotional repression.[81]

His preaching of the law, and the response which it evoked, should be seen in proper perspective against the general background of Wesley's teaching. Indicating the place which he gave to the law in his preaching, Dr Sargant quotes the following passage from Wesley:

'I think the right method of preaching is this. At our first beginning to preach at any place, after a general declaration of the love of God to sinners, and his willingness that they should be saved, to preach the law, in the strongest, the closest, the most searching manner possible.

'After more and more persons are convinced of sin, we may mix more and more of the gospel, in order to beget faith, to raise into spiritual life those whom the law hath slain. I would not advise to preach the law without the gospel, any more than the gospel without the law. Undoubtedly both should be preached in their turns; yea, both at once, or both in one. All the conditional promises are instances of this. They are law and gospel mixed together.'[82]

Now unless one is familiar with the theological controversies of the eighteenth century it is all too easy to miss the significance of the first part of this passage. The 'general declaration of the love of God to sinners, and His willingness that they should be saved', may not sound particularly novel to us, but to the majority of Wesley's hearers it was revolutionary doctrine, or even heresy. These words were no mere stock introduction to Wesley's sermons; rather they were a manifesto of his most distinctive teaching. The word 'general' was not meant to convey anything vague, but quite the reverse. When Charles Wesley sang of Christ as 'the general Saviour of mankind' he was not dealing with vague generalities, but proclaiming what was so often forgotten or explicitly denied in his day—that Christ is a *universal* saviour, the saviour of all who will receive him, and not merely of the select or elect few whom God had predestined for salvation. This was the declaration for which Wesley was renowned or notorious, according to one's point of view; it was the whole purport and tenor of his teaching, the constant background against which his proclamation of both the law and the gospel was made and understood.

In quoting the above passage from Wesley, Dr Sargant adds the quite gratuitous footnote: 'The "law" in this context includes the certainty that hellfire awaits the unsaved sinner'[83]; and, of course, if the passage had any relevance at all to this argument it would depend on the appropriateness of this footnote, rather than on anything actually quoted. However, once again Dr Sargant has misled both himself and his readers by taking his quotations at second hand. The passage is quoted from Tyerman's *Life and Times of Rev. John Wesley* and comes originally from a fairly long letter of Wesley's written probably to Ebenezer Blackwell, and reproduced in full in Volume XI of his Collected Works. The main purpose of the letter is to warn the recipient against a particular form of so-called gospel preaching current at the time, which was apparently devoid of ethical content, and therefore produced only an ephemeral emotional reaction without any permanent change of character or conduct.[84] Had Dr Sargant bothered to refer to this letter in full he would have discovered some interesting facts. First of all, Wesley explicitly says what he means by the preaching of 'the "law" in this context': 'By "preaching the law", I mean explaining and enforcing the commands of Christ, briefly comprised in the Sermon on the Mount.'[85] There is in fact no mention of hell, or the threat of future punishment anywhere throughout the whole letter, and although we do not deny of course that Wesley believed in hell, it is quite obvious from his letter that his paramount interest in preaching the law was something quite different. As against those who would preach either all gospel or all law, he insists that at every stage, both are needed together. Set in the context of God's universal love, the law is needed to convince the unconverted of his need, but it is also just as truly needed, along with the gospel, as a 'means of feeding and comforting believers'—and this latter point is Wesley's main concern in this letter. The fine blend of ethical preaching, salvation by grace alone, and the liberating power of the gospel is brought out in this passage, for example:

'But when these grow in grace and the knowledge of Christ, the wise builder would preach the law to them again; only taking particular care to place every part of it in a Gospel light, as not only a command, but a privilege also, as a branch of the glorious liberty of the sons of God. He would take equal care to remind them, that this is not the cause, but the fruit of their acceptance with God; that other cause, "other foundation can no man lay, than that which is laid, even Jesus Christ"; that we are still forgiven and accepted, only for the sake of what he hath done and suffered for us; and that all true obedience springs from love to him, grounded in his first loving us. He would labour, therefore, in preaching any part of the law, to keep the love of Christ continually before their eyes; that thence they might draw fresh life, vigour and strength, to run the way of his commandments.'[86]

Again and again this theme is reiterated throughout the letter.

It is 'the law grafted upon, tempered by, and animated with, the spirit of the Gospel'[87] that Wesley advises 'every Preacher continually to preach', and the setting of all this in the context of God's love is brought out again in the closing passage in which he says of a certain Methodist congregation:

'From the beginning they had been taught both the law and the Gospel. 'God loves you; therefore love and obey him. Christ died for you; therefore die to sin. Christ is risen; therefore rise in the image of God. Christ liveth evermore; therefore live to God, till you live with him in glory.'[88]

Dr Sargant's footnote to the passage quoted from this letter then, appears to tell us much more on his own *a priori* assumptions than about Wesley's advice about preaching.

We may well feel today that Wesley's teaching on ethical issues sometimes tended to be too moralistic in tone. Moralism has always been one of the worst enemies of morality, and all the more so because the two are so often mixed up together and mistaken for each other. Freedom and spontaneity are of the essence of genuine morality; where coercion begins morality ends. We cannot *make* people be good; we may make them conform to certain standards of outward conduct, but no matter how ethically admirable these standards may be in themselves, insofar as a person's conformity to them is not an expression of his own freedom, it ceases to be moral. Moralistic coercion can of course be of many kinds, ranging through physical force, social pressure, fear of hell, threat of emotional rejection, deliberate psychological manipulation, and sheer weight of suggestion and moral injunction. Such coercion may be built into a personality during the early years, and is often recognized by psychotherapists as the domination of a more or less ruthless super-ego which may have to be broken down before any genuinely moral personality can emerge.

Wesley can hardly be accused of the more crude and obvious forms of moralistic coercion, but modern readers of his sermons and tracts may well feel that he did harp a little too much on moral issues. Dr Sydney Dimond points out certain repressive and moralistic features of Wesley's own upbringing,[89] and while the nature of his conversion and subsequent experience of grace

I

seem to show that he was himself almost entirely delivered from this moralism, it may well be that something of its shadow lingered on, to influence the form in which some of his ethical preaching was cast.

However, there are much more clearly attested facts which must be taken into consideration also. The eighteenth century in England witnessed a widespread moral degradation, coarsening of manners, sensual extravagance and social corruption which were very largely a violent reaction and revolt against the rigid moralism of the previous century. Morality by legislation, social pressure and repression had been thoroughly attempted in Cromwell's England, just as it had been in the previous century in Calvin's Geneva; and in the anti-Puritan reaction that began with the Restoration and carried on unabated well into the next century not only was this repressive moralism swept aside, but because most men had lost the capacity to distinguish between the two, morality itself was in danger of being completely discredited and denied. Already there was abroad a specious form of revivalism which proclaimed salvation by faith alone, and the worthlessness of good works either before or after justification in such a way as to open the door to licence under the misnomer of liberty; and it was largely to erect a bulwark against this Antinomianism, as he called it, that Wesley laid such stress on the law in his preaching. As Dr Sugden observed in his prefatory note to Wesley's sermons on the Law:

'But to preach to unlettered and ignorant Christians that they were "free from the law" inevitably led to the most monstrous practical abuses; and some of them claimed even freedom to take the property of others and to commit adultery, to say nothing of other sins such as gluttony, drunkenness, idleness and the like.'[90]

Under these circumstances clear and strong moral teaching was certainly needed, but much recent writing seems to show that in our day, we are ourselves still too much involved in the confused reaction against Victorian moralism to be able to judge the moral teaching of the Evangelical Revival objectively, or to distinguish fairly between its genuine and necessary morality on the one hand and its residue of moralism on the other. Certainly Wesley and his followers were not sufficiently detached from the events of their day to get all this in perspective, and it would have been remarkable indeed if, in their efforts to defend morality, they had escaped completely the taint of moralism with which it was so commonly confused. The fact that they did so largely escape it, is, I would suggest, a sheer miracle of grace.

It was in fact the effective proclamation of saving grace that protected the Evangelical Revival in its full vigour from the worst effects of moralism; for it is only when moral concern loses vital touch with the means of grace that make it possible for man to be genuinely good, that it is faced with intolerable frustration, and tempted to resort to some form of coercion, and thus to degenerate into moralism. Some such fate as this probably did overtake the movement at different times in its later history. But despite the apparently moralistic tone of some of Wesley's sermons, I believe the contemporary records show us that during his lifetime and for some time after, the liberating grace of God was so offered and received that for many thousands of people genuine goodness flowered as a spontaneous expression of a new life in Christ, without much trace of moralistic compulsion.

We have already noted a certain inconsistency in Wesley's attitude towards the concept of tyrannical or despotic sovereignty as applied to God. By effectively discrediting the doctrine of the double decree and thereby demolishing the arbitrariness of God's justice and the uncertainty of his mercy, Wesley unwittingly did more (for the English speaking world at least) than anyone else to undermine the whole authoritarian concept of God. Yet, as we have seen, he did not entirely escape such a concept himself, and the outlines of the authoritarian God still appear in much of his own teaching; particularly where it strikes modern man as being tinged with moralism. Despite its early promise of liberty, the Protestant Reformation had issued in an authoritarian theology; partly, no doubt, by way of its legacy from mediaeval Catholicism which had been influenced by the concept of the despotic ruler, but reinforced also by the characteristic personality structure of the Reformers themselves, and the sociological conditions operative at the time.[91]

Authoritarian theology and moralistic ethics are linked by a certain inner logic. The essence of moralism is the effort to inculcate goodness by coercion or law. Calvin's God was primarily a sovereign and only secondarily a saviour, a lawgiver in essence and a lover by condescension. Whatever else may have been said about mercy and grace, the final sanctions of such a God were the sanctions of force—of almighty power and arbitrary decree. Luther was less consistent and less obtrusive than Calvin in his authoritarianism, but his thought was nevertheless constantly haunted by the hidden God, the *Deus Absconditus*,

'that secret and to be feared will of God . . . which will is not to be curiously enquired into, but to be adored with reverence as the most profound secret of the divine Majesty, which he reserves unto Himself and keeps hidden from us.'[92]

There was of course a more Christocentric side of Luther's theology also, and a wonderful recognition of the fatherhood of God. But on the whole it was Calvin's more rigid and consistent authoritarian doctrine of the divine sovereignty that dominated Protestant thought down to the eighteenth century. It is against this background of Reformation theology that we must assess the teaching of John Wesley, because the element of moralism in his system was undoubtedly connected with the traces of this authoritarian view of God which he retained and never completely harmonized with his own more profound teaching about the divine mercy.[93]

VIII

Except for a brief period when Charles seemed to be in danger of coming under the influence of the Moravian quietist teaching, the two Wesley brothers were in remarkable accord in matters of doctrine, and Charles Wesley's hymns were the perfect vehicle for expressing the evangelical insights of the whole movement, and in that way, nearly as influential as John's preaching. Dr Sargant's remark that these hymns 'were addressed to the religious emotions rather than to the intelligence'[94] displays no more understanding of his sources than one would expect. Certainly there is much vigorous religious emotion in these hymns, much joy and gratitude to God, much love to God and man, but they are also well packed with doctrine and the intellectual content of the faith. Charles Wesley's great Christmas hymns,[95] for example, are favourite expressions of Christian joy and praise; they do not rely on the pretty trimmings of some traditional hymns but are filled with the theology of the Incarnation. There is a great deal of the love of God in Charles Wesley's hymns, but very little indeed about hell.[96]

Battle for the Mind is deservedly a very widely read book, but it has done a great deal of disservice by presenting to a large number of readers a picture of Wesley the preacher which has no historical foundation, and is all the more seriously misleading because it will seem to many intelligent lay readers to be backed by the authority of both scholarship and science. To discredit Wesley at this stage matters very little, but the reflections this inevitably casts on the movement and what the movement stands for, are far more serious. One wonders how many thousands of readers who know nothing of the work of John Wesley have accepted in good faith Dr Sargant's unwitting caricature. Psychiatrists for example, to whom the subject is naturally of some interest, while they may differ from Dr Sargant's viewpoint, can hardly be blamed for assuming that he has at least got his facts right.[97] At least two such writers in recent years have been misled by taking Dr Sargant's undocumented version of Wesley, the hellfire preacher, at its face value. Dr Jerome D. Frank, discussing religious revivalism in his book *Persuasion and Healing*, says 'Great evangelists of previous eras, like Jonathan Edwards and John Wesley, dwelt on the horrors of damnation . . . ',[98] citing the American edition of Dr Sargant's book as his sole authority for this and other statements about Wesley. Reference has already been made to Dr J. A. C. Brown's book *Techniques of Persuasion*. Although he treats his subject from a different psychiatric viewpoint, this writer seems to have depended on Dr Sargant for some of his source material. Especially in the chapter on 'The Nature of Religious Conversion' in which he mentions Sargant, and reproduces almost verbatim[99] a summarized form of his remarks on Wesley from Chapter 5 of *Battle for the Mind*.

Over sixty years ago the agnostic historian Sir Leslie Stephen attempted to explain the phenomena of the Evangelical Revival along somewhat similar lines to those of Dr Sargant's book. The comment that was later made by Sir Arnold Lunn, on what he called 'this feeble caricature of a solution', is worth quoting:

' . . . men are seldom reformed by fear. Throughout the Middle Ages the horrors of Hell formed the staple topic of Mediaeval sermons, but there were few cases of men being thrown into "fits of excitement" by such sermons and still fewer cases of such fits proving an important crisis in their lives.

'Facts, as I said before, are stubborn things. Had Leslie Stephen checked his theory by the facts he would have discovered that Wesley only preached one sermon on Hell, whereas he preached rather more than forty thousand times on his favourite theme, the love of God freely offered to all mankind.'[100]

Perhaps that is the best summary of our answer to Dr Sargant under this head: 'Facts are stubborn things.'

FOOTNOTES AND REFERENCES

1. There are innumerable biographies of Wesley. Some recent and not so recent that may be recommended: *Life of John Wesley* by John Telford (1899), *Wesley and His Century* by W. H. Fitchett (1906), *Son to Susannah* by Elsie Harrison, Ivor Nicholson & Watson 1937, and Penguin Books 1944, *John Wesley and the Eighteenth Century* by Maldwyn Edwards, George Allen & Unwin 1933, *John Wesley* by Ingvar Haddal, Epworth Press 1961, *John Wesley, Anglican* by Garth Lean, Blandford Press 1964. Three appreciative books by Roman Catholic writers: *John Wesley in the Evolution of Protestantism* by Maximin Piette, Sheed & Ward 1937, *John Wesley* by Arnold Lunn, Cassell & Co. 1929, and *John Wesley and the Catholic Church* by John M. Todd, Hodder & Stoughton 1958, and also *Methodism* by Rupert E. Davies, Epworth Press and also Penguin Books 1963.

2. *Op. cit.*, Vol. VI, p. 77, by H. W. V. Temperley. Quoted by J. W. Bready in *England Before and After Wesley*, Hodder & Stoughton 1938, p. 180.

3. *Essays and Reviews*, p. 35. Quoted by J. W. Bready, *op. cit.*, pp. 180-1.

4. Southey, Robert, 1820, *The Life of Wesley*.

5. Bowen, Marjorie, *Wrestling Jacob*, William Heinemann Ltd., London 1937.

6. Knox, Ronald, *Enthusiasm*, Oxford University Press 1950, Chs. XVIII-XXI.

FACT AND FICTION135

7. Knox, op. cit., pp. 422-58.
8. Battle for the Mind, Ch. 5.
9. Op. cit., p. xii (10).
10. Ibid., p. 76 (83).
11. Ibid., p. xxii (19).
12. See above, Ch. 4.
13. Sargant, op. cit., pp. xxii (18-19).
14. See below, Ch. 7.
15. Sargant, op. cit., p. 78 (84).
16. See below, pp. 103, 109.
17. 'An Extract of John Nelson's Journal' in Wesley's Veterans, Vol. III, Charles H. Kelly, London 1912, pp. 11-12.
18. The Journal of the Rev. John Wesley A.M., Standard Edition edited by Nehemiah Curnock, Charles H. Kelly, London 1912 —hereinafter referred to as Journal—Vol. II, p. 223, June 17, 1739.
19. Southey, op. cit., Chs. vi and vii.
20. Knox, op. cit., Ch. XXI. See also his preface, pp. v-vi. The comparison which Knox made between Methodism and such sects as the Montanists, Donatists, Anabaptists etc. has of course been made before, but I cannot help thinking that his particular critical bias has led him to give too much weight to accidental similarities and too little to important differences. The word 'enthusiasm' in a religious sense is an emotive term, confused in Wesley's day and worse in ours. When we examine the variety of movements which Knox assembled under this title, it seems that the only really significant thing they all had in common was their failure to recognize the authority of Rome. (Cf. the last paragraph in Knox's Preface, p. v.)
21. Marjorie Bowen, op. cit., pp. 244-53.
22. Dimond, Sidney G., The Psychology of the Methodist Revival, Oxford University Press, London 1926, p. 83.
23. Winchester, C. T., The Life of John Wesley, The MacMillan Company, New York 1906, p. 88.
24. Journal, Vol. III, p. 13.
25. Ibid., p. 14.
26. Ibid., Vol. II, pp. 211-13, June 5, 1739.
27. All the sermons are included in the various editions of Wesley's complete works.

28. An Annotated edition of the Standard Sermons (the Forty Four) together with nine other sermons commonly associated with them, was edited by Dr E. H. Sugden and published by the Epworth Press in 1921 in two volumes.

29. See the lengthy quotations from Jonathan Edwards and Charles Finney, Sargant, *op. cit.*, pp. 136-45 (131-8).

30. In Sugden's edition of the Standard Sermons there are two references to 'Hell' in the Index. Indexes of course, are not exhaustive, but they do give some indication of the contents. Lest Sugden's index be suspected of reflecting the unconscious bias of a twentieth century editor, it should be mentioned that in the 1829-31 edition of Wesley's Complete Works, published only forty years after his death, the Index to the fourteen volumes, comprising over 7,000 pages, lists only eleven references to 'Hell'.

31. Davies, Rupert E., *Methodism*, Epworth Press, and Penguin Books 1963, Epworth edition p. 72, Pelican edition p. 94.

32. *Ibid.*, Epworth p. 74, Pelican pp. 96-7.

33. Sargant, *op. cit.*, p. 78 (84).

34. See John Todd in *John Wesley and the Catholic Church*, Hodder and Stoughton 1958, pp. 144-5.

35. Quoted in *John Wesley, Anglican* by Garth Lean. Blandford Press, London 1964, p. 46.

36. This is Sermon XV in the Works Vol. V, p. 160, and is included in the 'Fifty Three' (Sugden's edition).

37. Dimond, *op. cit.*, p. 115.

38. See Letter DCCCVIII to Miss Bishop, April 17, 1766, in which Wesley discusses the nature of heaven : 'But what is the essential part of heaven? Undoubtedly it is to see God, to know God, to love God.'—Works Vol. XIII, p. 29.

39. Robinson, J. A. T., in *Honest to God*, S.C.M. Press, London 1963, p. 16.

40. Strawson, William, B.D., M.Th., *Jesus and the Future Life*, Epworth Press, 1959, p. 143.

41. *Op. cit.*, pp. 143-4.

42. *Ibid.*, p. 150.

43. *Ibid.*, p. 147.

44. *Ibid.*, p. 149.

45. *Ibid.*, *loc. cit.*

46. *Ibid.*, p. 150.

47. At this point in the discussion we are concerned with the problems presented by the traditional teaching about hell, for the Christian *conscience*, rather than the intellect. However, it is usually objected to the idea of hell as consequence rather than as punishment (i) that this would detract from the sovereignty of God. I think this objection springs from a mistaken idea of the divine sovereignty that is mentioned below. (ii) That it would depersonalize the relationship between God and man; that hell as consequence would be far less personal than hell as punishment. But surely the weakness of this objection is that any form of everlasting punishment must be so grossly out of all proportion to even a lifetime of full-time sinning that it would represent the ultimate in depersonalization of the sinner. We are far less likely to be depersonalized by the inevitable and self-inflicted consequences of our own sinning than what we would be under the limitless vengeance of an angry God.

48. Baillie, John, *And the Life Everlasting*, Oxford University Press, London 1934, p. 245.

49. Strawson, *op. cit.*, p. 148.

50. *Ibid.*, p. 155.

51. *Ibid.*, *loc. cit.* Cf. Leckie, J. H., D.D. *The World to Come and Final Destiny*, T. & T. Clark, Edinburgh, 2nd Edition 1922, p. 113.

52. Richardson, Alan, D.D., *An Introduction to the Theology of the New Testament*, S.C.M. Press, London 1958, p. 74.

53. Cf. Guy, H. A., B.A., B.D., *The New Testament Doctrine of The Last Things*, Oxford University Press 1948, p. 53, and Baillie, *op. cit.*, pp. 241 ff.

54. Strawson, *op. cit.*, p. 155.

55. Robinson, J. A. T., *In the End, God*, James Clark & Co., London 1950, pp. 32-3.

56. Tertullian, *De Spectaculis*, quoted in Baillie, *op. cit.*, p. 242.

57. Leckie, *op. cit.*, p. 118.

58. *Ibid.*, pp. 118-19.

59. *Ibid.*, p. 119.

60. Matthews, W. R., M.A., D.D., *God in Christian Thought and Experience*, Nisbet & Co., London 1930, p. 226.

61. These words appear in Wesley's famous sermon on 'Free Grace' (Sermon CXXVIII, p. 356, Vol. 7 of *The Works of the Rev. John Wesley* A.M., 10th edition, John Mason, London 1849— hereinafter referred to as *Works*). This sermon should be read in full to understand the full force of Wesley's opposition to the Calvinist doctrine of the Double Decree.

62. From Wesley's Sermon on 'Hell'—see below.

63. *Op. cit.*, *Works*, Vol. 8, p. 46.

64. *Op. cit.*, *Works*, Vol. 5, p. 449. This sermon is No. XXXII in the Standard Sermons.

65. This is Sermon No. LXXIII, *Works*, Vol. 6, p. 360 ff.

66. See the Preface to the Second Series of Sermons, *Works*, Vol. 6, p. 175.

67. Wesley also has some rather tortuous exegesis of the obscure reference to being 'salted with fire' in his comments on Mark 9.49 in his 'Notes on the New Testament', in order to try and solve this problem of how physical bodies would endure endless physical fire.

68. *Op. cit.*, *Works*, Vol. 6, p. 366.

69. Cf. Doughty, W. L., in *John Wesley, Preacher*, Epworth Press, London 1955, p. 106.

70. The Sermon Register is included in Wesley's *Journal*, Vol. VIII, pp. 169-252.

71. *Journal*, Vol. V, p. 314.

72. Doughty, *op. cit.*, p. 106.

73. See above, p. 107.

74. See below, Ch. 8.

75. Davies, *op. cit.*, Epworth p. 76, Pelican p. 99.

76. See above, p. 102.

77. Fitchett, Dr W. H., *Wesley and his Century*, Geo. Bell & Sons, London 1906, p. 188.

78. Otto, Rudolf, *The Idea of the Holy*, translated by John W. Harvey, 5th (Revised) Impression, Oxford University Press 1929, Chs. IV-VI.

79. Dimond, *op. cit.*, p. 201.

80. Cf. Sermon No. XXXIV in the Forty Four Standard Sermons.

81. For the importance of this distinction see above, Ch. 4.

82. Quoted by Sargant, *op. cit.*, pp. 80-1 (86), from Wesley in L. Tyerman's *Life and Times of the Rev. John Wesley* M.A.

83. Sargant, *op. cit.*, p. 80, footnote 3 (86, footnote 1).

84. *Op. cit., Works*, Vol. XI, pp. 466-72.

85. *Ibid.*, p. 466.

86. *Ibid.*, p. 467.

87. *Ibid.*, p. 469.

88. *Ibid.*, p. 471.

89. Dimond, *op. cit.*, pp. 82-3.

90. Sugden, *op. cit.*, Vol. II, p. 37.

91. See Erich Fromm, *The Fear of Freedom*, Routledge and Kegan Paul, London 1942, pp. 53-88.

92. Martin Luther, *De Servo Arbitrio* LXIV (H. Cole's translation). Quoted by H. Maldwyn Hughes, *The Christian Idea of God*, Duckworth 1936, p. 69.

93. It has been pointed out (for example by G. C. Cell in *The Rediscovery of John Wesley*, Henry Holt & Co., New York 1935) that Wesley was more of a Calvinist than his opponents realized. He was an Arminian, but never a Pelagian. In their estimate of 'natural man' and his complete inability to do anything for his own salvation apart from sovereign saving grace, both Arminius and Wesley were as profoundly Augustinian as Calvin himself, but they refused to link the Augustinian view of man with the Augustinian view of grace as irresistible force.

94. Sargant, *op. cit.*, p. 78 (84).

95. See *The Methodist Hymn Book* (1933), Nos. 82, 117, 134, 135, 141, 142, 242, 902. Cf. also Rupert Davies, *op. cit.*, Pelican pp. 110-21.

96. I owe this point to the late Dr Alan Kay who was kind enough to read through the original articles on which this essay is based, and to add several comments from which I have profited.

97. *The Lancet* of April 27, 1957 (p. 870) carries a review of *Battle for the Mind* in which the reviewer refers (*inter alia*) to 'the hellfire threats of Wesley', and suggests that those who disagree with certain features of the book 'will find it hard to refute Dr Sargant's facts and main conclusion'.

98. Frank, Jerome D., *Persuasion and Healing*, Oxford University Press, London, and the John Hopkins Press, Baltimore, 1960, p. 78 and footnote (5) to this chapter—Notes p. 240.

99. Brown, *op. cit.*, p. 233.

100. Lunn, Arnold, *John Wesley*, Cassell & Co., London 1929, pp. 15-16.

CHAPTER 7

TRAVAIL AND TRIUMPH

As we undertake a more detailed consideration of the more violent and bizarre reactions to John Wesley's preaching, it will be of some value to get this whole matter into historical focus against the general background of the Evangelical Revival. Because of their particular interest in these strange phenomena, writers like Dr Sargant and the late Monsignor Ronald Knox may easily leave in the minds of their readers the impression that this sort of thing was a typical and more or less everyday occurrence wherever Wesley preached. This impression is, of course, quite misleading, as a fair examination of Wesley's *Journal* will reveal. The Evangelical Revival continued to be a vital and effective religious movement under the leadership of John Wesley for upwards of fifty years, but most of its more spectacular manifestations were confined to the early period between the years 1739 and 1743. Of the *Journal* entries for this period Dr Sydney Dimond writes as follows:

'In some instances the whole congregation is described as breaking forth into tears or cries or groaning, but, apart from these general statements, I have examined two hundred and thirty-four individual cases enumerated and reported on during the years 1739-43. Out of eighty-five cases of persons who "dropped as dead", fifty-six occurred in Bristol, nineteen in London, seven in Newcastle and three in Cornwall. Two cases of persons struck blind (psychogenic blindness) are reported from Newcastle. Convulsive tearings, violent trembling, groaning, strong cries and tears, and other physical effects are frequently recorded throughout the second and third volumes of the *Journal*. There are fourteen cases of madness and restoration, and nine cases of incurable insanity. From the distribution of these peculiar phenomena it is apparent that they occurred largely among the more primitive and less civilized types, in the neighbourhood of Bristol and

Kingswood, and at Gateshead Fell and Chowden, which Wesley characterizes as "the very Kingswood of the North".[1]

In this conveniently concentrated form the list looks formidable enough, but spread out in the context of Wesley's prodigious labours during these years, it gives a somewhat different impression. I have carefully examined the *Journal* covering this period, and there are less than twenty occasions recorded when a large number or a whole congregation was affected. In most instances there was no sign of the spread of physical symptoms or other highly emotional reactions by crowd contagion at all, and only a handful of people, or sometimes even a single individual was affected, in a very large crowd. There was nothing, for example, to parallel the wild outbursts of religious enthusiasm and mob hysteria that were a feature of the New England revival of about the same period. On the contrary, all the manifestations of mob violence associated with Wesley's own preaching were decidely anti-Methodist, and often deliberately stirred up or organized by the clergy who were opposed to him. They were certainly not outbursts of religious fervour among those swayed by his eloquence.[2] Taking in both the group manifestations and the two hundred and thirty-four individual cases which Dr Dimond mentions, there are recorded in the *Journal* a total of seventy different occasions on which these phenomena occurred between 1739 and 1743. But during this period Wesley was preaching between twelve and fifteen times per week, sometimes to smaller groups, but usually to congregations of several hundred people, and often to crowds running into the thousands, and the *Journal* and *Diary* record a total of some three thousand preaching occasions. Thus it will be seen that during the five-year period of their greatest frequency, these strange reactions to Wesley's preaching appeared on the *average* about once every three and a half weeks, or on less than three per cent of the occasions on which he preached.[3] For some reason or other, after 1743, while the Revival itself went on unabated, the incidence of these violent reactions declined quite sharply; however, they did reappear for shorter periods in later years and there were occasional manifestations right up to 1788.

Outbursts of involuntary, and more or less violent physical, symptoms and emotional reactions have often been associated

with religious revivals in their early stages. As the Rev Richard
Watson, one of Wesley's early biographers, wrote:

'It may be laid down as a principle established by fact that whenever a zealous and faithful ministry is raised up, after a long
spiritual dearth, the early effects of that ministry are not only
powerful, but often attended without extraordinary circumstances; nor are such extraordinary circumstances necessarily
extravagancies because they are not common.'[4]

An attitude of superficial contempt may quite easily sweep all
this aside as a lot of morbid nonsense, without realizing its significance or appreciating the immense 'variety of religious
experience' even at this level.[5]

There were two distinctive features of the Methodist Revival
with regard to these strange accompaniments. First, there was
the cautiously objective attitude of Wesley himself towards
them. He was certainly intrigued and even impressed by their
long term effects, and after carefully observing these strange
occurrences for some time he made a number of attempts in his
Journal to account for them; although he probably did not work
out a completely straightforward explanation even to his own
satisfaction. But he was always careful to insist that however
the agonies or other physical symptoms experienced by some of
his converts were to be accounted for, such things were never by
themselves to be taken as a sign of conversion or justification,
nor regarded as being in any sense essential to the process of
salvation.

Secondly, as Dr Sydney Dimond observed,

'The distinctive feature of Wesley's work when it is viewed in
relation to the history of revivals, is the marked *ethical* quality
both in his preaching and in his life, which made the emotional
disturbances in the vast majority of cases a decisive force in the
formation of a higher type of character.'[6]

Writing to his brother Samuel, who had expressed uneasiness at
some of the things he had heard, Wesley said in May 1739:

'I have seen (as far as a thing of this kind can be seen) very many persons changed in a moment from the spirit of fear, horror, despair to the spirit of love, joy, peace; and from sinful desire, till then reigning over them, to a pure desire of doing the will of God. These are matters of fact, wherof I have been, and almost daily am, an eye or ear witness. . . . And that such a change was then wrought appears (not from their shedding tears only, or falling into fits, or crying out: these are not the fruits, as you seem to suppose, whereby I judge, but) from the whole tenor of their life, till then many ways wicked; from that time holy, just and good.

'I will show you him that was a lion till then, and is now a lamb; him that was a drunkard, and now is exemplarily sober; the whore-monger that was, who now abhors the very "garment spotted by the flesh". These are my living arguments for what I assert . . . '[7]

Four years later, Thomas Butts, a trusted friend of Wesley, in a pamphlet produced in answer to some of the slanderous charges levelled at the Methodists, wrote:

'As to persons crying out or being in fits, I shall not pretend to account exactly for that, but only would make this observation upon it. It is well known that most of them that have been so exercised, were, before, persons of no religion at all; but they have since received a sense of pardon, have peace and joy in believing, and are now more holy and happy than ever they were before. And if this be so, no matter what remarks are made on their fits.'[8]

Under Wesley's preaching a great number of people passed through some form of spiritual struggle and crisis that issued in their conversion, with a marked and permanent reformation of character and a general increase in personal contentment and efficiency. Those who exhibited physical symptoms or other violent emotional signs of their struggle, were not regarded by Wesley as being radically different from the rest. In every case he felt himself preaching to men and women in bondage to sin and death, who could be set at liberty and born again by the grace of God. The violence of their birth pangs, while they were of considerable psychological interest, and aroused all manner of puzzled speculation and adverse comment, were of no particular theological significance in themselves. Those whose deliverance was accompanied by such symptoms were not considered to be in a class apart, nor does the end result of their conversion appear to have been any different from what happened in the more normal cases.

In some cases the hearers began to be troubled in mind ('cut to the heart', Wesley called it) and quickly passed into a more or less violent agony of body and mind expressed in crying, and sometimes in shrieking and roaring, and occasionally the struggle would reach the proportions of violent trembling or bodily convulsion. Sometimes, though not always, the general condition would grow worse till the sufferer collapsed in unconsciousness. However in other instances there was no outward sign of struggle at all, but the hearer would simply drop down as dead without any warning. During the period of struggle or unconsciousness (either of which might last some time) Wesley and some of the others present would pray earnestly for the afflicted person's release—not only from the torments of the moment, but from the powers of sin and darkness in general. It is quite important to notice this fact—that the relief sought was not merely from the present distressing symptoms, but from what was conceived as a long standing condition from which all men suffered, and of which the present distress was, in some puzzling way, simply an acute manifestation having all the appearances of a crisis. In most cases the release came before very long, and was immediately evident in peace and joy, and (what was considerably more important) subsequently worked out in a truly changed life. Of course, not all these results were permanent, but a very large proportion of them were, and I doubt whether there has been any other revival movement in the whole history of the Church, of which the permanent results have been more carefully investigated by both promoters and critics, or the long standing effects been more impressively documented.[9]

It will be worthwhile to examine for ourselves some of the reports which Wesley has given us in his *Journal*, of the more peculiar and violent reactions to his preaching. Seven of these accounts are quoted in *Battle for the Mind*,[10] and on closer examination we shall see that in most of them only one or two people in a large crowd were affected; in only one instance were these reactions spread throughout the crowd by the sort of emotional contagion which Dr Sargant mentions. Furthermore, in view of our discussion in the previous chapter, it will not be surprising to discover that there is even less evidence of hellfire preaching. In four out of the seven accounts cited, Wesley has in fact given us some details of his preaching on that occasion, but Dr Sargant does not mention these; they do not include any suggestion of the terrors of hell.

Such occurrences were common in Wesley's ministry at Bristol in April and the following months of 1739, and under his entry for April 17th he records:

'Thence I went to Baldwin Street and expounded, as it came in course, the fourth chapter of Acts. We then called upon God to confirm His word. Immediately one that stood by (to our no small surprise) cried out aloud with the utmost vehemence, even as in the agonies of death. But we continued in prayer till "a new song was put in her mouth, a thanksgiving unto our God". Soon after, two other persons (well known in this place, as labouring to live in all good conscience towards all men), were seized with strong pain, and constrained to "roar for the disquietness of their heart". But it was not long before they likewise burst forth into praise to God their Saviour. The last who called upon God, as out of the belly of hell, was John Ellis, a stranger in Bristol. And in a short space he also was overwhelmed with joy and love, knowing that God had healed his backslidings.'[11]

The fourth chapter of Acts which Wesley was expounding on this occasion relates the trial of Peter and John, their defiance of the authorities and the manifestation of the Holy Spirit's power. The lesson was apparently chosen because it was the one appointed for the day. It has no particular reference to the fear of hell, of course, although it is possible that Wesley may have applied its descriptions of the Spirit's manifestations to interpret some of the happenings both wonderful and weird that were becoming a feature of his Bristol ministry.

The recovery from collapse or despair was nearly always made in the context of prayer, and sometimes the whole event took place in such a setting. From the *Journal* of 1749 we may cite an instance of this, during Wesley's third visit to Ireland. He relates

K

how he 'had continued in prayer with the whole congregation' for some time, and goes on:

'When I had at length pronounced the blessing, no man stirred, but each stayed in his place till I walked through them. I was soon called back by one crying out "My God! My God! Thou hast forgotten me." Having spoken this, she sunk to the earth. We called upon God in her behalf. The cries both of her and of several others, mourning after God, redoubled. But we continued wrestling with God in prayer till He gave us an answer of peace.'[12]

Sometimes, as appears from the records, the collapse was more sudden and dramatic. Wesley notes in his *Journal* of September 1743 that at a Society Meeting at St Ives in Cornwall,

' . . . two women who came from Penzance fell down as dead, and soon after cried out in the bitterness of their souls; but we continued crying to God in their behalf, till he put a new song in their mouths. At the same time, a young man of the same place, who had once known the peace of God, but had sinned it away, had a fresh and clear manifestation of the love of God.'[13]

The *Journal* of November 1742 records this sort of reaction mixed with others at Newcastle:

'There seemed in the evening to be a deeper work in many souls than I had observed before. Many trembled exceedingly; six or seven (both men and women) dropped down as dead; some cried unto God out of the deep; others would have cried, but their voice was lost; and some have found that the Lord is "gracious and merciful, forgiving iniquity, and transgression and sin".'[14]

Release did not always come immediately; sometimes the person concerned would be in some travail for days. At Kingswood in January 1740, during an administration of the sacrament of Holy Communion, ' . . . a woman who had been before much tempted of the devil, sunk down as dead. One could not perceive, by any motion of her breast, that she breathed, and her pulse was hardly discernible . . . '[15] It was not until the following

Sunday, when Wesley had been preaching on the text 'ye are saved by faith', that this woman 'was now made partaker of this salvation; being above measure filled with the love of God, and with all peace and joy in believing'.[16]

We have already noted how Dr Sargant followed up his fanciful description of Wesley's technique as a hellfire evangelist with a somewhat inappropriate quotation from the *Journal* of one of his converts, but the descriptions of violent conversions which he cites from Wesley's own *Journal*, on the following page of *Battle for the Mind*, are no more useful for this purpose either. The first of these is taken from the *Journal* entry of June 22, 1739:

'While I was speaking one before me dropped down as dead, and presently a second and a third. Five others sunk down in half an hour, most of whom were in violent agonies. "The pains" as "of hell came about them, the snares of death overtook them." In their trouble we called upon the Lord, and He gave us an answer of peace. One indeed continued an hour in strong pain, and one or two more for three days; but the rest were greatly comforted in that hour, and went away rejoicing and praising God.'[17]

Whether Wesley's expressions 'the pains as of hell'[17]and 'the snares of death' were meant to indicate in this case, the actual *content* of these people's agony, or whether they were more or less stock phrases quoted to suggest the *degree* of anguish, we have no way of deciding. There are of course indications of a quite profound fear of death and hell already in the minds of some of the people who came to hear Wesley preach; and while, as we have seen already, he made no real attempt either to implant or exploit such a fear it was, without doubt, sometimes part of the tremendous burden and bondage from which people broke free forever, under his ministry. Anyway, this particular incident is one for which Wesley himself has supplied the details of his preaching. In the same paragraph of the *Journal*, and immediately preceding the passage quoted above, Wesley related:

'In the afternoon I preached at the Fishponds, but had no life or spirit in me, and was much in doubt whether God would not lay me aside and send other labourers into His harvest. I came to the society full of this thought; and began, in much weakness, to explain, "Beloved, believe not every spirit, but try the spirits, whether they be of God". I told them they were not to judge of the spirit whereby anyone spoke either by appearances, or by common report, or by their own inward feelings. No, nor by any dreams, visions, or revelations supposed to be made to their souls; any more than by their tears, or any involuntary effects wrought upon their bodies. I warned them all these were, in themselves, of a doubtful, disputable nature; they might be from God, and they might not; and were therefore not simply to be relied on (any more than simply to be condemned), but to be tried by a farther rule to be brought to the only certain test—the Law and the Testimony. While I was speaking . . . ' (Here follows the passage set out above, and quoted by Dr Sargant.)[18]

This passage is worth quoting, of course, not only for its lack of hellfire, but because it provides valuable evidence of Wesley's own level-headed attitude towards the strange phenomena we are trying to understand.

The next passage which Dr Sargant quotes,[19] concerns the strange case of a woman who while 'sitting at work', 'about ten in the morning', was 'seized with grievous terrors of mind, attended with strong trembling', but was relieved at the society meeting in the evening. Others are mentioned in the same *Journal* entry as being variously disturbed and relieved, including one 'who had been mourning many months, without any to comfort her'. On this occasion the *Journal* gives us no details whatsoever of Wesley's preaching either during or preceding the events related; although, as in many other cases cited in the *Journal*, the reference to this woman 'who had been mourning many months' definitely suggests that at least one who was set at liberty was the victim of a long standing depression, and was not merely whipped into a frenzy of fear by the terror of the preaching, or the technique of the preacher on that occasion.

The third quotation from Wesley's *Journal* on this page of *Battle for the Mind* concerns several incidents that took place when he was preaching at Newgate Prison. No doubt in order to save space, Dr Sargant has abbreviated the quotation. He begins to quote not at the beginning of the entry but from the sentence 'Immediately one, and another, and another sunk to the earth; . . . ', and half way through the paragraph there is an omission, indicated in the usual manner by a series of dots. The omissions are unfortunate, because, as comparison with the full entry will show, they both contain significant details of Wesley's preaching on these occasions. Here is the full entry as it appears in the *Journal* for Thursday, April 26, 1739. I have put square brackets round the portions that are *not* included in Dr Sargant's quotations:

['While I was preaching at Newgate on these words, "He that believeth hath everlasting life", I was insensibly led, without any previous design, to declare strongly and explicitly that God willeth "all men to be" thus "saved"; and to pray that, "if this were not the truth of God, He would not suffer the blind to go out of the way; but, if it were, He would bear witness to His word . . . "] Immediately one, and another, and another sunk to the earth; they dropped on every side as thunderstruck. One of them cried aloud. We besought God on her behalf, and He turned her heaviness into joy. A second being in the same agony, we called upon God for her also; and He spoke peace unto her soul. [In the evening I was again pressed in spirit to declare that "Christ gave Himself a ransom for all". And almost before we called upon Him to set His seal, He answered.] One was so wounded by the sword of the Spirit that you would have imagined she could not live a moment. But immediately His abundant kindness was showed, and she loudly sang of His righteousness.'[20]

The significance of these incidents will be further discussed in the next chapter, but in the meantime we simply note that they appear to have occurred not in response to hellfire preaching, but when Wesley was expounding his favourite theme of God's desire to save *all* men.

Many of Wesley's hearers were of course sceptical about the genuineness of these reactions, and others were strongly opposed to his teaching. The first account which Dr Sargant quotes from the *Journal* includes the case of a woman who was closely observed by her physician while undergoing violent reactions.

The physician was at first 'much afraid that there might be fraud or imposture' in some of the happenings of the past few days, but when 'one whom he had known many years . . . broke out "into strong cries and tears" . . . '

'He went and stood close to her, and observed every symptom, till great drops of sweat ran down her face and all her bones shook. He then knew not what to think, being clearly convinced it was not fraud nor yet any natural disorder. But when both her soul and body were healed in a moment, he acknowledged the finger of God.'[21]

The parallel which Dr Sargant draws between this case and some of those reported by Grinker and Spiegel[22] is of more significance than he seems to realize, and will be further discussed in the next chapter. On the day following the incident Wesley relates how a number of people in his congregation began to cry out, much to the disgust of others present, and one of the highly critical bystanders found himself similarly overwhelmed:

'Many were offended again, and, indeed, much more than before. For at Baldwin Street my voice could scarce be heard amidst the groanings of some and the cries of others, calling aloud to Him that is "mighty to save". I desired all that were sincere of heart to beseech with me the Prince exalted for us, that He would "proclaim deliverance to the captives". And He soon showed that He heard our voice. Many of those who had been long in darkness saw the dawn of a great light; and ten persons, I after-wards found, then began to say in faith, "My Lord and my God".

'A Quaker, who stood by, was not a little displeased at the dissimulation of these creatures, and was biting his lips and knitting his brows, when he dropped down as thunderstruck. The agony he was in was even terrible to behold. We besought God not to lay folly to his charge. And he soon lifted up his head, and cried aloud. "Now I know thou art a prophet of the Lord".'[23]

An even more striking example of the conversion of the sceptic is the strange case of John Haydon the weaver who, being present on this occasion, ' . . . was quite enraged at this; and, being unable to deny something supernatural in it, laboured beyond measure to convince all his acquaintances that it was a delusion of the devil'.[24] The next day, about midday, he was reading a borrowed copy of Wesley's sermon on 'Salvation by Faith', and we may take up Wesley's own account of the incident again at this point:

'In reading the last page he changed colour, fell off his chair and began screaming terribly, and beating himself against the ground. The neighbours were alarmed and flocked together to the house. Between one and two I came in, and found him on the floor, the room being full of people, whom his wife would have kept without; but he cried aloud, "No; let them all come; let all the world see the just judgment of God." Two or three men were holding him as well as they could. He immediately fixed his eyes upon *me*, and, stretching out his hand, cried, "Aye, this is he who I said was a deceiver of the people; but God has overtaken me. I said it was all a delusion; but this is no delusion." He then roared out, "O thou devil! thou cursed devil! yea, thou legion of devils! thou canst not stay. Christ will cast thee out. I know His work is begun. Tear me to pieces if thou wilt; but thou canst not hurt me." He then beat himself against the ground again, his breast heaving at the same time, as in the pangs of death, and great drops of sweat trickling down his face. We all betook ourselves to prayer. His pangs ceased, and both his body and soul were set at liberty.'[24]

According to Nehemiah Curnock who edited the Standard Edition of Wesley's *Journal*, the paragraph of Wesley's sermon which John Haydon was reading when he became violently affected was the following:

'For this reason the adversary so rages whenever salvation by faith is declared to the world; for this reason did he stir up earth and hell to destroy those who first preached it; and for the same reason, knowing that faith alone could overturn the foundations of his kingdom, did he call forth his forces and employ all his arts of lies and calumny to affright Martin Luther from reviving it.'[25]

As Curnock remarks, 'The quotation is not from a sermon preached by a fiery evangelist to a street mob, but from the great sermòn Wesley preached in the University Church of Oxford.'[25] We are not necessarily committed to Wesley's belief in a literal Satan rampant, in order to appreciate the historical and psychological truth of this passage, and the reference to the 'raging of the adversary' in Apostolic and Reformation times apparently spoke rather directly to John Haydon's condition, not only to suggest the deeper meaning of recent events at Bristol, but also to bring to light the hidden turmoil of his own soul.

Dr Sargant is particularly interested in this type of conversion where the person involved had been previously a strong critic or an indignant sceptic, and he quotes three such cases from Wesley's Journal,[26] all concerning people who, like John Haydon and the Quaker referred to above, took exception to the violent reactions of others. It will be recalled that the general theme in this chapter of Battle for the Mind is that Wesley's converts were overwhelmed by violent emotion, and reduced to a state of collapse and high suggestibility in which they could be easily induced to accept new beliefs and behaviour patterns. For the most part Dr Sargant claims that this was brought about by Wesley's technique of hellfire preaching, although as we have seen, he has nothing to substantiate this claim but his own repeated assertions. However, he also has a secondary line of argument, suggesting that in some cases the emotion aroused was not the fear of hell but violent anger.

It will be noted that there is a slight shift of ground here. Wesley could hardly be said to have deliberately aroused this anger as he is alleged to have deliberately aroused the fear of hell. The conversions that allegedly resulted from anger then, Dr Sargant seems to imply, were not so much a deliberate result of Wesley's 'highly successful technique' as an unwitting by-product of it. However, on this line of argument, these conversions would still come within the general Pavlovian formula of 'Stress — Breakdown (Cortical Inhibition) — Reconditioning' which he propounds to explain religious conversion and brainwashing as essentially the same type of process. Here is Dr Sargant's own explanation:

'As Pavlov's experimental findings in dogs and experiences in the treatment of war neuroses would lead one to expect, the effect of getting too emotionally involved, either positively or negatively with Wesley's preaching was to increase markedly the likelihood of being converted. It often happened, quite unexpectedly for the person concerned, that when he had been roused to the greatest pitch of indignation and anger by the proceedings, he suddenly broke down and accepted every belief demanded of him. For it has been shown in previous chapters that anger, as well as fear, can induce disturbances of brain function which make a person highly suggestible and reverse his conditioned behaviour patterns, or even wipe the "cortical slate" clean.'[27]

In the interests of clarity three comments should be made on the last sentence in this passage:

(a) I have been unable to find, in the previous chapters of Dr Sargant's book, either explanation or evidence of anger as a form of emotional involvement which increases suggestibility. The only material that appears even remotely relevant is a passage in the Introduction where he relates how the deliberate use of suggestion to stimulate fear or anger in a patient under the influence of drugs was often useful to facilitate the abreaction of these emotions.[28] However, this is quite a different matter.

(b) The release of pent up emotion in the treatment of the victim of battle neurosis on the one hand, and the type of conversion we are discussing on the other, are both examples of emotional abreaction. However, the part which is played by anger in the first case, is quite different from the way it features in the second. In the case of Dr Sargant's patient we have a person suffering from various debilitating symptoms, but *not consciously angry*. Nevertheless, he is the victim of *repressed anger*—blind, terrified, hating anger against the enemy, aroused in the heat of battle, and probably an even more violent and rebellious anger against the army and his immediate superiors who have thrust him into this situation of ghastly terror and imminent death. Denied adequate expression by the circumstances of battle, and also because it conflicts with other powerfull elements in the personality of the normal soldier, such as loyalty and fear of desertion, this anger has been driven into the unconscious—i.e. repressed. In that condition, right outside the present awareness of the patient, it is responsible for his debilitating symptoms. In the course of treatment, as Dr Sargant describes it,[29] the patient is put into a highly suggestible condition—not by anger, it should be noted, but by the use of barbiturate drugs or ether. Only then, when he has already been made suggestible by these other means, is it possible to make him accept the sort of suggestions that are calculated to intensify his repressed anger to the point where it may burst through the repressing barrier, into consciousness again.[30] What was brought to light or abreacted then, was mainly the repressed anger and allied emotions, and with this the debilitating symptoms disappeared.

Now when we turn to the type of conversion we are considering—such as that of John Haydon or the Quaker mentioned above, or the three other examples cited by Dr Sargant from Wesley's Journal, we are dealing with quite a different situation. In each of these cases we start off with a person who does not display any obviously debilitating symptoms but is quite consciously angry or indignant, and giving free expression to these feelings. When abreaction occurs we have no reason to believe that what is poured out is predominantly repressed anger, but what is brought to light is the acceptance of what was previously repudiated by the conscious personality. The end result then is not the dispersal of debilitating symptoms, but a radical change of outlook, and sometimes of the whole way of life.

I would suggest then that it is a gross over-simplification to ignore all these important differences. It confuses the issue completely, to regard anger as a causative factor in the conversions, simply because in a quite different way it was one of the causative factors in the abreactive treatment of battle neuroses.

(c) Dr Sargant succeeds in overlooking all these differences because, as I have already pointed out, he consistently fails to take into account the psychodynamics of either repression or abreaction, but prefers instead to interpret both processes as examples of breakdown under stress, according to the simple Pavlovian formula. I have already argued at some length, that to treat the dispersal of neurotic symptoms by abreaction as analogous to the wiping out of conditioned behaviour patterns by imposed stress is to confuse two entirely different, and indeed opposite, processes.[30] Exactly the same objection must be made against Dr Sargant's attempt to explain abreactive conversion along Pavlovian lines also. This point will be taken up in more detail in the next chapter, because it is the real source of his failure to understand the nature of religious conversion and the abreactive phenomena that sometimes accompanied it under Wesley's preaching.

The classic example of a sudden conversion in which the convert switches without any warning from an attitude of more or less violent opposition to one of involvement in what was previously repudiated is, of course, the case of St Paul; 'breathing out threatenings and slaughter' against the Christians on the way to Damascus.[31] Dr Sargant considers that this confirms his belief 'that anger may be no less powerful emotion than fear in bring about sudden conversion to beliefs which exactly contradict beliefs previously held', and he suggests that Paul's anger reduced him to a condition of 'total collapse, hallucinations and an increased state of suggestibility'.[32] This seems to me to be a very forced and unnatural account of the matter. The more usual—and I think more likely, explanation is not that Paul's anger caused his conversion, but on the contrary, that it was his conversion that caused his anger. In other words his frantic outburst of persecuting zeal against the Christians was really a sort of desperate and unavailing attempt to repudiate the Christian convictions that had already formed in the unconscious depths of his own mind. Dr C. G. Jung pointed this out many years ago:

'It is only when the preparation is complete, that is to say, when the individual is ready to be converted, that the new view breaks forth with great emotion. St Paul had already been a Christian for a long time, but unconsciously; hence his fanatical resistance to the Christians, because fanaticism exists chiefly in the individuals who are compensating for secret doubts.'[33]

As against this perfectly feasible explanation, it is very hard to believe that Paul, or for that matter, John Haydon, the Quaker (or any of the other people whose cases are quoted in Battle for the Mind) were actually reduced to a state of 'transmarginal inhibition' and collapse through the vehemence of their anger; particularly in view of the fact that their abreactions in some cases occurred when they had been for some time out of direct contact with the source of annoyance, or powerful suggestion. To sum the matter up then : our investigation of the conversion of St. Paul and of the angry critics mentioned in Wesley's *Journal*, and our consideration of Dr Sargant's comments, give us no reason to account for this type of conversion in terms of high suggestibility induced by violent anger; no more does our general investigation of Wesley's methods give us reason to account for the other conversions in terms of a similar state induced by hellfire preaching. In later chapters we shall discuss in a more positive way the network of causes which led to abreactive conversions under Wesley's preaching, but in the meantime there are other features of these phenomena which must be looked at.

Reference has already been made to two incidents quoted in *Battle for the Mind* involving violent reactions on the part of Wesley's hearers when he was preaching on the theme of universal salvation and God's offer of forgiveness to *all* who would repent.[34] Since this was one of his favourite themes it is not surprising that it recurs on quite a number of such occasions. The first of the three accounts dealing with the reaction of hostile critics, which Dr Sargant quotes from the *Journal*,[35] probably falls into this category; the *Diary* entries for that day seem to indicate that on the occasion when mother and daughter were affected, Wesley was expounding Luke 7.41 'When they had nothing to pay he frankly forgave them both'.[35] This central teaching of Wesley's movement was attacked from two different directions, and there are accounts of people being violently affected during discussion of these particular issues. At Oxford, in March 1739, Wesley's teaching on justification by faith and the assurance of forgiveness was under fire; a number of people seem to have been in conflict between the liberating announcement of free grace and forgiveness for the undeserving on the one hand, and the agonizingly frustrating idea of earning one's own salvation by good works on the other. Wesley relates how he visited (in response to her invitation to dinner) a certain Mrs Compton who was 'above measure enraged at this *new way*', and writes in the *Journal* :

'Finding argument to be of no other effect than to inflame her more and more, I broke off the dispute, and desired we might join in prayer, which she so far consented to as to kneel down. In a few minutes she fell in an extreme agony, both of body and soul, and soon after cried out with the utmost earnestness, "Now I know I am forgiven for Christ's sake". Many other words she uttered to the same effect, witnessing a hope full of immortality.'[36]

Mrs Compton's conversion appears to have been no merely passing experience because two years later, the *Journal* still records a Methodist Society meeting at her place in Oxford.[37]

A couple of days later Wesley encountered a certain Mr Washington who was busily going round his people reading from Bishop Patrick's 'Parable of the Pilgrim' to 'prove that we were all under a delusion, and that we were to be justified by faith and works'. After several other chance encounters Wesley met him again, together with a like-minded companion, at Mrs Compton's place in the evening, 'earnestly labouring to pervert the truth of the gospel', and in his *Journal* he recounts the following:

'To prevent his going on, as the less evil of the two, I entered directly into the controversy, touching both the cause and the fruits of justification. In the midst of the dispute one (Mrs Mears) who sat at a small distance felt, as it were, the piercing of a sword, and before she could be brought to another house, whither I was going, could not avoid crying out aloud, even in the street. But no sooner had we made our request known unto God than He sent her help from His holy place.'[38]

In a parallel account of this incident, in a letter written to George Whitefield,[39] Wesley adds that Mrs Mear's husband was also 'set at liberty soon after' on the same evening, and the lady in whose home the latter part of these things took place also 'fell into a strange agony both of body and mind' from which she was delivered after about an hour's prayer 'having remission of sins and knowing that her Redeemer liveth'.

A few weeks later, at Bristol, Wesley's teaching about salvation was being attacked again; this time not from a Catholic ('faith and works') point of view, but from the standpoint of Calvinism and its doctrine of a limited Atonement—intended by God to apply only to the 'elect' whom he had chosen for salvation. Thus Wesley relates in his *Journal*:

'At Newgate another mourner was comforted. I was desired to step thence to a neighbouring house, to see a letter wrote against me, as a "deceiver of the people", by teaching that God "willeth *all men* to be saved".'[40]

He had thus far deliberately refrained from controversy on this issue, but a week previously had received a letter which had been passed round for some time in Bristol before despatch, accusing him of 'resisting and perverting the truth'[41] in this matter. It is clear from Wesley's own communication to James Hutton a few days later, that it was the combined effect of these two letters that finally influenced him to publish his famous sermon on 'Free Grace' and so bring the controversy with Calvinism out into the open.[41] During the discussion which ensued on Wesley's reading of the second letter mentioned above, when he was no doubt defending his teaching that 'God willeth all men to be saved', he relates the following:

'One who long had asserted the contrary was there, when a young woman (Jenny Worlock) came in (who could say before, "I know that *my* Redeemer liveth") all in tears, and in deep anguish of spirit. She said she had been reasoning with herself how these things could be, till she was perplexed more and more; and she now found the Spirit of God was departed from her. We began to pray, and she cried out, "He is come! He is come! I again rejoice in God *my* Saviour." Just as we rose from giving thanks, another person reeled four or five steps, and then dropped down. We prayed with her, and left her strongly convinced of sin, and earnestly groaning for deliverance.'[40]

The explicit declaration of a universal atonement was much to the fore in Wesley's preaching at Bristol during the next few weeks, and in the *Journal* for May 12th he records:

'In the evening while I was declaring that Jesus Christ had

"given Himself a ransom for all", three persons almost at once sunk down as dead, having all their sins set in array before them. But in a short time they were raised up, and knew that "the Lamb of God who taketh away the sin of the world" had taken away their sins.'[42]

A few days later, the same emphasis on atonement and forgiveness is recorded with similar results:

'While I was declaring at Baptist Mills, "He was wounded for our transgressions", a middle-aged man began violently beating his breast and crying to Him "by whose stripes we are healed". During our prayer God put a new song in his mouth. Some mocked and others owned the hand of God: particularly a woman at Baptist Mills, who was now convinced of her own want of an Advocate with God, and went home full of anguish; but was in a few hours filled with joy, knowing He had "blotted out" all her "transgressions".'[43]

Apparently in response to the same kind of preaching, an even more violent reaction affected a number of people a few nights later. Wesley relates it thus:

'In the evening I was interrupted at Nicholas Street, almost as soon as I had begun to speak, by the cries of one who was "pricked at the heart", and strongly groaned for pardon and peace. Yet I went on to declare what God had already done, in proof of that important truth, that He is "not willing that any should perish, but that all should come to repentance". Another person dropped down, close to one who was a strong asserter of the contrary doctrine. While he stood astonished at the sight, a little boy near him was seized in the same manner. A young man who stood up behind fixed his eyes on him, and sunk down himself as one dead; but soon began to roar out and beat himself against the ground, so that six men could scarcely hold him. His name was Thomas Maxfield. Except John Haydon, I never saw one so torn of the Evil One.'[44]

This time, however, the reaction spread through the crowd and there was a general disturbance. Whether the phrase 'emotional contagion' is by itself sufficient to account for this sort of phenomenon we shall discuss later. Wesley's account continues:

'Meanwhile many others began to cry out to the "Saviour of all", that he would come and help them, insomuch that all the house (and indeed all the street for some space) was in an uproar. But we continued in prayer, and before ten the greater part found rest to their souls.'[45]

Despite the general confusion it appears that Wesley attended to those who were affected, individually. The *Diary* entry notes that by eight o'clock eleven were comforted. He was also called from supper to attend to one person, and at midnight to another, and the last entry in the *Journal* for the day states 'I think twenty-nine in all had their heaviness turned into joy this day'.[46]

Another occasion on which quite a large number of people were affected is one which is partly related in *Battle for the Mind* amongst the cases which involved the reaction of hostile critics. Again, in view of Dr Sargant's general claims about Wesley's preaching, it is worthwhile to quote the full entry from the *Journal*, for purposes of comparison:

'In the evening I went to a society in Wapping, weary in body and faint in spirit. I intended to speak on Romans iii.19, but could not tell how to open my mouth. And all the time we were singing my mind was full of some place, I knew not where, in the Epistle to the Hebrews. I begged God to direct, and opened the book on Hebrews x.19: "Having therefore, bretheren, boldness to enter into the holiest, by the blood of Jesus; by a new and living way which He hath consecrated for us, through the veil, that is to say, his flesh . . . let us draw near with a true heart, in full assurance of faith; having our hearts sprinkled from an evil conscience, and our bodies washed with pure water". While I was earnestly inviting all sinners to "enter into the holiest" by this "new and living way" many of those that heard began to call upon God with strong cries and tears . . .'[47]

Then follows the passage that is quoted by Dr Sargant, leading up to the sudden involvement of the critic:

' . . . Some sunk down, and there remained no strength in them; others exceedingly trembled and quaked; some were torn with a kind of convulsive motion in every part of their bodies, and that so violently that often four or five persons could not hold one of them. I have seen many hysterical and many epileptic fits; but none of them were like these in many respects. I immediately prayed that God would not suffer those who were weak to be offended. But one woman was offended greatly, being sure they might help it if they would—no one should persuade her to the contrary; and was got three or four yards when she also dropped down, in as violent an agony as the rest . . . '[48]

However we account for what happened to the woman who was 'offended greatly' there is certainly nothing in the passage as a whole to suggest that the original disturbance was caused by either violent anger or fear of hell. The closing part of this *Journal* entry shows Wesley apparently not greatly carried away by the excitement, but carefully checking the results:

' . . . Twenty-six of those who had been thus affected (most of whom during the prayers which were made for them, were in a moment filled with peace and joy) promised to call upon me the next day. But only eighteen came; by talking closely with whom I found reason to believe that some of them had gone home to their homes justified. The rest seemed to be waiting patiently for it.'[49]

Charles Wesley did have occasional violent outbursts from his hearers which he treated with little patience, but apart from the Wesleys the only other preachers of the revival who evoked such reactions to any extent were three other Anglican ministers, the Rev William Grimshaw, and the Rev John Berridge of Everton and his neighbour the Rev William Hicks.[50] Wesley included in his *Journal* several long accounts written by someone else, concerning the strange revival that burst out at Everton in May 1759 under Berridge and Hicks.[51] Although comparatively shortlived, the outbreak of emotional reactions there seems to have exceeded both in violence and variety anything that was seen under Wesley's own preaching, although the end result in terms of liberation was usually the same. While not involved in

L

this himself, Wesley visited Everton and closely questioned numbers of people who had experienced visions and trance states;[52] in his *Journal* he observed that such 'outward symptoms' had attended 'the beginning of a general work of God' in various places,

' . . . but after a time they gradually decrease, and the work goes on more quietly and silently. Those whom is pleases God to employ in His work ought to be quite passive in this respect, they should choose nothing, but leave entirely to Him all the circumstances of His own work.'[53]

When he returned six months later he found that there had been a strong reaction against such things, and this time the *Journal* records:

'The danger *was* to regard extraordinary circumstances too much, such as outcries, convulsions, visions, trances; as if these were essential to the inward work, so that it could not go on without them. Perhaps the danger *is* to regard them too little, to condemn them altogether, to imagine they had nothing of God in them, and were a hindrance to His work.'[54]

The two cases of psychogenic blindness in Newcastle that are mentioned by Dr Dimond in his summary, are unfortunately only briefly described in the *Journal*. Jung claimed that in his experience, psychogenic blindness was ' . . . always due to an unwillingness to see, *i.e.* to understand and accept, what is incompatible with the conscious attitude'.[55] After noting that the work of God at Newcastle had not, by that time, gone so deep as in other places, and very few there had any thorough conviction of sin or deliverance, Wesley continues:

'I found the first witness of this good confession. Margaret H— (oh how fallen since then!) told me that the night before, her sight (an odd circumstance) and her strength were taken away at once. At the same time the love of God so overflowed her soul that she could not speak or move.'[56]

It appears from the first parenthesis that this conversion was not lasting. The *Journal* then continues:

'James R— also gave an account today that in going home the day before, he lost his sight in a moment, and was forced to catch hold of some rails for fear of falling. He continues under strong conviction, longing for the salvation of God.'[57]

The subsequent reversal of the conversion in the first case and the continuing conflict in the second, are both compatible with Jung's interpretation of psychogenic blindness. We are not told anything of the subsequent history of these people; but since this was such an uncommon type of reaction in Wesley's experience, it seems to me unlikely that he would have passed over it so lightly if their blindness had remained permanent. It is probable that in both these cases the blindness was a temporary affliction (as in the case of St Paul) which disappeared when the emotional conflict that it symbolized was resolved one way or another.

We have no way of assessing the incidence of serious mental illness in Wesley's day. Even today it is not always easy to define true madness. In the eighteenth century when psychiatry in the modern sense had not even begun, it was much easier to think of it simply in terms of deviation from the social norm. In the absence of any reliable criteria of diagnosis a person could be declared mad simply because his principles or beliefs were radically different from those of his fellows, in a way which they felt to be annoying or inconvenient or which implied a reproach on their own pattern of living. Thus there are several instances quoted in the Journal of new converts who appear to have been sent to bedlam by irate relatives, for no other reason than that they had taken the first steps towards real sanity in a society that was itself in rather a poor state of mental health.

In a day when the stock treatment for mental illness was blooding and blistering it is not surprising that numbers of people thus afflicted came to hear Wesley preach, or joined themselves to the Methodist societies in search of some more profound deliverance from their very real troubles. Amongst these, as the Journal shows, were many people suffering from chronic states of depression, some of them quite profound, whose conversion effected their deliverance from these conditions. Sometimes the convert, formerly depressed, passed into a state of mild elation for a time, something like the swing to a state of hypermania which is a feature of the less serious forms of manic depressive psychosis. However the rather down to earth discipline of the Methodist societies, with its stress on practical goodness rather than elevated feelings, usually brought this under control. There were people whose psychoses appear to have flowered under Wesley's preaching, and a number of cases which involved strange agonies and bizarre struggles without any successful outcome; but both the historical and psychological evidence seem to suggest that these were unsuccessful developments of existing illnesses, not that anything in Wesley's preaching actually *caused* these people's psychoses or sent them mad. The first example of violent reactions to his preaching which is recorded in Wesley's *Journal* concerns a certain Mrs Randal who had not responded successfully to medical treatment for a long standing distress. Wesley describes the incident thus:

'We were greatly surprised in the evening, while I was expounding in the Minories. A well-dressed, middle-aged woman suddenly cried out as in the agonies of death. She continued so to do for some time, with all the signs of the sharpest anguish of spirit. When she was a little recovered, I desired her to call on me the next day. She then told me that about three years before she was under strong conviction of sin, and in such terror of mind that she had no comfort in anything, nor any rest day or night: that she sent for the minister of her parish, and told him the distress she was in: upon which he told her husband she was stark mad, and advised him to send for a physician immediately. A physician was sent for accordingly, who ordered her to be blooded, blistered, and so on. But this did not heal her wounded spirit. So that she continued much as she was before: till the last night, He whose word she at first found to be "sharper than any two-edged sword" gave her a faint hope that He would undertake her cause, and heal the soul which had sinned against Him.'[58]

A few weeks later, in a letter to George Whitefield, Wesley describes the sequel to this incident:

'We prayed that God who had brought her to the birth, would give her strength to bring forth, and that He would work speedily, that all might see it, and fear, and put their trust in the Lord. Five days she travailed and groaned, being in bondage. On Thursday evening our Lord got Himself the victory, and from that moment she has been full of love and joy, which she openly declared at the same society on Saturday last.'[59]

Over six months later, Wesley reports in the *Journal* that he was 'glad to see Mrs Randal',[60] and recalls her deliverance in a way which suggests that it had proved to be lasting. I think a fair examination of the *Journal* will show that generally speaking, Wesley himself was not responsible for the abnormal or psychotic condition exhibited by some of his hearers, but under God he *was* a means of restoring many of them to sanity.

We have now examined from Wesley's *Journal* over twenty accounts of these violent reactions to his preaching, in a variety of circumstances. Before venturing to discuss these incidents in the light of our modern understanding of similar or related abreactive phenomena, it will be useful first of all, to examine in more detail, Wesley's own attitude towards them.

Wesley's unbridled curiosity about nearly every subject under the sun has often been adversely noted by his critics, but it is surely important to recall that curiosity is the parent not only of credulity but also of science; and there was more of the genuinely scientific attitude in Wesley's curiosity than is sometimes realized. By temperament he was a thoroughgoing empiricist and even a pragmatist; he had an insatiable interest in facts —all kinds of facts—and a bias in favour of procedures that worked, even if he didn't know exactly why they worked. Yet, despite his empirical bias we must admit that no man who lived so much on horseback, even though he were a genius like Wesley, could possibly have been a careful observer of the wide variety of natural phenomena and current events on which he commented. He often tended to generalize from particular instances or insufficient evidence, or to rely too uncritically on other people's accounts of things. But in respect of the various religious phenomena of the Evangelical Revival he had no need to make such hasty judgment. He carefully observed these things over a period of many years, often closely questioned those concerned, noted the long-term results and compared them with similar happenings in other places and movements.

Because Wesley refused to strain the empirical facts he

encountered, through the philosophical sieve of eighteenth century deism and naturalism, he had to maintain his own interpretation of these facts in the midst of the criss-cross of public controversy, and he was much too able a controversialist to lay himself open to the charge of a merely naïve or dogmatic supernaturalism. Wesley's explanations *were* of course frankly supernaturalist; he believed in God—a God actually at work in the world and in human lives. Taught to him by both the Bible and the Church his belief was, in that sense, dogmatic; but its immense logical cogency that gave it strength and passion arose from his daily experience of a redeeming God reaching down into the broken sinful stuff of humanity to make men whole. Like the empiricist he was, Wesley considered that he made no claims in this direction which he could not substantiate by producing the living evidence.

It seems fairly safe to assume also, that Wesley had to overcome in himself a strong natural aversion to the sort of bizarre manifestations of emotion that we have considered in this chapter. It is hard to imagine this rather fastidious little Anglican clergymen, who liked 'everything done decently and in order', being anything but disgusted at the unseemly goings on at Bristol in 1739. Yet, by the grace of God, he seems to have achieved towards these happenings an attitude of emotional detachment which we would do well to emulate. It is true that the very thought of people crying, roaring, fainting or convulsing in a religious meeting is highly revolting to our sensibilities; but there are many things, for example in the modern practice of medicine, which are equally revolting to a layman undisciplined in such things, and fortunately this does not prevent the doctor accepting them as a necessary accompaniment to the total process of healing.

For John Wesley and his contemporaries these violent reactions posed three questions: 'Are they genuine?' 'If so, are they a necessary or significant part of the process of salvation?' and 'Do they arise from natural causes, or are they due to some supernatural agency?' It was often claimed by Wesley's critics that the victims could help it if they would, and sometimes only the sudden involvement of the critic himself would convince him that the whole affair was not a fake. No doubt there are strong motives in us all for wishing to deny the very possibility of a personality being genuinely overwhelmed by emotion, and it was no doubt the imminence of just such an occurrence in the lives of some of the critics themselves that strengthened their defensive denial to the point of vehemence. There were others, however, who denied the genuineness of these reactions out of ignorance of the facts, or because such happenings, if genuine, seemed to threaten their naturalistic assumptions.

Wesley, on the other hand, was firmly convinced that the majority of these emotional reactions were genuine. In this he was undoubtedly wiser than his critics not only because he was better informed about the facts both within and beyond his own movement, but also because he did not feel obliged to fit them into the rather restricted view of human personality that was current in eighteenth century naturalism. In this respect modern psychology of course agrees that emotional abreaction is a genuinely involuntary affair.

However, Wesley's rather permissive attitude to these things was bound to arouse criticism, and although there is little evidence to justify the suspicion expressed by both Whitefield and his brother Charles, that he actually encouraged these emotional reactions, the point is that he did very little to discourage them either. Charles himself sternly discouraged such outbursts and spoke darkly of imitation and counterfeit, concluding on the whole that when they were not mere exhibitionism, they must be a device of the devil to hinder the preaching of the gospel.[61] Southey concluded that John's less suspicious attitude was due to his credulity,[62] but this is a rather superficial judgment. Wesley knew full well that some of these reactions were probably counterfeit, but he was not so touchy about being fooled as his brother was. 'The shadow is no disparagement of the substance,' he said, 'nor the counterfeit of the real diamond';[63] he knew how subtly these could be mixed up together and was apparently willing to be imposed on at times, rather than run the risk of unwittingly rejecting one person genuinely in the birth pangs of a new life. As Richard Watson said of Wesley in his reply to Southey, he

'... concluded that in ignorant and inexperienced persons much good principle may be mixed with fancy and oblique feeling ... He had "compassion on them that were ignorant" as well as

"out of the way" . . . Many a spirit in danger both from
ignorance and its own peculiar constitution was saved by his
confiding charity which . . . assured to every enquirer patient
attention, and sympathetic counsel, forbearance for their weaknesses, and respect for their assumed sincerity.'[64]

Even if he were sometimes a 'fool for Christ's sake' I think we
can safely conclude that regarding the genuineness of these
emotional outbursts, Wesley was not nearly so naïve as some of
his less discerning critics have supposed.

When we turn to the second of our two questions—'Are these
emotional reactions a necessary or significant part of the process
of salvation?' we find that throughout his ministry Wesley
maintained sincerely, and in a sense quite consistently, that they
were not. In an early letter to his brother Samuel which we
have already quoted,[65] he stated that these things were merely
incidental to a work of grace which was to be judged solely in
terms of changed lives, 'till then in many ways wicked; from that
time holy, just and good'. His encounter with the French
Prophets sharpened his aversion to a religion that valued
emotional experience before ethical fruits, and he warned his
people that these emotional upheavals were 'in themselves of a
doubtful disputable nature' and that 'they might be from God,
and they might not; and were therefore not simply to be relied
on (any more than simply condemned), but to be tried by a
farther rule to be brought to the only test—the Law and the
Testimony'.[66] He felt that the whole process of salvation could
never be divorced from actual moral change of personality and
life, and no mere emotional upheaval, be it ever so impressive,
could ever be a necessary or sufficient sign of the new birth.

Yet despite these pronouncements, some of his critics were not
satisfied that Wesley had stated his *real* attitude towards the
emotional outbursts at all; although they found it very difficult
to make out their case without misrepresenting what he had
actually written. This is the burden of Wesley's complaint
against a certain Rev Mr H. who accused him in 1764 of having
laid down in his *Journal* 'some marks of the new birth, not only
doubtful, but exceptionable; as, particularly, where persons
appeared agitated or convulsed under the ministry'.[67] The same
issue had been taken up by Dr Thomas Rutherforth, Regius

Professor of Divinity at Cambridge, in a pamphlet written the previous year but which, for some reason or other did not come to Wesley's notice until 1768; Wesley replied in a long letter observing that he is frequently misrepresented or misquoted by his critics, and when he appeals to what he has actually published on the subject, he is accused of evasion. He had little difficulty in winning the formal argument against Dr Rutherforth, and showing that nothing which the Professor had been able to quote showed that Wesley ever regarded the emotional upheavals as anything more than 'something which may accidentally attend' the new birth; and he reiterated this point with some vehemence. 'But what does all this prove?' he wrote,

' . . . just what I said before; I speak of them as "outward symptoms which have often accompanied the work of God". Often I say, not always, not necessarily: they may, or they may not. This work may be without these symptoms, and those symptoms may be without this work.'[69]

However, if Wesley could justly claim that he was misunderstood and even misrepresented, it must also be said that he in his turn did not understand his critics either. Dr Rutherforth had a point, even if he didn't know how to put it, and Wesley didn't know what he was getting at. The question they were discussing was in fact quite an ambiguous one, and neither Wesley nor his critics succeeded in defining the issue with sufficient precision to save them from talking at cross purposes. In asking whether the emotional outbursts are a necessary or significant part of the process of salvation, it is important to decide whether the matter is being discussed (a) in terms of the theological definition of the process of salvation, or (b) in terms of the individual psychology of a particular convert. This is the sort of distinction that comes more readily to the modern mind that it did to the controversialists of the eighteenth century.

In theological terms Wesley consistently answered our question in the negative, insisting that the emotional symptoms were nothing but accidental accompaniments of salvation; and he did this for pastoral, rather than apologetic, reasons. He was anxious that no one should imagine that he had come to saving faith in Christ simply because of certain emotional experiences ('those symptoms may be without this work') and that on the other hand, no one in whom a genuine work of grace had begun should doubt its reality because it was not accompanied by emotional upheaval ('this work may be without those symptoms').

However, what puzzled Dr Rutherforth, and many other readers of his *Journal* was, that having stated this explicitly and repeatedly, Wesley continued to treat such reactions whenever he encountered them, as though they were in fact something of considerable interest and importance. It is impossible to read Wesley's *Journal* without gaining this clear impression, and this point which Dr Rutherforth and some of his contemporaries could never quite get their finger on, was taken up in more recent times by Monsignor Ronald Knox.[70]

In dealing with a variety of people day by day Wesley was often obliged to give an answer to our question not merely in theological terms, but in terms of (b) above—i.e. in terms of the individual psychology of a particular person confronting him; and he was not prepared to dismiss out of hand, any experience that was felt to be significant by the person concerned. Thus, while he would do his utmost to prevent anyone from trying to build his faith on experiences which were of a doubtful, disputable nature, and would therefore insist that these were merely incidental to the process of conversion *as such*, he also knew intuitively that these emotional upheavals, when they did occur, were seldom a mere incidental to the person concerned; that they must not be swept aside, but must be taken seriously as something which had to run their course or be worked through if this person's conversion were to be achieved. Modern pastoral insights show the wisdom of this attitude, but in the eighteenth century it must have seemed to many that Wesley's practice was exasperatingly inconsistent with his pronouncements. Both parties, of course, suffered from the lack of any adequate psychology of individual differences, and if Wesley himself failed to see the apparent discrepancy between these two attitudes, his critics also failed to see their ultimate harmony.

However, Wesley's answer to our third question would probably be no more acceptable to most moderns than it was to many of his contemporaries. For when these emotional reactions were genuine, as they very often were, he maintained that whatever secondary influence natural conditions may have had on them, they were ultimately due to some agency from right outside the natural order of things—either God or the devil. At first he toyed with the idea that they might be sent or at least permitted, as special signs of God, to convince the sceptical;[71] but he soon realized that the sceptics were not going to be convinced anyway, and he dropped the idea. He dismissed with scorn the various rather lame attempts that were made to account for these phenomena as natural effects due to the heat and closeness of the room,[71] or the influence of imagination, or animal spirits, and he also rejected at this stage, the suggestion that they were a mere delusion of the devil.[72] Somewhat more thoughtfully perhaps, Dr Hales, the philosopher and scientist with whom Wesley was on friendly terms, spoke of the 'sympathetic nature of all violent emotion',[73] just as Southey was later to refer less graciously to emotions that were as 'infectious as the plague',[74] or we would speak today of emotional contagion or mob psychology. However, Wesley was not impressed by this type of explanation, because it does not really get to the point. It may partly explain the spread of emotion in a crowd, but it does not by itself, tell us why this kind of emotion should be generated in the first place, why it should happen under the preaching of the gospel, or what was even more important to Wesley, why it should so often issue under these circumstances, in a striking moral change of personality that persisted as a permanent and growing effect long after any element of emotional contagion had gone. This type of explanation, which is still sometimes offered today, is not so much untrue as beside the point.

Southey's Life of Wesley was much influenced by his own latitudinarian views, and although he did not particularly stress hellfire preaching, he spoke of 'a powerful doctrine preached with passionate sincerity' that 'produced a powerful effect on weak minds, ardent feelings and discordant fancies',[75] thus offering an explanation not very different in principle from Dr Sargant's formula of breakdown under stress, the inadequacy of which was easily pointed out by Dr Tyerman.[76] Southey said that Wesley 'like Mesmer and his disciples . . . had produced a new disease, and he accounted for it by a theological theory instead of a physical one.[77] But as Richard Watson pointed out, he was 'very cautious not to describe the future effects, being probably aware that, were he to proceed to the consequent holy lives and peaceful deaths of many of the patients the "new disease" would have too much the appearance of "saving health" to support his theory.'[78]

Southey also pointed to what we should call today the psychosomatic factor, remarking that 'As men are intoxicated by strong drink affecting the mind through the body, so are they by strong passions influencing the body through the mind'.[79] But like the emotional contagion phrase, this merely underlines the obvious without in the least explaining why these particular strong passions were brought to light under Wesley's preaching.

Had there been current in the eighteenth century a depth psychology with a secular bias, Wesley might have had much more ingenious arguments to rebut; but as it was, the various naturalistic explanations put forward by his critics were so obviously beside the point or too small to fit the facts, that we cannot blame him for treating them with scant respect. At the very most, all they could show was that in some of these emotional outbursts nature was mixed with grace—a fact of which Wesley himself was already well aware.[80] However, despite his tendency to look for divine intervention in the course of common events, we must not assume that in seeking some supernatural explanation for these strange phenomena, Wesley was simply invoking a God in the gaps that were left in eighteenth century thinking. He was much too concerned with the central realities of salvation to build too much on these outward signs which he himself described as being of a 'doubtful, disputable nature'. In his experience the miracle of man's salvation was wrought out day by day in a discernible and progressive change in their character and condition of life, and if the more spectacular events seemed to require some supernatural explanation it was mainly because they so often accompanied the beginning of this process of spiritual liberation which was so manifestly a work of God.

In 1739 Wesley corresponded with the Rev. Ralph Erskine who was at that time involved in a secession from the Church of Scotland and had experienced similar, though less violent, reactions to his own preaching. Erskine suggested that these represented something of a spiritual conflict between God and the devil within the soul of the convert.[81] Although Wesley had at first rejected any attempt to write off these upheavals as mere works of the devil, he seems to have responded to this suggestion of dynamic conflict, since it would account for both the obviously repulsive and evil aspect of the symptoms, and for the moral and spiritual good that eventually came out of them. In 1743, after carefully questioning a number of people who had been violently affected at Chowden, he commented, 'These symptoms I can no more impute to any natural cause than to the Spirit of God. I can make no doubt that it was Satan tearing them, as they were coming to Christ.'[82] He seems sometimes to have wavered towards a more ambiguous view that 'they may be from God; they may be from nature; they may be from the devil',[67] but continued observation seemed to confirm his sense of a diabolic resistance to a work of grace.

Yet, aware as he was of the obvious link between these bodily symptoms and strong emotion, he had to try and account for these emotions also, in terms of the immediate situation created by his preaching. We have already seen the way in which fear of hell or ultimate loss, was one element though by no means the major one, in the existential choice which Wesley put before his hearers. He saw no reason either to exaggerate this or to hide it, and casting around for something in his own proclamation that would help to account for these distressing emotions, it was probably inevitable that like Dr Sargant, he should look first in that direction. Thus, the year after the Chowden incidents (1744) we find him writing in his 'Farther Appeal to Men of Reason and Religion':

'For how easy is it to suppose, that a strong, lively, and sudden apprehension of the heinousness of sin, the wrath of God, and the bitter pains of eternal death, should affect the body as well as the soul, during the present laws of vital union, should interrupt or disturb the ordinary circulations, and put nature out of its course!'[83]

But, unlike Dr Sargant, Wesley's thinking did not stop here. For these emotional reactions were not only linked to distressing bodily symptoms soon to pass off, but also followed by a lasting spiritual liberation, and in his last and most considered pronouncement on the subject we find him allowing for direct diabolic agency in some cases, but in others, linking these violent symptoms with the total proclamation of saving grace, rather than merely with its more sombre themes:

'Upon the whole, I declare once for all (and I hope to be troubled no more upon the subject), I look upon some of these bodily symptoms to have been preternatural or diabolical, and others to have been effects which in some circumstances naturally followed from strong and sudden emotions of mind. These emotions of mind, whether of fear, sorrow, or joy, I believe were chiefly supernatural, springing from the gracious influences of the Spirit of God which accompanied His word.'[84]

Of course, Wesley's simple supernaturalism is hardly satisfactory from a modern point of view. His thinking was much more influenced by the world view of the Bible than that of modern man, and therefore more at home with Hebrew conceptions in which the idea of intermediate causes hardly occurs. He did have some rudimentary idea of intermediate causes, particularly the psychomatic factors, but he had no way of understanding the psychological mechanisms that were at work. Much as we may regret it, we can hardly blame him for failing to anticipate by two centuries the findings of modern depth psychology. Nevertheless, when these are taken into account, I believe a good case can be made to support the view that in assigning the creative upheavals, and the more permanent results, of the Evangelical Revival to 'the gracious influences of the Spirit of God which accompanied His word', Wesley was, in the profoundest sense, not mistaken.

FOOTNOTES AND REFERENCES

1. Dimond, Dr Sidney G., *The Psychology of Methodism*, Epworth Press, London 1932, p. 81.
2. Cf. Ch. II of *More About the Early Methodist People* by Dr Leslie F. Church, Epworth 1949, Ch. VIII in *John Wesley, Preacher* by W. L. Doughty, and frequent references in Wesley's *Journal*, Vols. II and III.

3. This is an overall average for the five-year period during which most of the violent reactions occurred, but their distribution during that period was, of course, very uneven. There were times when they occurred almost daily, followed by weeks or even months when there is no record of such happenings at all. The reason for treating this period separately is that after 1743 the intervals became much longer, and the occurrences more isolated, and by the early 1760s they were rare.

4. Watson, Richard, *The Life of the Rev. John Wesley* (*The Works of the Rev. Richard Watson*, 5th edition, 1845), p. 89.

5. If we compare, for example, the violence of the Anabaptists at the time of the Reformation, the barking and tree climbing of the Kentucky camp meetings, the quaking of the early Friends, the glossolalia of the Irvingites, the trance states of the French prophets, the wild excitement of the New England Puritans, and the tearful outcries of the eighteenth century Scottish secessionists, any adequate attempt to account for the differences among this wide variety of phenomena would have to take into consideration not only the theology of the preachers, but also the psychological condition of the hearers; and therefore the sociological conditions prevailing in the communities concerned for some time before the revival began.

6. Dimond, Dr Sidney G., *The Psychology of the Methodist Revival*, p. 135.

7. *Journal*, Vol. II, pp. 201-2.

8. *Letter from a Private Person to his Pastor concerning the People called Methodist* T.B.—quoted by Doughty, *op. cit.*, p. 135, and also by Dr Sargant, *op. cit.*, p. 102 (104).

9. Cf. Bready, J. W., *England Before and After Wesley*, H. & S. 1938, and R. F. Wearmouth, *Methodism and the Common People of the Eighteenth Century*, Epworth 1945, for well-documented accounts of the ethical and social effects of the Evangelical Revival, and Leslie F. Church, *op. cit.* and *The Early Methodist People*, Epworth 1948, for a wealth of contemporary evidence of spiritual transformations of both personal and social significance.

10. Sargant, *op. cit.*, p. 81 (86-7).

11. *Journal*, Vol. II, p. 180.

12. *Journal*, Vol. III, p. 406.

13. *Journal*, Vol. III, p. 89.

14. *Journal*, Vol. III, p. 52.

15. *Journal*, Vol. II, p. 332.

16. *Journal, loc. cit.*
17. *Journal,* Vol. II, p. 226, Sargant, *op. cit.,* pp. 79-80 (85).
18. *Journal, loc. cit.*
19. Sargant, *op. cit.,* p. 79-80 (85).
20. *Journal,* Vol. II, p. 184. Cf. abbreviated version in Sargant, *op. cit.,* p. 80 (85).
21. Sargant, *op. cit.,* p. 75 (81), *Journal,* Vol. II, p. 186.
22. Sargant, *loc. cit.*
23. *Journal,* Vol. II, pp. 186-7.
24. See Wesley's letter to his brother Samuel, May 10, 1739, quoted in footnote, *Journal,* Vol. II, p. 190, and fuller account *ibid.,* pp. 189-91.
25. *Journal,* Vol. II, p. 190, f. 1. The Sermon quoted is No. 1 in the Standard Sermons.
26. Sargant, *op. cit.,* pp. 81-2 (87). Incidentally, in the following passage and throughout his book Dr Sargant fails to make what is an elementary distinction for Methodists—the distinction between conversion and sanctification. The source of his confusion seems to have been William James' mistaken treatment of the passage from Wesley which Dr Sargant has borrowed from him and quoted on pp. 82-3 (87-8). James, who himself had the quotation at second hand from Tyerman, treats it as a discussion of conversion (*Varieties of Religious Experience,* Fontana Library edition, p. 229) whereas reference to its original source in Wesley's sermon 'On Patience' (No. LXXXIII, *Works,* Vol. VI, pp. 495 ff.) shows that Wesley was discussing something altogether different.

Conversion (Wesley preferred the term 'New Birth') is the turning of the sinner to God to accept forgiveness, reconciliation and justification. Sanctification (according to Methodist usage of that term) is the moral change that follows upon this, as its consequence—a change towards perfect love. This change, Wesley held, begins with the new birth; but thereafter he sometimes spoke of as a gradual development or 'growth in grace', and sometimes as a change that was completed some time before death in a more or less instantaneous experience which Methodists sometimes described as 'the second blessing'. It was this latter type of experience that Wesley was referring to in the passage quoted—*not* the new birth or conversion.

The evidence for this moral transformation in the direction of 'perfect love' is far too impressive to dismiss, and one can accept the reality and importance of such a change without believing with Wesley that it is normally completed instantaneously, or that it is ever complete at all in this life. (On this whole subject, see Harald Lindstrom, *passim*, *Wesley and Sanctification*.

However, Dr Sargant's references to 'sanctification' throughout his book are really beside the point, as the violent symptoms with which he is concerned were associated with the convert's original turning to God and not with the process of sanctification either gradual or sudden.

27. Sargant, *op. cit.*, p. 81 (86-7).
28. *Idem.*, p. xxi (18).
29. *Idem.*, pp. 45-50 (56-60).
30. See above, pp. 62-3.
31. Acts 9.1-19.
32. Sargant, *op. cit.*, pp. 104-5 (105-6).
33. Quoted by R. H. Thouless in *An Introduction to the Psychology of Religion*, Cambridge 1928, p. 189.
34. See above, p. 149.
35. Sargant, *op. cit.*, pp. 81-2 (87). *Journal*, Vol. II, p. 232.
36. *Journal*, Vol. II, p. 147.
37. *Journal*, Vol. II, p. 477, Diary entry for July 21, 1741.
38. *Journal*, Vol. II, pp. 148-9.
39. *Journal*, Vol. II, pp. 152-3.
40. *Journal*, Vol. II, pp. 188-9.
41. This first letter was received on April 26th, and no doubt provoked Wesley's sermon in Newgate prison on that date, the effects of which we have already noted (above, p. 149). See Wesley's letter to James Hutton, May 8, 1739, appended as a footnote to the *Journal*, Vol. II, p. 184.
42. *Journal*, Vol. II, p. 198.
43. *Journal*, Vol. II, pp. 199-200.
44. *Journal*, Vol. II, p. 203.
45. *Journal*, Vol. II, pp. 203-4.
46. *Journal*, Vol. II, p. 204.
47. *Journal*, Vol. II, p. 221.
48. *Journal*, Vol. II, pp. 221-2, and Sargant, *op. cit.*, p. 82 (87).
49. *Journal*, Vol. II, p. 222.
50. John Cennick, one of Wesley's local preachers records at least one striking instance of violent reactions to his own preaching (see letter from Cennick September 12, 1739, quoted in L. Tyerman's *Life and Times of the Rev. John Wesley M.A.*, Vol. I, p. 263). Cennick later parted company with Wesley.

M

The one recorded instance of such reactions to George Whitefield's preaching in England is noted in Wesley's *Journal*, Vol. II, pp. 239-40.

51. *Journal*, Vol. IV, pp. 317-22, 333-43.

52. *Journal*, Vol. IV, p. 347.

53. *Journal*, Vol. IV, pp. 347-8.

54. *Journal*, Vol. IV, p. 359.

55. Quoted by R. H. Thouless, op. cit., p. 190.

56. *Journal*, Vol. III, p. 51.

57. *Journal*, Vol. III, p. 52.

58. *Journal*, Vol. II, pp. 131-2.

59. *Journal*, Vol. II, p. 145.

60. *Journal*, Vol. II, p. 272.

61. See quotation from Charles Wesley's *Journal* for June 4, 1743, in Doughty, op. cit., pp. 134-5.

62. Southey, op. cit., p. 128.

63. *Journal*, Vol. IV, p. 360.

64. Watson, Richard, *Observations on Southey's Life of Wesley*, pp. 427-8.

65. *Journal*, Vol. II, p. 202.

66. *Journal*, Vol. II, p. 226.

67. Letter CCIX, *Works*, Vol. 12, pp. 227-8.

68. 'A Letter to the Rev. Dr. Rutherforth', *Works*, Vol. 14, pp. 329-41, especially sections 8-12.

69. *Ibid.*

70. Knox, Ronald, op. cit., Ch. XXI.

71. *Journal*, Vol. II, p. 202.

72. *Journal*, Vol. II, pp. 222-3.

73. Quoted by Tyerman, op. cit., Vol. I, p. 265.

74. Southey, quoted by Tyerman, op. cit., Vol. I, p. 265.

75. *Ibid.*

76. Tyerman, loc. cit.

77. Southey, op. cit., p. 128.

78. *Observations on Southey's Life of Wesley*, pp. 438-9.

79. Southey, loc. cit.

80. Cf. *Journal*, Vol. III, pp. 43-4.

81. See letter from the Rev Ralph Erskine, quoted in *Journal*, Vol. II, p. 231.

82. *Journal*, Vol. III, p. 69.

83. *Works*, Vol. 8, p. 127.

84. 'A Letter to the Rev. Dr. Rutherforth', para. 12.

PART III

INTERPRETATION

CHAPTER 8

WORD AND WILDERNESS

I

As we have seen, Dr Sargant regards the more violent phenomena that accompanied Wesley's preaching as examples of the
process of emotional abreaction, and thus far we must agree with
him. By way of illustration he quotes Grinker and Spiegel's
description of the abreaction of war experiences, induced by the
use of barbiturate drugs:

'The terror exhibited . . . is electrifying to watch. The body
becomes increasingly tense and rigid; the eyes widen and the
pupils dilate, while the skin becomes covered with a fine perspira-
tion. The hands move compulsively . . . Breathing becomes
incredibly rapid or shallow. The intensity of the emotion sometimes becomes more than they can bear; and frequently at the
height of the reaction, there is a collapse and the patient falls
back in the bed and remains quiet for a few minutes. . . . '[1]

Whatever obvious differences there were in the circumstances
leading to such behaviour, or in the actual details of the reaction,
we are undoubtedly dealing here with the same general type of
psychological experience as that which many of Wesley's hearers
underwent in the process of their conversion—viz. the sudden
and dramatic release of emotion previously pent up or repressed.
Furthermore, again despite obvious differences, there is an unmistakable parallel between the two results. In both cases the
discharge of emotion was followed by a more or less permanent
liberation of the personality—in the case of the war neurotic,
from debilitating symptoms, and in the case of Wesley's converts, from an unsatisfactory or often vicious manner of life.
  Now the clue to Dr Sargant's misunderstanding and misrepresentation of the work of John Wesley is his failure to appreciate

the real nature of emotional abreaction.[2] As we have seen already, abreaction is essentially a process of recovery and conscious acting out of strong emotions previously aroused by some immediate or long standing situation, but denied adequate expression because they came into conflict with other more powerful elements, or more basic needs, in the personality. Such emotions when they cease to be acknowledged by the conscious personality, do not merely cease to operate, but are held in the unconscious; they are repressed but still dynamically active, and often force an indirect and unrecognized expression in debilitating symptoms or compulsive behaviour. In effective abreaction these distortions of personality disappear, because the emotions to which they gave partial and indirect expression are no longer repressed; instead they are given expression in a way that is consciously accepted and integrated with the personality as a whole. However, Dr Sargant's fixed aversion to depth psychology makes him incapable of understanding this; he seems to be trying to tell us that emotional abreaction is simply a violent response to immediate stimulation and strain—a breakdown essentially similar in principle to that experienced by Pavlov's dogs under the extremes of experimental stress. Thus, faced with the accounts in Wesley's *Journal*, of the more spectacular outbursts of the Evangelical Revival, he has to invent for us the quite unhistorical picture of Wesley the hellfire preacher who allegedly put his hearers under such an extreme of stress as to stimulate this welter of violent emotion. On the other hand, when we understand the real nature of these abreactive phenomena, as something right outside the simple Pavlovian formula of breakdown-under-stress, we shall have no need to do this sort of violence to the facts of history. The historical Wesley with his own peculiar doctrinal emphases, and the historical situation in which he worked, will in fact, quite adequately account for these things.

We have already seen in Chapter 4, that where emotion is under repression, the possibility of a healing abreaction taking place will depend finally on the relative strength of the repressed emotion on the one hand, and those other forces within the personality which keep it repressed, on the other. Change in the strength of these two factors relative to each other may be brought about in a variety of ways—either by lowering the strength of the repression (by the use of drugs, for example), or by building up the strength of the repressed emotion by means of suitably penetrating and powerful suggestion, or by simultaneously applying both methods. However, whichever one of these methods is used, it is quite important to recognize that when abreaction does occur, the flood of emotion that is poured out is not merely the result, or *product* of the method used, or a response to any present stimulation. Any emotional stimulus employed merely acts as a primer, or perhaps we should even say a detonator which helps to release repressed emotion which for some reason or other is already there.[3] Without this powerful charge of repressed emotion, no amount of stimulation would produce an emotional abreaction. There would be nothing to abreact.

This point is extremely important, and should be made quite clear: the emotional reactions and subsequent behaviour of Pavlov's dogs are understandable in terms of the immediate stress situation in which they were placed. They were simply a response (in terms of the dogs' normal psychophysical make up) to the abnormal stresses applied at the time. However, when we consider some of the cases mentioned by Dr Sargant we are dealing with a very different kind of reaction. For example we quote the following:

'Among the patients . . . was a soldier in a tank regiment whom we could bring to the point of emotional collapse, under ether, only by persuading him that he was trapped in a burning tank and must try to get out at all costs.'[4]

Now the abreactive outburst of this patient is not merely a response to the immediate fear stimulus that was applied during treatment, in the same sense as the collapse of Pavlov's dogs was a response to the immediate stress situation. It seems fairly obvious that the emotional stimulus applied by the psychiatrist simply served to trigger off, as it were, the full outburst of emotion, and that this outburst was something much greater than the normal response to this kind of immediate stimulus. It was the sudden release of the repressed emotions of terror that were originally aroused in the traumatic experiences of battle, but hitherto denied adequate expression. It is this fact which makes the experiences of Dr Sargant's patients genuine abreactions, whereas those of Pavlov's dogs were not.

Applying these differences to the matter of terrifying preaching, it is certainly conceivable that under the right conditions a powerful and convincing hellfire preacher could terrify his hearers. But this in itself would not be emotional abreaction. If he continued the process with equal success he could probably even bring some of his congregation to a state of collapse, not very different in principle from those of Pavlov's dogs. But again, this would not be emotional abreaction. Only if, in some way or other, the preacher managed to set free a whole flood of emotion that was not merely a normal response to present stimulation, but the outpouring of *repressed* emotion from the past, would we have a genuine abreaction. Dr Sargant tries to account for the genuinely abreactive response which many people made to Wesley's preaching by suggesting that he simply terrified his hearers into collapse by means of hellfire preaching. But this is not only historically untrue, but also psychologically quite inadequate.

I believe that both the psychological and historical evidence will support the view that Wesley's preaching was not the cause or source of the violent emotions poured out at all, but in some way it *was* the immediate precipitating cause that set them free. The effect of his preaching was to release large quantities of repressed emotion which, for a variety of reasons (which we shall examine shortly) was already there in the minds of the people affected; and long before they heard Wesley preach, or came under the influence of the Evangelical Revival at all. Furthermore, as in the case of all successful abreactions, the sequel was not the debilitating collapse of breakdown under stress, but a healing liberation of personality. When the surgeon's lance opens up an infected wound, we do not hold the surgeon responsible for the poisonous discharge which is released. That is, we do not blame him for the poison, but give him credit for releasing it. Unpleasant though it may be, we realize that this has to be done before inner cleansing and healing can take place. I do not think we shall understand either the more spectacular features of the Evangelical Revival or its long term effects unless we realize that under Wesley's preaching, something very like this was actually going on in the souls of many people.

If we accept the fact that the more violent reactions to Wesley's preaching were not a mere response to something immediately terrifying, but genuine abreactions of repressed emotion, then it becomes relevant to ask two more questions: 1. Why were so many of the people to whom Wesley preached subject to this kind of deep psychological infection?—i.e. why had so many of them repressed large and explosive quantities of violent emotion? and 2. What was there distinctive about the preaching of John Wesley that so often opened up the wound as it were, and released all this pent up emotion in ways that were not only immediately sensational, but ultimately healing? To both these questions I believe there are relatively straightforward answers that arise out of a study of the facts.

II

Carlyle's terse description of the condition of England during the first half of the eighteenth century was 'Stomach well alive, soul extinct',[5] and Mark Pattison says:
'The historian of moral and religious progress . . . is under necessity of depicting the same period as one of decay of religion, licentiousness of morals, public corruption, profaneness of language—"a day of rebuke and blasphemy".'[5]

The same year that John Wesley was converted (1738) the restrained and eminently rational Bishop Berkeley was warning Magistrates and Men in Authority of a collapse of English morals and religion 'to a degree that has never been known in any Christian country' and went on to say:

'Our prospect is very terrible and the symptoms grow worse from day to day. . . . The youth born and brought up in wicked times without any bias to good from early principle, or instilled opinion, when they grow ripe, must be monsters indeed. And it is to be feared that the age of monsters is not far off.'[6]

J. W. Bready, in his study of the period, cites a list of the most well known contemporary writers who in one way or another endorsed this verdict; and another list of prominent historians of more recent times and widely divergent points of view whose opinions concurred with Berkeley's view that this period in

England was one of extraordinary social and moral degeneration.[7]

In some form or other the disease afflicted every level of English society, and Bishop Secker spoke of the 'dissoluteness and contempt of principle in the higher part of the world' (and the) 'profligate intemperance and fearlessness of committing crimes in the lower'.[8] The gloomy story of the senseless luxury, corruption and greed, the arrogant contempt for the poor, and the shameless scrambling for preferment which were rampant among the so-called higher orders of society, both clerical and lay, is too well known to need repetition. There were, fortunately, some very notable exceptions to this in both Church and Government. But it was among the common people of England that Wesley gained an immediate and sometimes dramatic response—among the great unchurched, and sometimes almost uncivilized, masses of the poor, and it is therefore in their condition of life that we are mostly interested.

The social and economic upheaval which has been traditionally known as the Industrial Revolution probably did not reach its full vigour for another twenty years, but by the time Wesley began to preach in the fields, in the market places and at the pitheads, the face of England was already beginning to change. London was rapidly expanding, and many agricultural labourers and small properietors were being forced off the land by Enclosure Acts, and there was a steady drift of population from the country to the growing towns and industrial villages.[9] This was attended with all the evils of haphazard and unplanned urbanization, to a degree which we who live in a welfare state find hard to imagine. Dr J. H. Plumb describes urban conditions at this time, particularly as they were endured by the poor:

'The first noticeable thing about these towns would have been the stench. There was no sanitary system; an open cesspool in the court often served the richer inhabitants; the poor, as with Eastern peoples today, made a public convenience of every nook and cranny. The unpaved streets were narrow, often only six feet wide; at Bristol they were too narrow for carts, and sledges had to be used for moving goods. The houses of the poor were one or two room hovels, frequently only made of weatherboard with a pitched roof, placed back to back; or they were the houses of the rich, deserted because their owners were seeking more salubrious suburbs—ramshackle warrens of filth, squalor and disease. Most cellars were inhabited, not only by people but also by their pigs, fowls, sometimes even by their horses and cattle. All tradesmen and craftsmen used the street as their dustbin, including butchers who threw out the refuse of their shambles to decay and moulder in the streets. . . .

'All houses and cellars were desperately overcrowded—ten to a room was common in Manchester. It was reported that often the rooms were without furniture and lacking even beds. Disease was rampant and unchecked: smallpox, typhus, typhoid and dysentery made death a commonplace.'[10]

The artisan and journeyman class — although restricted in political power, nursing bitter grievances against the government, and subject to the insecurities and anxieties of fluctuating trade—often fared comparatively well; but below them in the social scale, the hordes of the labouring poor who were congregating in the large towns, had neither economic security nor political rights,[11] and usually lived in conditions of abject poverty, squalor and disease. Even for those who were fortunate enough to get work in the factories, life was 'bitter and hard' and living conditions usually 'desolate and drab'.[12] These were the people whose 'hard, lean faces and shrunken bodies gave a sense of bitter despair to many of Hogarth's prints of London life',[13] and these were the people who in places like London, Bristol and Newcastle formed the bulk of Wesley's audiences, and among whom he observed the wildest emotional reactions to his preaching.

From such appalling conditions many of the poor took refuge in almost compulsive gambling, drinking and violence, or in the most brutalized forms of 'sport' such as bear-baiting, bull-baiting or cock-fighting which enjoyed huge popularity. Immorality was rife and mob violence was common and much feared by the authorities. Dr Plumb speaks of London at that time as 'a city, above all, of crime and turbulence and hard living'[14] and Dr Dorothy Marshall describes the brutalizing effects of such social conditions as follows:

'Overcrowding made every kind of sexual laxity almost normal. Extreme poverty made thieving and bullying the only alternatives to starvation. Overcrowding, poverty, and ill-health together with monotonous food and over-long hours of work, often found compensation in drunkenness, in a love of brutal sports, and in a violence that broke out again and again when the pressure became too great. It was a hard, harsh world for the mass of English people, and one singularly devoid of pity. Disease, violence, early or sudden death were too common.'[15]

In the face of widespread lawlessness and violence, the only answer of the authorities—and it was not a very effective one—was to intensify the repressive savagery of the law and the penalties imposed for offences against property or public order. These were the days of the stocks and of the press-gangs, of deportation under terrible conditions, of filthy overcrowded prisons, and the almost daily public hangings at Tyburn, for a variety of offences. By 1740 a child could be hanged for stealing a handkerchief,[16] and starving men were being hanged because they rioted for food for their families.[17] In his life of Wesley, Professor Winchester describes the reaction of 'decent' people towards the lawless rabble of the poor:

'Wherever any form of industry called together large numbers of ignorant, unskilled workmen, the restraints of orderly society were almost entirely removed; the colliers of Yorkshire and the miners of Cornwall were little better than hordes of wild men. For this lawless mass of humanity that surged about the foundations of society, decent order-loving folk had only hatred and threats of punishment. Philanthropy was hopeless of them. . . . The Church seemed powerless to take religion to them; it was certain they would never come to the Church.'[18]

It needs little imagination to picture the psychological condition of many of those born and reared in such a bitter, brutal and hopeless environment. Deprived as children of even the minimum of material or emotional security, their personalities must have been subject to every kind of emotional warping and poisoning from their earliest days, and into this mould would be poured all the hopelessness and bitter resentment of the years to come. It is true, of course, that the most significant repressions—those that concern the most primitive and powerful emotions of hatred (rejection thwarted love), destructive aggression, and the consequent fear and guilt that these arouse—occur in early childhood, long before any developed sense of social injustice could arise. Nevertheless, the social conditions under which people live will powerfully affect the quality of their family life and relationships, and thus the psychic well-being of their children and their vulnerability to deep repression in early childhood and subsequent emotional damage in later life. While the full bitterness of eighteenth century life among the poor would be felt directly only by those who were old enough to understand, yet through them, these same emotions would bear on the next generation at the most vulnerable stage in their lives. The hatred and resentment of children aroused in the first place against the lovelessness of brutalized, over-worked, love-starved parents would thus provide in many cases the typical nucleus of deep repression, and so very much of their later experience of the rejection and harshness of society would but serve to build up the intensity of these emotions on the one hand, and the strength of their defensive repressions on the other.[19] Grown to a twisted kind of maturity, many would find an outlet for some of these savage emotions in the risky business of mob violence and crime, but for many others all this welter of hatred, thwarted aggression, guilt and fear would have to remain forced out of consciousness and driven deep within their own souls. Emotional conflict, partly arising out of social conditions, is a common factor in human experience. For very many people, if not satisfactorily resolved, it is more or less 'successfully' contained by means of repression, and the stability of society is thereby preserved. It is only when social conditions become, as they had for the poor of eighteenth century England, so utterly inimical to human welfare and happiness that emotional repression may reach an intolerable degree for many people, and the stability of society be threatened by outbreaks of violence and other pathological behaviour.

III

Although social conditions under which so many of Wesley's hearers lived go a long way towards explaining the phenomena of widespread and heavy emotional repression among them, the story is not complete until we consider also the appalling weakness of the Church at that time. One of the important social functions of religion is to enable people to cope with emotional conflict in more satisfactory ways than by continued repression —to satisfy emotional needs that would otherwise be thwarted. To provide a pattern of meaning and purpose in life which makes the inevitable privations and tensions of earthly existence tolerable without retreat into neurotic reaction, and opportunities for emotional expression in a community where this will be understood, accepted and used to promote the maturity and freedom of its members. Above all, to provide a way of dealing with the facts of anxiety and guilt which robs them of their compulsive and destructive power in the individual and, therefore, of their tendency to produce deep neurotic resentments and anxiety in his children. When these normal functions of religion really operate in people's lives they can amount to a form of preventive hygiene against emotional repression and neurotic character distortion, which is effective even under the most adverse of external conditions. However, religion in England during the early part of the eighteenth century was at such a low ebb that it had not for a long time been fulfilling this function, and for the hard pressed masses of the poor, there was nothing to take its place.

The eviction of the Puritan clergy in 1662 and of the Non-Jurors in 1690 had crippled the Established Church by depriving her of a quarter of her ministers—and those by far the most devout and able. As J. W. Bready says:

'With this second tragedy the Church found herself shorn of both left and right wings. Zealous priest and flaming prophet were now cut off. The "moderate", "reasonable" men, the time-servers, self-seekers and pluralists—these all were left: but the wings of faith were gone. Had the "National" Church studied how best to extinguish all spiritual fire within the realm and to crush all crusading initiative, she could have devised no better plan than these two tragic expulsions.'[20]

The parochial system which had been suitable enough in a relatively stable society, was totally inadequate to meet the needs of a moving population and the rapidly developing industrial centres. But the suppression of Convocation by royal decree in 1717 had robbed the Church of any power of effective self-criticism and reform just at the very time when these were sorely needed. While some of the eighteenth century bishops, like Berkeley and Butler, were great scholars and good men, many others were not. With a cynical and open worldliness, they used their high office in church and state simply for purposes of political intrigue, personal enrichment and social ostentation and luxury. Bishoprics and the richer parish livings were regarded as prizes to be competed for, or rewards handed out by the government in return for political support. There were many faithful and conscientious parish priests, especially in the country areas, but all too often parish life was plagued by the practice of pluralism. This was the accumulation of several livings in the hands of one man who collected the combined income, but made no attempt at pastoral oversight in most of them. At best he would sometimes appoint a grossly underpaid and ill-equipped curate to do what he could. This was a very real part of the eighteenth century background, and helps us to see the significance of John Wesley's preaching and the response it evoked among the poor people of England.

Along with these quite unusual moral and practical weaknesses of the Church, her message was also strongly influenced and restricted by the intellectual climate of the times. The eighteenth century was predominantly the age of rationalism—of a vigorous but somewhat superficial confidence in the power of human reason, and reason alone, to solve all mysteries and satisfy all human needs. The fashionable philosophy of Deism denied the whole idea of revelation, and reduced God to the status of a benign but decidely remote being who never intervened in human affairs, and religion to a mere matter of good taste, commonsense and moderation in all things. Christian apologists like Butler and Berkeley were better scholars than the Deists, and easily outstripped them in argument, but they met their opponents on their own essentially rationalist terms, their own religion was characterized by the same pathological dread of emotion and enthusiasm and the exaltation of the unexciting virtues of moderation and prudence.

No doubt the dispute between Deists and Christians went right over the heads of the labouring poor, but, nevertheless, its most serious feature was not really the debate about revelation but the amazing failure of both parties to understand the emotional needs of man and, as a consequence, their complete failure to provide any religion that could touch the lives of the masses at all. Dr Plumb sums the matter up thus:

'But the greatest danger to the Church lay not only in its refusal to reform but in its attitude to life. The way to success was in discretion and man-pleasing and the worldly virtues became heavenly ones. The most popular sermon in the eighteenth century was Tillotson's on the text: "His commandments are not grievous", in which he stresses that if a man applies the same principles he uses in business or commerce to his moral life, he will be sure—of what? A *place* in heaven. Evil and guilt, sin and redemption—the whole personal drama and appeal of religion— was forgotten or rationalized away and the eupeptic optimism of politicians pervaded the teaching of the Church. It was not a religion which had much appeal to the men and women living brutal and squalid lives in the disease-ridden slums of the new towns and mining villages. They needed revelation and salvation.'[21]

Outside the established church, English Dissent had passed its heroic age. Although its academies were probably providing the best higher education in England at the time, its religion was running out either into a fairly arid rationalism, or else to Calvinism with its strictly limited doctrine of salvation.

Thus, in the early part of the eighteenth century, the poor people of England knew much of the harshness of the world and the severity of the law, but had little access indeed to the healing of grace. The foregoing sketch of the period is no doubt oversimplified; kindness was not absent from the common life, nor was philanthropy dead in either church or state. Nevertheless these ameliorations scarcely touched the hard core of the problem. And, at the period when social conditions must have generated the most bitter and violent emotions among the poor, the Christian forces at work in England were singularly unable either to change these conditions or to provide the means of emotional hygiene which would have offset their worst psychological effects. It is no coincidence then, that the outpouring of violent emotion which was sometimes a feature of early Methodism followed on a period of one-sided rationalism and long neglect of the emotional factors of religion. As we have seen already, Richard Watson noted that such a sequence of events had not been uncommon in the past, and in his study of Jonathan Edwards, for example, Professor Perry Miller has pointed out a similar rationalistic background to the much more violent outbursts of the New England revival.[22]

Between the harsh social conditions we have described on the one hand and the rationalistic degeneration of religion on the other, there is ample to account for the widespread and rather dangerous degree of emotional repression among the labouring poor by the time Wesley first went out to met them with a gospel of universal redemption. Dr Guntrip's reference to 'the fact of love embittered to a stifling, choking hate by frustration of all really human needs, hopes and goals'[23] could surely have been applied to many of these people. It is little wonder if some of them exhibited the most violent and repulsive reactions, as repressions began to crumble and all the pent up mess of distorted emotion was released. Referring to the 'taut neurotic quality of life in eighteenth century England, Dr Plumb writes:

'At no point did the Anglican or Dissenting churches of the day touch this inner tragedy of man, which was the emotional core of Methodism. But Methodism gave far more than emotional release; it brought a sense of purpose and a field for the exercise of both will and power.'[24]

IV

At this point then, we are led to consider the second of our two questions. What was there distinctive about Methodism, and the preaching of John Wesley in particular, that induced the healing abreaction of so much of this repressed emotion?

It has already been pointed out that Wesley himself did not regard converts who reacted violently as being in a class apart from the others—the majority whose conversions were just as real, though less spectacular at the time. The differences were incidental, but there was only one criterion of reality — the ethical and spiritual transformation of the convert, characterized by the experience of forgiveness and reconciliation with God, and a spontaneous and practical love towards his fellow men.

N

Our attention in this study has been focused on the more spectacular reactions and bodily symptoms of the Evangelical Revival. We must not, however, lose sight of the fact that these were only the more unusual and obviously noticeable form of a psychological process which, in other and more typical ways, was characteristic of the movement as a whole. A reading of Wesley's *Journal* suggests that the outpouring of repressed emotion often occurred without being accompanied by any of the violent or spectacular symptoms we have been examining. The radical and lasting transformation of personality, in the case of many converts who apparently experienced no *particular* occasion of emotional upheaval at all, plainly suggests the more gradual but no less significant dissolution of repression and successful working through of conflicts hitherto unrealized, such as may often occur in the process of psychotherapy.[25] Thus, the more violent reactions conveniently bring into sharper focus for us a major element in the Evangelical Revival—viz. the overcoming of emotional repression and the consequent liberation of personality, which, taken over the whole period, usually went on in ways less exciting but no less important. In seeking to understand what lay behind the more sensational factors to which our attention has been drawn, we are also looking for the psychological elements which made the Evangelical Revival as a whole an astonishingly effective religious movement, at a time when other movements largely failed.

It is not difficult to discover these elements. The most distinctive and important emphasis in the teaching of John Wesley and the hymns of his brother Charles, that played an equally effective part in spreading the message of the revival, was their insistence on the unswerving, unconditional and universal love of God for all men. 'The unchanging and changeless mercy of the Divine love'[26] was their constant theme. When John first went to Bristol at Whitefield's invitation 'and proclaimed in the highways the glad tidings of salvation', it was on the text 'The Spirit of the Lord is upon me, because He hath anointed me to preach the gospel to the poor, to proclaim deliverance to the captives . . . to set at liberty them that are bruised' that he preached to three thousand people in the open air.[27] Two days later it was 'I will heal their backsliding, I will love them freely'.[28] A few weeks later there were ten thousand at Rose

Green as he proclaimed that 'The Son of Man is come not to destroy men's lives but to save them.'[29] And so it went on. Wesley's preachers took up the same theme with him, and as Dr Wearmouth says, 'From 1739 onwards, with a crescendo of interest, the poor and oppressed in Britain listened in multitudes to the Methodists' pulsating and passionate proclamation of the Everlasting and All-Embracing Mercy.'[30] Certainly there were the sombre notes in John Wesley's preaching and sometimes references of topical and passing interest, but through them all this one great theme ran like a golden thread, and as Richard Green put it, 'Men could not hear Wesley preach and yet doubt whether God loved them and desired their salvation; or whether He had opened up a way to Himself for all.'[31]

Love, said John Wesley, is

' . . . that attribute which God peculiarly claims, wherein he glories above all the rest. It is not written "God is justice" or "God is truth": (although he is just and true in all his ways:) but it is written "God is love", love in the abstract without bounds; and "there is no end of his goodness". His love extends even to those who neither love nor fear him. He is good, even to the evil and unthankful; yea, without any exception or limitation, to all the children of men. For "the Lord is loving" (or good) "to every man, and his mercy is over all his works".'[32]

Less calmly perhaps, but with the same considered conviction, he cried in his famous sermon on 'Free Grace', 'No scripture can prove that God is not Love'. This message which the Methodist preachers proclaimed throughout England, Charles Wesley taught the people to sing, and writing of 'The Evangelical Doctrines of Charles Wesley's Hymns' Dr Ernest Rattenbury says

'"Arms of Love" outstretched to save men reveal the chief fact in the nature of God—His Love. Here we come to the very heart of Charles Wesley's gospel. He preached in the most literal and unqualified way that God is Love. "Pure universal love Thou art" was the discovery of "Wrestling Jacob"; that line in the great hymn was always printed in capital letters to distinguish it from everything else Charles Wesley said about God. The

notion of God's love in which he had been well instructed from
his youth upwards was discovered by him, in his own experience,
to be the central and commanding fact about God.'[33]

But this love of God which provided the central core of the
Wesleys' proclamation was no mere vague benevolence or sentimental indulgence. On the contrary it was always and everywhere 'sovereign saving grace' offered to all men. As Dr
Maldwyn Edwards has written of the 'Joint Manifesto' of John
and Charles Wesley,

'They did not sacrifice or minimize any of the essential insights
of Luther and Calvin. Both as interpreters of the Bible and as
children of their age, they were able to conceive of God as lifted
far above all rule and authority and power and dominion. He
rules from his throne as King of Kings, and upon his strong
selective activity we utterly depend. John and Charles Wesley
gladly accepted the reformers' solemn bowing of the knee to
God.'[34]

Yet, 'their new distinctive contribution lay in their understanding of love in relation to God's nature and purpose'[35] and 'their
bold and original move of recognizing the sovereignty of God
but declaring it to be the sovereignty of love. The King is the
Father; His power is the power of love'.[36] Of course all this is
new only in the sense in which the New Testament is 'new', and
Dr Edwards traces the various influences that led the Wesleys to
rediscover it, including their indebtedness to Lutheran, Moravian, Anglican and Catholic devotional writers; and, most significantly I think, to their general sensitivity (despite their own
personal politics) to the emerging ideas of democracy.[37] However, the importance of its rediscovery can hardly be overestimated. Here again was Deity without despotism, sovereignty
without savagery, a high doctrine of God calculated not to reduce
men and women to a state of anxious dismay before his 'dreadful
decree' or sullen resentment at his 'inscrutable will', but to lift
them up and give them a new dignity and joy as sons and
daughters of the Most High.

For this was redeeming love that encompassed within it all
the sovereign power of God, and could therefore treat with full

seriousness and depth the sin and tragedy of man on the one hand, and the glorious possibilities of his new being on the other. And could do this consistently, without degenerating into judicial tyranny or mere sentimentality. This consistent understanding of the divine love as always and everywhere a movement of saving grace, was, as Rupert Davies has reminded us, 'the centrepiece of the whole Wesleyan theology'.[38] It was worked out in terms of a salvation that was never a merely extrinsic transaction, but which changed man in the centre of his being, healing his lovelessness by reconciling him to God; giving him the conscious assurance that he was 'ransomed, healed, restored, forgiven' and begetting within him a spontaneous and continuing love towards his fellows that was nurtured in a distinctive kind of fellowship, and expressed in practical goodwill to all men.[39] In his 'Earnest Appeal to Men of Reason and Religion' Wesley wrote:

'We see, on every side, either men of no religion at all, or men of a lifeless formal religion. We are grieved at the sight; and should greatly rejoice, if by any means we might convince some that there is a better religion to be attained—a religion worthy of God that gave it. And this we conceive to be no other than love; the love of God and of all mankind; the loving God with all our heart and soul, and strength, as having first loved us, as the fountain of all the good we have received, and all we ever hope to enjoy; and the loving every soul which God hath made, every man on earth, as our own soul.

'This love we believe to be the medicine of life, the never-failing remedy for all the evils of a disordered world, for all the miseries and vices of men. . . .

'This religion we long to see established in the world, a religion of love, and joy, and peace, having its seat in the inmost soul, but ever showing itself by its fruits, continually springing forth, not only in all innocence (for love worketh no ill to his neighbour), but likewise in every kind of beneficence, spreading virtue and happiness all around it.'[40]

None of this was novel, as Wesley repeatedly pointed out. It was simply New Testament Christianity as set out in the formularies of the Church of England. But under the preaching of the revival it ceased to be mere theory; it did happen and its happening changed the face of England.[41]

The whole of Wesley's gospel then, began and ended in love, and when on his deathbed he asked that his sermon on the Love of God should be printed and spread abroad for all men to read, it was not the sort of sentimental gesture which one might forgive a dying man, but the simple 'amen' to over fifty years' ministry spent in proclaiming that theme to all who would listen. Summing up his chapter on the 'Joint Manifesto' of the Wesleys, Dr Maldwyn Edwards says:

'If every true revival is, in essence, the recapturing of some neglected dogma, then the Methodist revival swept through the earth because two brothers discovered afresh the deathless love of God and the sweep of that love in the heart of the believer and in the family of the Church.'[42]

If this emphasis has since been absorbed back into the common stock of Christian teaching, and no longer appears particularly distinctive, we need to be reminded that, as the London *Times* remarked on the centenary of Wesley's death, ' . . . all this was not commonplace in 1738. Much of the very essence of Christianity, as at least all evangelical Christians conceive it, had passed out of the religious life.'[43] Only as we see the Wesleyan proclamation of the love of God against the background of contemporary religion in England will we appreciate fully its psychological significance for the common people. By comparison, other religious movements current at the time completely failed to reach the masses, because they were either too shallow or too narrow.

V

We have already noted something of the way in which the rationalistic temper of the age invaded and restricted the teaching of the established Church. Outside the Church, it is not surprising that Deism which was anti-Christian in tone, and whose God was vaguely benign but far, should have nothing to say in terms of redemptive love. Within the Church of England, the Latitudinarians who were more or less the active spiritual heirs of the Cambridge Platonists (though with little of their mysticism) rose in able defence of the faith. But although they performed a useful task of intellectual apologetics, they were really no more effective in proclaiming the saving love of God to the masses than their avowedly rationalistic opponents. In fact neither party to this high level intellectual dispute seems to have been much concerned with such a thought. As Professor Cragg says, of the Latitudinarians,

'Everything they said or did was moderate in tone; their religion was genuine but never ardent; they stood for a temper rather than a creed. Their outlook was reasonable and dispassionate, magnanimous and charitable. Their virtues easily degenerated; their goodwill subsided into mere complacency.'[44]

The condition of religion in England in the early part of the eighteenth century is described by Williston Walker in these words:

'The end of the struggles of the seventeenth century has been marked by a general spiritual lethargy in the establishment and among Dissenters alike. Rationalism had penetrated all classes of religious thinkers, so that even among the orthodox, Christianity seemed little more than a system of morality supported by divine sanctions. . . . There were able preachers, but the characteristic sermon was the colourless essay on moral virtues. Outreaching work for the unchurched was but scanty. The condition of the lower classes was one of spiritual destitution.'[45]

The almost complete lack of any compelling sense of the divine mercy reaching out to meet the deep need of sinful men, at this time, is brought out in a letter from John Gambold to Charles Wesley early in 1738:

'But if you speak of faith in such a manner as makes Christ a Saviour to the uttermost; as discovers a greater pollution in the best of us than we could before acknowledge, but brings a greater deliverance from it than we could before expect—if anyone offers to talk at this rate, he shall be heard with the same abhorrence as if he was going to rob mankind of their salvation.'[46]

There is no doubt, I think, that the Latitudinarians for all their magnanimity and broad humanity had no profound sense of sin and redemption, and anything they had to say about the love of God was consequently far too shallow to be of much use to the common people.

By way of vivid contrast, it was Wesley's very emphasis on human sinfulness that gave his proclamation of the divine love for sinners depth and immediate relevance to his hearers. To assume, as Dr Sargant seems to have done, that Wesley had to evolve a technique for producing an artificial sense of sin for his gospel of salvation to appear relevant, is to display a rather amazing ignorance of the real condition of his audience. Most of the common people to whom Wesley preached were steeped in sin, and the awareness of sin already. They may not have used the word, or always thought of their condition in those terms, but they were in daily contact with the viciousness and corruption of human nature both in themselves and in their world, and they knew exactly what Wesley was talking about. He spoke to their condition. Nor, in spite of their tough exterior, were they strangers to a morbid sense of guilt either.[47] The long period of Puritan ascendancy allied with the forces of law and order in England had left a mixed legacy which included a fairly heavy deposit of moralistic guilt feelings in the minds of many people. This is the sort of thing that tends to become incorporated of course, into social conventions and parental attitudes, and so to perpetuate itself as a slowly diminishing quantity for several generations after its original source has dried up. Puritanism, as a movement may have been spent; but a great deal of the senseless vice at all levels of eighteenth century society was largely an irrational and ineffective protest against these half buried guilt feelings that it had left behind—feelings that could seldom be tolerated in the full light of consciousness, because men had no satisfactory way of dealing with them. No doubt it was among the poorer classes who were more frequently on the wrong side of the law, or threatened with its condemnation, that these moralistic guilt feelings were most pronounced. The pathology of the upper classes was more urbane. Had Wesley's audiences been from amongst the well-to-do, the conventionally good-but-not-too-good, the cultured and educated classes, they would have laughed at his gospel. After all, their repressions, inhibitions and

blind spots were relatively comfortable because of their privi-
leged position in society. They wanted nothing of Wesley's talk
of sin and salvation, and the only love of God that they were
interested in was a sort of vague benevolence on the side of the
status quo that would leave them and their children after them,
well-to-do, conventional and cultured—sinners unaware and un-
redeemed. But the poor people of England to whom Wesley
preached could not manage many comforting illusions, and the
only gospel they could receive was the proclamation of a love
that was deep enough to deal with their real need—with the
problems of sin and guilt.

It is important to realize that in Wesley's proclamation of the
love of God there was not the slightest hint of blackmail or
coercion. Nowhere did Wesley ever suggest that God loves men
if they are good, or if they are sorry, or if they decide to accept
a particular brand of salvation. The love of God was always
unambiguously prior to any of these things, and it was unconditional. Because of the strong ethical emphasis in the preaching
of Wesley, those unversed in either the history of theology or
the experience of salvation have sometimes misunderstood the
place he gave to good works. For Wesley, good works were the
fruit of salvation, made possible by the liberating grace of God
at work in the life of the convert. But they were never the prior
condition of salvation, and certainly not something which God
would require of a man before he would love him and seek his
salvation. God's love towards man was unconditional and completely reliable, and was preveniently at work for the salvation
of the sinner long before he became aware of it or was able to
make any response. Yet, because man's salvation (justification) is
the rebuilding of a genuinely personal and mutual relationship,
it would not happen automatically without man's consent, and
it could never be coerced. The grace of God was not irresistible
but always sought man's free response of faith, a faith which
was simply the sinner's choosing to accept and rely on a love
which he could do nothing to either earn or deserve. This choice
itself, God would enable, but would never force. Many whom
God loves might remain unsaved, but if they did, it would only
be because of their own choosing; no man would ever fail of
salvation because God did not love him or desire him to be
saved.[48]

Wesley's distinctive stress on prevenient grace and his insistence on justification by faith alone, as against those who taught the prior need for good works as well, were important features of his proclamation of the love of God. No other kind of gospel could possibly have won a response from people caught in the web of degradation and hopelessness. Although it may seem strangely sombre and severe to the modern mind, Wesley's stress on the sinfulness of men was not in itself at all distinctive. It was essentially the teaching of the Reformers, and had played an important part in the Calvinism that dominated English religion during the period of the Commonwealth, and was still by no means a spent force. But this alone would have produced no evangelical revival, for the revival of religion came as a response to something that *was* distinctive in eighteenth century England—Wesley's rediscovery and re-publication of the unconditional and undeserved love of God for the sinner—'Amazing love, immense and free'. Secure in such a love as this, men could run emotional risks that they were quite incapable of before; the old hard outer shell began to crumble, and inner defences and barriers could be let go and, to use John Gambold's terms, they began to 'discover' (i.e. uncover) in themselves 'a greater pollution than they could before acknowledge' and to find 'a greater deliverance from it than they could before expect'.[49]

VI

While Wesley's proclamation of the love of God went to much greater depths of human need than Latitudinarianism could reach, it was in contrast and in conflict with Calvinism that the most characteristic feature of his message developed — viz. its vigorous and sometimes almost ebullient insistence on the infinite breadth of God's love, as a love which reaches out to every man, so that in his mercy God wills all men to be saved. This was in the clearest contrast, of course, with the Calvinist teaching that God wills only the salvation of the elect, whom he saves by irresistible grace, and wills the rest of mankind to be damned.

To all outward appearances Calvinism was a declining force in English church life at this time. Its close association with the Puritanism of the Commonwealth period naturally tended to discredit it rather heavily in the minds of a generation that was doing its best to forget the Commonwealth and repudiate its social ideals. But the influence of a religious movement, both positive and negative, persists long after the movement itself has gone out of fashion. We still meet many people today with no conscious interest in religion whatsoever, who display not only some unmistakeable signs of a Christian morality but also, unfortunately, elements of a pseudo-Christian moralism, both of which are part of their legacy from the intentionally Christian upbringing of their forebears two or three generations back. In like manner, I am convinced that in eighteenth century England, while the current rationalism passed right over the heads of the masses, Calvinism, despite its outward decline, was at a much deeper, level, one of the dominant religious influences in their lives. I am not suggesting, of course, that the masses were all good Calvinists at heart—far from it. Nevertheless, Calvinism still dominated them, because it was Calvinism against which many of them were inwardly in rebellion. Their 'image' of God was a Calvinist image—the God of stern moralism who saved or damned by arbitrary decree and irresistible force, and their revolt against such a God was expressed in their almost compulsive anti-moral behaviour and their wholesale rejection of religion.[50]

It is probably difficult for most people today to appreciate the full significance of the Wesleys' controversy with the Calvinists over the doctrine of the double decree, since this particular doctrine has long since ceased to be a living issue; except for certain conservative-evangelical groups now somewhat removed from the mainstream of Church life. The logic of the Calvinist position went something like this: man's salvation depends entirely on God, and is not achieved by anything man can do for himself. Now it is obvious that some men are saved and others are not, and since man contributes nothing to his own salvation it must be God, and God alone, who chooses to save some ('the elect') and to damn others ('the reprobate'). This divine choice is not made in response to man's merit, since this would be salvation by works. Nor is it made in response to man's faith, since saving faith itself is entirely the gift of God which he bestows on those whom he has chosen for salvation. God's election of some to salvation and some to damnation is entirely arbitrary and depends on nothing but his own sovereign will. It follows that the choice once made is both irresistible and irreversible. In Calvin's own words:

'Predestination we call the eternal decree of God by which He has determined in Himself what He would have to become of every individual of mankind. For they are not all created with a similar destiny; but eternal life is fore-ordained for some, and eternal damnation for others. Every man, therefore, being created for one or other of these ends, we say he is predestined either to life or to death.'[51]

God's predestination of the reprobate, Calvin himself described as a 'dreadful decree', but he and his associates nevertheless followed this aspect of the doctrine through with unflinching logic. Of those predestined to hell before they were born Calvin wrote:

'God speaketh to them that they may be the deafer; he gives light to them that they may be the blinder; he affirms instruction to them that they may be more ignorant; and uses the remedy that they may not be healed.'[52]

And Theodore Beza, his successor at Geneva, frankly admitted 'We believe, though it is incomprehensible, that it is just to damn such as do not deserve it.'[53] However much it was usually offset by much more humane practice, this doctrine, essentially unchanged, had become part of the religious heritage of many of the people to whom Wesley preached; his terse summary of such teaching as he still encountered it, two centuries after Calvin, was perfectly fair: 'One in twenty (suppose) of mankind are elected; nineteen in twenty are reprobated. The elect shall be saved, do what they will; the reprobate shall be damned, do what they can.'[54]

Against this blasphemous travesty of the Gospel the Wesleys set themselves quite uncompromisingly. Charles ridiculed it ironically in his polemical hymns and verses, and although they had only an ephemeral value in themselves, Dr J. E. Rattenbury affirms that 'nothing did so much to destroy popular Calvinism in England as Charles Wesley's hymns; they made it incredible to the reason, and repulsive to the heart of decent people'.[55] But far more significantly, the controversy called forth his *Hymns on God's Everlasting Love* which have lived on, and include some of the finest proclamations of the love of God in all its depth and breadth, in the history of Christian literature, beginning with verses still in familiar use:

> Father whose *everlasting love*
> Thy only Son for sinners gave,
> Whose grace to *all* did *freely* move
> And sent him down *a world to save;*
>
> Help us Thy mercy to extol
> Immense, unfathom'd, unconfined;
> To praise the Lamb who *died for all,*
> The *general Saviour of mankind.*
>
> Thy *undistinguishing regard*
> Was cast on Adam's fallen race;
> For *all* Thou hast in Christ prepared
> *Sufficient, sovereign, saving* grace.

The italics were in the original edition of this hymn, and as Dr Rattenbury remarks, they 'indicate plainly the controversial character of the hymn from which these verses are selected, but the verses abide as a fine expression of truths of permanent value'.[56]

John was just as uncompromising as his brother in his rejection of predestinarian doctrine, and clear in his proclamation of the universal sweep of God's love and his desire to save *all* men. The suggestion that one could speak of God loving those whom he had foredoomed to hell he swept aside as utter nonsense.[57] Yet he was less scathing in controversy than Charles, and more inclined to be irenical if he could. Firstly, because he quite genuinely deplored acrimonious disputes over doctrine and desired a unity among Christians based on mutual toleration of different points of view, and secondly, because of his personal friendship with George Whitefield.

Whitefield, who actually commenced the open air preaching at Bristol and persuaded Wesley to take over from him on the eve of his return to America, held and taught the Calvinist view of a strictly limited offer of salvation. In practice, however, he was gloriously inconsistent, and the harshness of his theoretical

Calvinism was greatly softened by his enthusiastic proclamation of a gospel of salvation to all and sundry. Nevertheless, since we are considering the effect of Wesley's preaching in bringing about violent abreactions and breaking down emotional repression, it is not without significance that the only occasion on which anything like this happened under Whitefield's preaching in England was after he had been discussing the matter with Wesley, and in his presence so far forgot his Calvinism as to 'invite *all* sinners to believe in Christ'.[58] Of course the only evangelistic action that would be really consistent with strict Calvinist views would be to take no action whatsoever. If the elect are irresistibly destined to be saved, and the rest to be irresistibly damned, all the preacher's eloquence and passion are redundant for the former and quite futile for the latter. Fortunately for the Evangelical Revival, Whitefield and the other Calvinist preachers were seldom logical about this, but went on offering Christ with passion and with power to all who would listen, while holding to the theoretical belief that most of their hearers were rendered quite incapable, by God himself, of ever responding to their message, and that those who did respond would have been saved anyway. However, the danger of Quietism was quite real, and one of the most serious threats to the Methodist movement in its earlier phase was the doctrine of Stillness, imported in the first place from the Moravians but also highly congenial to some of the more consistent Calvinists.[59] According to this, since salvation is wholly the work of God, men should not have recourse to preaching or any other of the means of grace, but should simply be still and await the divine miracle which will happen if God so decrees.[60]

Despite his affection for Whitefield, Wesley found his teaching about election and predestination totally unacceptable and felt obliged himself to proclaim in the clearest possible terms God's universal love and desire to save all men. The two men agreed to differ, but it was inevitable that there should be a serious rift between them. Wesley might shrink from an open controversy which would give rise to unchristian recriminations; this would split the ranks of the Methodists and divert them from their real task, but he could not tolerate teaching that would cut the very nerve centre of his gospel, present a picture of God just as likely to harden men's hearts as to soften them, and possibly even encourage his people to neglect the ordinary means of grace. As we have seen already,[61] it was Calvinist activity among his people that finally goaded Wesley to publish his sermon on 'Free Grace' which came to be regarded as something of a manifesto. The Calvinists' interpretation of a few texts, Wesley claimed, was such as 'flatly contradicted all the other texts, and indeed the whole scope and tenor of Scripture'. He amply supports his own argument with scripture, but he makes it quite clear that what is at stake is not merely a matter of biblical exegesis, but the whole Christian conception of God. Here is one famous passage that is typical of his argument:

'This is the blasphemy clearly contained in the horrible decree of predestination! And here I fix my foot. On this I join issue with every assertor of it. You represent God as worse than the devil; more false, more cruel, more unjust. But you say you will prove it by Scripture. Hold! What will you prove by Scripture? That God is worse than the devil? It cannot be. Whatever that Scripture proves it cannot prove this; . . . No Scripture can mean that God is not love, or that his mercy is not over all his works.'[62]

Wesley and Whitefield were subsequently reconciled and remained friends until the latter's death, but neither of them gave way an inch in his respective doctrinal position. The controversy was carried on by lesser men who sometimes mingled theological argument with violently abusive personal attacks on Wesley. While Wesley did not reply in kind, and tried to avoid public controversy as much as possible, he was not inclined to be at all conciliatory in proclaiming his own message. In sermon after sermon, as well as in his brother's hymns, the doctrine of a universal atonement, i.e. of salvation freely and genuinely offered to all men for their responsible decision, was set forth. Indeed it was the very warp and woof of the whole Wesleyan message, the fabric on which all the other patterns of doctrine and devotion were developed. From time to time Wesley published controversial pamphlets on the subject, such as his long *Predestination Calmly Considered*[63] and the much shorter *Dialogue between a Predestinarian and his Friend*,[64] and in 1777 he commenced publication of the Arminian Magazine, a sixpenny monthly which, as its name indicates, was dedicated to the publication of 'some of the most remarkable tracts on the Universal Love of God and His willingness to save all men from sin'.[65]

Sunk in social and moral degradation and almost untouched by the Church, which seemed so often indifferent to their plight, it must have been very easy for many of the common people to feel themselves among the reprobate, irretrievably destined by God himself, for damnation. Their lives were hard, bitter, loveless and lost; and the tragedy of it all was that those who spoke so smoothly of the divine benevolence that ordered all things well had not the faintest conception of their need, while those who could expatiate so effectively on the depth of human wickedness and woe could bring only such a narrow and uncertain offer of salvation that the people were left even deeper in their hopelessness. But into their hopelessness came Wesley and his field preachers, taking the spiritual plight of these people very seriously, but sweeping aside every restriction on the love of God and proclaiming with passionate certainty

> Outcasts of men to you I call,
> Harlots and publicans, and thieves!
> He spreads His arms to embrace you all;
> Sinners alone His grace receives.[66]

This was an astonishing gospel, and produced astonishing results. Against Christianity merely as law and judgment and hell, the hardened sinner was more than proof. To the God who saved or damned by arbitrary decree he could turn a heart of stone, but before the offer of the divine mercy 'immense, unfathomed, unconfined' his stony heart was broken. As Mrs Elsie Harrison puts it,

'To souls bound fast in the dungeon of Giant Despair, with the shackles of John Calvin upon them, such a gospel of liberation broke all the prison bars. Flames of hell, eternal damnation, the nightmare of the reprobate, all were conquered in that unconquerable love of God.'[67]

The most sombre note in Wesley's preaching was not the threat of hell, but the reality of human sin and need, which as we have seen, only served to deepen his proclamation of the divine love. It is not denied that hell played some part in his preaching. We may disagree with his views on this theme today, but given the limitations of eighteenth century biblical interpretation, it is difficult to see what else he could have believed; and believing what he did, he would have been singularly lacking in human love and concern if he had not warned men to flee from the wrath to come. Yet, as we have seen, this was not at all a distinctive note in Wesley's preaching such as would account for the distinctively different response it evoked; there were others who proclaimed the terrors of hell much more effectively than he did. For, quite contrary to what Dr Sargant would have us believe, I think we shall have to conclude that in the gospel which the Wesleys preached and sang, it was not the fear of hell but the love of God which broke men's hearts and cracked their repressions, often letting loose a pent up flood of buried emotion—in those paroxysms of cleansing and relief that must have been very unpleasant to behold, but sometimes had to occur if these people were ever to find the splendid sanity and joyous love of new men and women in Christ.

FOOTNOTES AND REFERENCES

1. *War Neuroses in North Africa. The Tunisian Campaign* (*January - May* 1943) by R. R. Grinker and J. P. Spiegel. Quoted by Sargant, *op. cit.*, p. 74 (81).
2. See above, Ch. 4.
3. 'There' is of course a figurative term. It does not imply any literally *spatial* locality. The concepts of depth psychology are sometimes criticized by logical purists because they are expressed in spatial terms. However, no depth psychologist takes such language literally. Spatial terms used symbolically are the only language we have to describe certain aspects of human experience, and their use in this way is of course much older than modern psychology.
4. Sargant, *op. cit.*, p. 50 (61).
5. Both these quotations are from Bready, J. W., *England Before and After Wesley*, p. 41.
6. Quoted by Bready, *op. cit.*, p. 19, from Berkeley's 'Discourse Addressed to Magistrates and Men in Authority', p. 41 f.

o

7. Bready, *op. cit.*, p. 19. Historians mentioned include Lecky, Stephen, Ranke, Macauley, Green, Trevelyan, Halévy and Temperley.

8. Quoted by Professor G. R. Cragg in *The Church in the Age of Reason*, p. 129, The Pelican History of the Church, Vol. 4, Penguin Books 1960.

9. Cf. Dr J. H. Plumb on the structure of English Society 1714-42 in *England in the Eighteenth Century* (1714-1815), The Pelican History of England, Vol. 7, Penguin Books 1950, p. 11 and pp. 19-20. The table on p. 82 also shows how the process of Enclosure which changed the face of rural England and hastened the growth of the urban poor, began to quicken in tempo in the period immediately prior to the Evangelical Revival.

10. Plumb, *op. cit.*, p. 12.

11. *Idem.*, pp. 16-17.

12. *Idem.*, p. 89.

13. *Idem.*, p. 16.

14. *Idem.*, p. 14.

15. Marshall, Dr Dorothy, in *Eighteenth Century England*, Longmans 1962, p. 243.

16. Plumb, *op. cit.*, p. 17.

17. See *Methodism and the Common People of the Eighteenth Century* by Dr R. F. Wearmouth, Epworth Press, London 1945, Ch. 3 and especially p. 78. The whole of this chapter should be read to gain a clear picture of the appalling savagery of the law which bore heavily on the poorer classes. Cf. also Dr Maldwyn Edwards in *John Wesley and the Eighteenth Century*, Epworth 1933, p. 174.

18. Winchester, C. T., *The Life of John Wesley*, The Macmillan Coy., New York 1906, p. 76.

19. On the interaction of social conditions and inter-personal relations in the family cf. Erich Fromm: 'Freud has shown that the early experiences of the child have a decisive influence upon the formation of its character structure. If this is true, how then can we understand that the child, who—at least in our culture—has little contact with the life of society, is moulded by it? The answer is not only that the parents—aside from certain individual variations—apply the educational patterns of the society they live in, but also that in their own personalities they represent the social character of their society

or class. They transmit to the child what we may call the psychological atmosphere or the spirit of a society just by being what they are—namely representatives of this very spirit. *The family thus may be considered to be the psychological agent of society.' — The Fear of Freedom*, p. 245.

20. Bready, *op. cit.*, p. 25.

21. Plumb, *op. cit.*, pp. 44-5. On the condition of the Church generally during this period, and its tendency towards rationalism cf. Bready, *op. cit.*, Chs. 1-3, and Cragg, *op. cit.*, Ch. 9.

22. Perry Miller, *Jonathan Edwards*, William Sloane Associates, USA, 1949.

23. See above, p. 52 and f. 8, Ch. 4.

24. Plumb, *op. cit.*, p. 95.

25. See above, Ch. 4, p. 57.

26. Wearmouth, *op. cit.*, p. 192.

27. Wesley's *Journal*, Vol. II, pp. 172-3.

28. *Idem.*, p. 174.

29. *Idem.*, p. 205.

30. Wearmouth, *op. cit.*, p. 192.

31. Green, Richard, *John Wesley, Evangelist*, Religious Tract Society, London 1905, p. 259.

32. 'Predestination Calmly Considered', para. 42, *Works*, Vol. 10, p. 219.

33. Rattenbury, Dr J. Ernest, *The Evangelical Doctrines of Charles Wesley's Hymns*, Epworth, London 1941, p. 125.

34. Edwards, Dr Maldwyn, *Sons to Samuel*, Epworth, London 1961, p. 87.

35. *Ibid.*

36. Edwards, Dr Maldwyn, *The Astonishing Youth*, Epworth, London 1959, p. 118.

37. *Sons to Samuel*, pp. 88-91, and *The Astonishing Youth*, p. 118.

38. *Methodism*, Pelican Edition, p. 99.

39. Cf. Maldwyn Edwards *Sons to Samuel*, Ch. 5; H. Lindstrom, *Wesley and Sanctification, passim*, Epworth 1946; and an important discussion of the influence of the Wesleyan Revival and its rejection of a merely 'extrinsic justification' by Louis Bouyer in *The Spirit and Forms of Protestantism*, The Harvill Press, London 1956—Translation by A. V. Littledale, pp. 179-88.

40. *Works*, Vol. 8, pp. 3-4.
41. For the widespread social effects of the Evangelical Revival, see J. W. Bready, *op. cit.*, and F. R. Wearmouth, *op. cit.*
42. *Sons to Samuel*, p. 116.
43. Quoted by Dr Henry Bett in *The Spirit of Methodism*, Epworth, London 1937, p. 100.
44. Cragg, *op. cit.*, p. 72.
45. Walker, Williston, *A History of the Christian Church*, T. & T. Clark, Edinburgh 1953, p. 507.
46. Letter from John Gambold, quoted by Bett, *op. cit.*, p. 110.
47. 'Morbid guilt' is used here in the sense of those essentially irrational and unrealistic guilt feelings produced simply by the disapproval of others, as distinct from realistic or moral guilt which involves actual wrongdoing. Both kinds of guilt, though of different origins, are, I believe, very closely intertwined in much human experience, and this was almost certainly the case in the lives of many of Wesley's hearers.
48. Cf. J. E. Rattenbury, *op. cit.*, p. 126: 'Wesley teaches that man is a rebel, but that God respects his will; He cannot force it, or he will not. There is no such thing as irrestible grace. A man who cannot resist would not be a man, but an automaton, hence God does not try to force him to assent; He loves him, reasons with him and pleads with him. This is the doctrine which Charles Wesley had inherited and formulated in verse in contradiction to that of Calvin's irresistible God and passive, helpless clay-man. God is striving always to win the man He never loves more than when he sins. The rebel can only be overcome by grace, but it is not irresistible grace. Man is subjected to the continual pleadings of the Holy Spirit, the spirit of love and righteousness.'
49. It is important to realize that the sense of sin that was so vivid in many of Wesley's converts was not a shuddering response to the divine wrath, but an opening up of the sin-sick soul to the divine mercy. After surveying the spiritual experience of the early Methodists, from their first-hand accounts, and bearing in mind, no doubt, some of its more violent expressions also, Dr Leslie Church had this to say: 'That an experience of such radiant joy should seem to begin in paroxysms of misery is in itself astonishing. But did it begin in penitence or is not Dr Barry right when he says "You cannot have any genuine sense of sin (in its full religious connotation) until you have seen some vision of God's glory"? That was surely how the

experience began. The early Methodists realized their sinfulness only when they had begun to realize the love of God in Christ Jesus.' — *The Early Methodist People*, Epworth 1948, p. 143.

The quotation from Dr F. R. Barry is from his book *The Relevance of Christianity* (Nisbet, London 1931), p. 190.

50. This interpretation of the psychological roots of much of the immorality and irreligion of eighteenth century English society is quite consistent with that already given above in terms of harsh social conditions, a brutal criminal code and alienation from the means of grace. Calvinism could hardly be blamed for the harsh social conditions, yet by the very irresistible nature of his working in the world Calvin's God must surely have been on the side of the *status quo*, and the savage, hopeless inner revolt of the poor against the social conditions they were powerless to change or escape, must surely have had deep emotional affinities with the revolt against a God whose equally unreasonable and inescapable decrees had already branded most of them for hell.

51. Quoted in *Portrait of Calvin* by T. H. L. Parker, S.C.M. Press, London 1954, p. 57.

52. Quoted in *John Wesley* by Sir Arnold Lunn, Cassell & Co., London 1929, p. 174.

53. Quoted in Lunn, *op. cit.*, p. 173.

54. Quoted in Lunn, *op. cit.*, p. 173.

55. Rattenbury, *op. cit.*, p. 121.

56. *Ibid.*, p. 134. The hymn quoted is No. 75 in the present Methodist Hymn Book.

57. See Wesley's *Predestination Calmly Considered*, sections 42-4, *Works*, Vol. 10, pp. 219-21.

58. Wesley's *Journal*, Vol. II, pp. 239-40. There were, of course, many conversions under Whitefield's preaching, and these must have involved the lowering of repression. However, it is reasonabe to assume that the more violent abreactive phenomena represented the breakdown of the harder and deeper repressions, and it is significant that these occurred under Wesley's preaching of a universal and unconditional divine love, and not under Whitefield's Calvinist doctrine.

Whitefield also had a highly successful ministry in America where, in contrast to the harsh, rigid and terrifying Calvinism of Jonathan Edwards, his own doctrine was mild and merciful. (See Bready, *op. cit.*, pp. 427-31.)

BATTLE FOR THE FREE MIND

59. See Wesley's *Journal*, Vol. II, Part iv.
60. Apparently such a wholly consistent attitude is not unknown among certain modern believers in strict Calvinism. See *Election and Biblical Evangelism* by Tom Rees (published by the author and obtainable from the Bookroom, Hildenborough Hall, Frinton-on-Sea, Essex).
61. See above, Ch. 7, p. 158.
62. *Op. cit.*, section 26, *Works*, Vol. 7, p. 366.
63. *Works*, Vol. 10, pp. 197-249.
64. *Works*, Vol. 10, pp. 250-6.
65. See Wearmouth, *op. cit.*, p. 192.
66. See Hymn No. 361 in the present Methodist Hymn Book.
67. Harrison, Elsie, *Son to Susannah*, Penguin Books 1944, p. 111.

CHAPTER 9

LOVE AND LIBERATION

I

The more violent emotional features of the Evangelical Revival have hitherto been difficult to understand, I would suggest, because until comparatively recent times we have had no psychological tools or concepts that were adequate for their interpretation. Those favourably disposed towards the movement have felt obliged to point out what is, after all, perfectly true—that these particular phenomena were not very common after the first few years; and they have thus been prepared, on the whole, to accept them as somewhat embarrassing and anomalous side-effects which, if they could not in honesty be hushed up, were at least not to be given undue attention. On the other hand, some of those who have not felt any particular loyalty to the principles of the Evangelical Revival have probably tended towards a rather unhistorical kind of explanation based on certain *a priori* assumptions rather than on documentary evidence, and have therefore tended to tell us what must have happened rather than taking note of what did happen.

It has been taken for granted that men and women break down only under stress of fear, whereas modern psychology shows us that there is more than one kind of breakdown, and that some kinds have nothing to do with any immediate threat of fear. However, with such an assumption firmly in mind, this kind of interpreter may be tempted to fasten on Wesley's references to hell, and to treat them in a quite unhistorical way. In contrast to twentieth century fashions this may seem to be a distinctive feature of his preaching; but when we examine the message of the Evangelical Revival and of Wesley in particular, in its own historical setting, the fear of hell is seen as a comparatively minor item. There were other dominant themes, notably its stress on the universal love of God for sinful man, which

215

sounded a quite distinctive note in his day. What modern depth psychology can show us is why this particular emphasis, at this particular time, served to bring about not only the more violent forms of abreaction with which we have been concerned, but also the more significant and permanent results of the Evangelical Revival.

We have seen already that the breakdown of psychological repression with the consequent release and expression of buried emotion, the satisfactory working through of hidden conflicts, and the reintegration into consciousness of previously buried aspects of personality together make up a total process which, in various forms, occurred to many people during the Evangelical Revival. However, this same process is also the major concern of all those forms of deep psychotherapy which are committed today to the more radical treatment of the psychoneuroses, rather than a mere suppression of their symptoms. The different forms of psychotherapy which have a common ancestry in the work of Sigmund Freud and are all based on what we have agreed to call 'depth psychology', in some ways present the appearance of a bewildering variety and confusion. Widely divergent theories have evolved about the elements in human nature which are dominant in emotional conflict; the different stages in human growth at which these conflicts have their origins, and the relative importance of biological and cultural influences; also, different conceptions of the structure of personality, and a variety of techniques for dealing with its ills. However, the situation is not nearly so confused as would at first appear, and despite divergency of theories, many psychotherapists can in practice quite easily adopt an eclectic approach to the treatment of their patients. This is so because certain broad and commonly accepted insights regarding the cause and cure of emitional illness have emerged within the movement as a whole.

One of the earliest comprehensive and constructive criticisms of the work of Freud was made by Dr Ian D. Suttie in his book *The Origins of Love and Hate*[1] published in 1935; in this he argued very persuasively that emotional illness 'is to be regarded as due to the frustrations, distortions and reactions of the *love* disposition in its first adjustments to family life',[2] rather than to the thwarting and repression of sexuality as such. The source of this love, which involved a need both to love and be loved, Suttie found in the original nurtural relationship between mother and child, which included both tenderness and a shared 'feeling-interest', and in a 'normal' human development this would eventually issue in 'Free "feeling-interest" relationships' between the adult and his social environment.[3] However, when development is subject to 'distortions and dissatisfactions of the love life'[4] at an early stage, 'the rage and anxiety evoked by thwarting is inhibited and goes to build up a sense of guilt'.[5] It is this thwarting of love in early childhood that Suttie held to be the real source of hatred in the personality, rather than attributing it to any independent destructive tendencies or 'death instinct' such as Freud had postulated. Hatred then, he considered, 'is just a standing reproach to the hated person, and owes all its meaning to a demand for love',[6] and he goes on to say:

' "Earth hath no hate but love to hatred turned, and hell no fury but a baby scorned", for hatred, except for a preferred rival or a rejecting lover does not seem to exist. At bottom therefore hatred is always ambivalent, always self-frustrated. It has no free outlet, can look for no favourable response, and this is why it is so important in Psychopathology.'[7]

He adds a significant footnote: 'In a measure it must undergo *automatic inhibition* or repression, and this process is already being dimly perceived by clinical analysis.'[7]
      Even at this time Suttie could say that

' . . . an examination of the various extinct and extant theories of psychotherapy will show that the trend and present consensus of opinion supports the view that psychopathy is a disturbance of the love life.'[8]

and he therefore saw psychotherapy as

'nothing but the *overcoming of the barriers to love and feeling oneself loved* . . . fundamentally an attempt to assist the patient in his love-quest and to set this upon lines more likely to achieve the desired results.'[9]

For Suttie, the relationship that developed between the therapist and the patient was far more important than either theory or technique and he wholeheartedly endorsed Ferenczi's dictum that 'It is the physician's love that heals the patient'.[10] Thus, though he felt obliged to criticize the theoretical formulations of Freud and his followers, he maintained that Freudian practice—quite inconsistent with its underlying theory, was in fact ' "Cure" by Love'.[11]

Unfortunately, Dr Suttie died soon after his book was published, and his work was never taken up by any particular school, although his general viewpoint appears to have been shared by some of his colleagues at the Tavistock Clinic. It is all the more significant then, that after the lapse of twenty-five years Professor Mace could say, in his editorial introduction to the Pelican edition of *The Origins of Love and Hate* that the general trend of psychotherapy since, has been in the direction that Suttie indicated.[12] In particular, there has been a growing recognition of the major role that is played by the deprivation of love in producing neuroses and character distortions; and conversely of the hygienic power of love in preventing them, and its unique therapeutic importance in bringing about their cure. Thus, writing not of any particular school of psychotherapy, but of the 'broad and general emphases which they all share', Professor C. A. Outler says:

'Psychotherapy has developed an impressive pile of evidence to show that the mass of human misery comes from the lack or the corruption of the love in their interpersonal relations—and an equally impressive demonstration that love is the chief restorative power in the remaking of psychic health and wholeness.'[13]

He points to 'the sovereign virtue of love in the making and remaking of human persons'[13] and to the fact that in the view of modern psychotherapy generally,

'The quality of love which a growing child receives from the significant adults in his life is the most important factor in his development; the quality of love in the therapist or counsellor is the most decisive factor in therapy.'[13]

While the importance of love in the developing experience of the child can hardly be over-emphasized, it is the plight of the emotionally sick and distorted adult that concerns us most directly in this study. In particular we are interested in the therapeutic situation as seen by depth psychology, for it is in this setting that there occurs the lowering of emotional repression which contributes to healing, and which has significant parallels in the experience of the Evangelical Revival. It is therefore revealing to discover that by common consent among psychotherapists, the most important healing factor in their work is the inter-personal relationship that develops between therapist and patient; which offers to the patient, within human limits, the very thing which Wesley offered as from God—an unconditional and completely dependable love.

The word 'love' may not very often appear in the psychotherapist's description of his own attitude towards the patient because, as we all know, it is an ambiguous word; and as Suttie pointed out long ago, for this and other reasons scientists are reluctant to introduce such a concept into their discussions. However, we shall not quibble over a word, for there is ample evidence to show that the basic attitudes which psychotherapists strive to adopt and the kind of relationship they try to establish with the patient come very near indeed to what the Christian faith *means* by 'love'. Dr S. H. Foulkes, a psychiatrist specializing in psychoanalysis and group therapy, writes: 'Certain basic attitudes are required of the psychoanalyst if he is to be in a position to play his part, such as a broad and deep tolerance and acceptance of the patient in every respect.'[14] The ideal therapeutic situation, says Dr Foulkes, is one in which the patient can express himself and his feelings with perfect freedom and yet be confident 'that he is fully accepted, whatever he may be or whatever he may disclose'.[14] This need for an unconditional *acceptance* of the patient by the therapist is of course one of the dominant themes of all forms of psychotherapy today (apart from those aiming at mere symptomatic relief or environmental adjustment). Dr Carl Rogers describes its significance for the patient (or 'client', to use his term):

' . . . the client moves from the experiencing of himself as an unworthy, unacceptable, and unlovable person, to the realization that he is accepted, respected and loved, in this limited relationship with the therapist. "Loved" has here perhaps its deepest and most general meaning—that of being deeply understood and deeply accepted.'[15]

It is the unconditional character of this 'acceptance' which is so important to the patient. Gradually he comes to trust the therapist—to know that the goodwill and acceptance he is being offered is completely dependable. He may arrive at this assurance only very slowly, and after having 'tried the therapist out' in a variety of ways, but sooner or later, if all goes well, he realizes that in this relationship, he can say, and do and be what he likes, and he will not be rejected. This experience of a completely secure ('anxiety-free') relationship, entirely free from the threat of rejection, almost literally takes him back beyond the range of his conscious memory; to a time in his life before emotional repression was forced upon him by the desperate fear of losing his precarious hold on the love of those he depended on completely for his life and security. In this unusually permissive and accepting situation emotional repressions begin to crumble away from within—because they are no longer necessary as a precaution against the possibility of losing love. Freud himself came later to place more stress on the fear of losing love, that Suttie had seen as the main source of repression. The hatred, resentment and primitive rage which are the natural reaction of the young child to the thwarting of his desire for love—these things are far too dangerous to be given direct expression. He fears— probably with good reason—that their expression would bring on him the awful penalty of still further rejection, and these destructive, negative emotions must therefore undergo what Suttie called 'automatic inhibition or repression'.

The possibility of this process being reversed through the therapeutic relationship will depend on 'the willingness of the patient and his emboldenment to relax his defences *against expressing his hate and so running a risk of being hated*'.[16] All this welter of negative emotion and buried hostility must be let back into consciousness again and given expression, sometimes violently explosively as in abreaction, but usually in the more prolonged and fluctuating process of negative transference towards the therapist himself. In the absence of drugs or other facilitants—which are of limited value—the patient will only be able to release these buried drives when he can bring himself to trust the accepting 'love' and goodwill of the therapist towards him as something completely reliable, a relationship '*which will be capable of surviving* the reproaches arising from repressed anxiety and rage and which therefore make repression . . . *unnecessary*'.[17]

Our investigation of the social conditions under which many of Wesley's hearers were brought up, and their almost inevitable brutalizing effect on family life, would suggest that the very emotions we have been considering, arising as a reaction to the deprivation of love in early childhood, viz. hatred, primitive rage, hostility and resentment were the ones most likely to be under heavy repression in the minds of many of the poor. Suttie wrote of the 'aimless states of anxiety and rage' that are aroused by love deprivation, and which are repressed before the child is old enough to be aware of the distinction between itself and its mother. He emphasized that at this stage these states are essentially *undirected* 'not anger *at anyone* any more than they are caused by *anything* that the child knows of'.[18] The violent, convulsive and irrational character of the abreactions that burst through their crumbling repressions, when into the love starved hearts of these people there came the amazing realization that God *loved* them—and would go on loving them, no matter what happened—seem to point to the release of such violent emotion, originally aroused and repressed at this early 'undifferentiating' stage. Karl Menninger, the noted American psychiatrist, has written :

'A convulsion—however produced—represents a sudden, uncontrolled, relatively unstructured release of enormous quantities of energy, expressed by muscular contractions and the obliteration of consciousness. It permits an episodic explosive emergence of aggressive impulses. It does not seem to be directed towards anything or anyone (as a rule), but seems to be a primitive expression of violent murder and violent suicide—like an enormous temper tantrum.'[19]

No doubt significant repressions occurred then, as now, at other stages during infancy, and involving emotions other than

those arising directly out of a deprivation of love. Yet the driving
force within the actual *repression* of these and any other
unacceptable emotion is probably the same—viz. the fear of
rejection or disapproval—i.e. *the fear of losing love*. This is
probably what Professor H. V. Dicks meant when he wrote that
' . . . every patient with mental illness was more afraid than
he could tolerate when he was a baby'.[20] The relevance of the
Christian message of the 'love that casts out fear' to this central
concern of psychiatry, ought to be obvious. Dr Paul Tournier,
the Swiss psychiatrist, has written :

'The proclamation of Jesus Christ is about the love of God, a love
which is all-inclusive and unconditional. And here we impinge
on one of the most important themes of modern psychology.
Freud has shown us, it may be remembered, that guilt is
awakened in the infant's mind by the fear of losing the love of
his parents; and also that all the traumas of his mental life are
connected with this doubt about being loved. The infant feels
that he is being rejected and no longer loved. The anxiety of
guilt is just this anxiety of being loved no longer. The child has
the impression that his parents' love is conditional; that they
will love him only on condition that he is good. . . .

'In every age men have projected precisely the same idea on
God. They picture God as one who loves them only on the condition that they are good, and who refuses them his love if they
become guilty. . . . This false idea of God still so widespread
among his people, is just what Jesus came to remove. He shows
us that God loves us unconditionally . . . '[21]

It was surely Wesley's rediscovery and reaffirmation of the love
of God for sinful man, in the spiritual barrenness of eighteenth
century England, in Tournier's phrase, 'a love which is all-
inclusive and unconditional', that touched men at the point of
their deepest need; and which accounts, more than anything
else, for the tide of spiritual liberation that followed his
preaching.

II

But here we raise a protest, or at least a sceptical query. It is this
expression 'sinful man' that sparks it off. Surely this is a phrase

that no psychotherapist would use, but similar expressions were often on Wesley's lips—which just goes to show that you cannot by any stretch of the imagination cast Wesley in the role of the psychotherapist—and certainly not of a 'non-directive' therapist! He talked far more than he listened, he gave advice—and worst of all he passed moral judgment and proclaimed the judgment of God in no uncertain terms. We have already noted that Wesley could, in fact, listen with remarkable patience and insight; and that in some of his pastoral contacts, and especially his attitude towards strange emotional outbursts he could be wonderfully permissive, but we must not use this to evade the real issue which is this: we have been suggesting that the unconditional love of God as proclaimed by Wesley, was analagous to the unconditional acceptance which the psychotherapist gives his patient. But was it? Was Wesley's God really 'permissive'? Did he not deal with man in terms of moral judgment, and is not this the very attitude which must be kept right out of the therapeutic relationship altogether, because it would completely destroy the 'permissiveness' that the patient needs if he is ever going to let go his repressions sufficiently for him to recover his lost integrity? These are searching questions that lead us into an area where there is much misunderstanding on both sides—into the discussion on the question of 'judgment'. We may perhaps usefully open it up by a sort of brief dialogue representing two different points of view.

From the point of view of psychotherapy we are repeatedly being told that we must refrain from making moral judgments when we counsel people. If we are really going to help them come to terms with themselves, and resolve their personality conflicts, we must abandon the point of view of moral judgment altogether; that the reason why so many people would rather unburden their souls to their doctor than to their minister is that the doctor does not judge them. Or, the reason why they find that their interviews with the psychotherapist enable them to bring out and face all sorts of things that they could not acknowledge before, is because his attitude is completely permissive and accepting, and he is not there to judge or condemn them, or shame them.

Now even when he is sympathetic towards psychotherapy and understands something of its rationale, the Christian is still likely to be a little unhappy about all this. He probably gets the rather uneasy feeling that the psychotherapist, though certainly not *immoral*, in his dealings with his patients anyway, tends to be *amoral*, or at least to give the appearance that he is lacking in a proper concern for morality in general, and the moral welfare of those he is trying to help.

As against this, however, I suspect that most psychotherapists do have a very deep and genuine moral concern for their patients. In particular, their respect for the patient's personal integrity and emerging freedom, and their desire to accept him unconditionally as a person, even though these may make them refrain from *talking* about morals, are in themselves *moral* attitudes of the greatest importance. Furthermore, the therapists are rather impressed with the fact that no one can be genuinely good unless he is free. Most of the people they deal with are not free but in bondage, and so often in bondage to an *imitation goodness*, a compulsive sort of moralism which has been forced on them as a sort of pattern, by emotional pressure and moral condemnation. They see their task as psychotherapists, then, to help people to become more free.

The Christian (if he is enlightened) will be grateful for this point of view and glad to be reminded by the psychotherapist of the moral importance of respect for personality, and how easily one may sin against it. He will also have considerable sympathy with the psychotherapist's efforts to set men free from inner bondage. Even though he may not be as well acquainted as the therapist with the extent and effects of compulsive moralism, he will know that there are 'moral' people who repel him, and that even Jesus had most of his opposition from the so-called 'good' people of his day. And he will agree, of course, that real goodness has to be free and spontaneous.

But having said all that, he still won't be satisfied with the psychotherapist's suggestion that moral judgments should be left right out of our efforts to help people in their personal difficulties. After all, he will say, while we recognize that a lot of guilt may be morbid, not all guilt is like that—there *is* such a thing as genuine guilt to be faced and repented of. There may be a lot of imitation goodness — either conventional or compulsive, but there is such a thing as real goodness, and real badness too; and the chances are that at least *part* of the sufferer's problem may be genuinely a moral issue. Even if the moral issue is all tangled up with other things and we have the uneasy feeling that neither of us can sort them out very well, still it is not very satisfactory to be told at the outset that moral issues have to be left right out of our consideration. We are all rather good at dodging moral issues anwway, and this apparently amoral attitude of the therapist suggests tacitly at least that morals don't matter, and may aid and abet the sufferer in evading some very real elements in his need. When a patient comes to a physician he probably doesn't understand the nature of his own illness, but he comes for a diagnosis and the appropriate treatment. We recognize that there may be some circumstances under which the physician may feel it unwise to *disclose* his diagnosis to the patient, but we would not think much of a physician who, 'out of respect for the patient' refrained from even *making* a complete diagnosis, for his own guidance, and then proceeded to base his treatment on this inadequate estimate of the patient's need. A Christian may well feel that in some cases a moral judgment is an essential element in an honest 'diagnosis', and he wants to make such judgments for the sake of the person concerned—so that his real need can be met, and not merely glossed over.

To this the psychotherapist may retort that it sounds all right in theory, but that in actual practice the Church has been very often sadly astray in her 'diagnosis' of moral factors; she has at various times condemned as wrong much of human behaviour which is, from a psychological point of view, wholesome and natural; she has tried to impose an essentially morbid moralism in the name of morality; and in some of the traditionally 'Christian' countries, the general effect of the Church's influence over several centuries, has been to greatly increase men's burden of guilt without doing much to help them cope with it. This has been so serious that in some continental countries, for example, they use the term 'ecclesio-genic neurosis' . . . And all this, mark you, in the name of moral judgment undertaken as an aid towards man's salvation.

The Christian, if he is wise, will not try to deny this or avoid its seriousness. (It is no part of Christianity to whitewash the history of the Church.) However, he will insist that honesty compels us to admit that there is another side to the story as well; that along with her blunders and her own misunderstanding,

P

and even betrayal, of the gospel the Church *has* stood time and time again, for a genuinely higher ethic. An ethic without which the world would have been immeasurably poorer, and that the Church's moral judgment, while being of considerable help to individual people has often been prophetic, and socially redemptive. Furthermore, he will point out that the psychotherapist's own work presupposes such a background and an essentially moral social context; that he is only able to maintain the luxury of a 'non-judgmental' point of view because he lives in a world where a host of other people—the Church included—are actively engaged to maintain moral standards, and to make moral judgments for that purpose.

For all the stern judgments that the non-judging psychotherapist feels bound to pass on the Church for her moralistic failures, he will probably admit that there has been, and still is, a more positive and healthy function of moral judgment for her to carry out in the community. But then he will probably add that this may be the Church's business, but it is not his. For his part he feels that he has ample evidence that moral judgments would only hinder the psychotherapist in his work of trying to help people, and that if the Church in her pastoral work is going to profit by the insights of psychotherapy, then she had better take notice of this point of view.

Here we may leave the dialogue in the meantime, because it has brought us to a very practical dilemma that often faces Christian pastors today. So long as psychotherapist and pastor consider they are doing quite different things, then what each privately thinks of the other's work may not be of much consequence, but when the Church begins in her pastoral practice to take serious note of psychotherapy, then the tension between these two viewpoints inevitably develops. Many pastors, no doubt, can ignore the psychotherapeutic point of view, while others have adopted it so completely and uncritically that it is difficult to find much that is distinctively Christian left in their pastoral dealing with their people. However, I suspect that many more experience a sort of alternating uneasiness about the more serious pastoral situations, fearing that if they introduce moral judgment they may be committing a serious psychological blunder, and if they omit it they may be failing in their plain religious duty.

However, even thus far, the dialogue has not been in vain, because I hope that it begins to be evident that in discussing the matter of moral judgment, the psychotherapist and the Christian are not talking about exactly the same thing. The psychotherapist is pointing to something that we *both* agree the Church should not do—but often has done, while the Christian is trying to point to something which he believes the Church *should* do—and often has done. We must now try to define this distinction much more clearly, both for the sake of the issue itself, and in order to meet the objection raised by our imaginary critic to the interpretation I have suggested of the effects of Wesley's preaching.

Discussing the meaning of 'acceptance' in the therapeutic relationship, C. G. Jung wrote 'The patient does not feel himself accepted unless the very worst in him is accepted too'.[22] I think that most psychotherapists would undoubtedly agree with this statement. Now it is true that Jung went on in the same passage to issue the usual warning about the harmful effects of passing judgment; but surely the very fact that he could speak of 'the very worst' in the patient, does imply judgment—and even 'moral' judgment in some sense. We cannot use words like 'better' and 'worse' without making a judgment. To this, Jung would probably have replied that what is involved here is not our judgment of the patient, but the judgment which the patient has already made on himself. Already, the patient has unwittingly driven out of consciousness (i.e. repressed) those aspects of his personality which he felt to be 'the very worst' in him—what Jung called *the shadow*. This repressed side of his personality he is able to accept back into his own consciousness, only as he feels intuitively that this too, 'the very worst in him', will be accepted by the therapist along with all the rest. To 'accept', of course, does *not* mean to 'approve'; it simply means that the therapist is prepared to face the fact that this, too, is part of his patient's personality. He accepts him *as he is*; his attitude does not say to the patient, 'now if you reform, if you break free from all these things that you see to be the very worst in you, or at least keep them well in the background—then I'll be glad to accept you'. That would be no help whatsoever. The patient will have to know in advance that he will be accepted unconditionally, before he can even begin to acknowledge the *shadow* and accept these repressed things back into consciousness, let alone grapple with them.

Unless the therapist conveys by his attitude that he is willing to accept the patient on these terms, he will never find enough security in the relationship to be able to let go his inner defences and repressions. This fact should not be very difficult for any of us to appreciate. In ordinary social intercourse most of us have known at some time or other how insecure we feel if we think we are being 'accepted' by someone on the basis of a false impression. It is probably this sort of feeling in an acute form that an emotionally disturbed patient has about the psychotherapist at first. He may feel 'Ah yes, he accepts me at this stage, but that's only because he doesn't really know what an awful person I am. If only he knew half as much about me as I know myself, he'd be disgusted; he'd give me up as hopeless'. Perhaps only slowly will he get the courage and confidence to run the risk of trying out the therapist with some of the 'awful things' he *knows* about himself . . . and if he meets with even a flicker of rejection, things may go no further. If, on the other hand he meets only a steady and unfailing acceptance on the part of the therapist, he may go much further until the really therapeutic part of the process begins to happen: when he is able to tell the therapist not only the 'bad' things he *knows* about himself, but the other 'bad' things too—the ones that have been hitherto such a threat to his own security that they have been repressed—hidden away even from his own awareness.

It is true that in being prepared to accept 'the very worst' in his patient the therapist is not so much passing judgment on him, as showing that in a sense he is willing, if necessary, to accept the judgment which the patient has passed on himself, but he will do this *without rejecting the patient himself*. It may well be that the judgment that the patient has passed on himself is far too severe, or even quite unrealistic in terms of any really objective moral standard. However, it will not usually help him if the therapist tries to reason with him on this issue, or to mitigate the severity of his own self-condemnation. This is an insight which he may gain later himself, but if the therapist tries to suggest to him that he is not after all quite so bad as he thinks he is, then the patient may easily experience this well meant manoeuvre as a form of rejection, or what for him amounts to the same thing—as a sign of a limited or conditional acceptance. He may well feel that the therapist is not giving him *unconditional* acceptance after all, but an acceptance which actually depends on the truth of this more favourable judgment. Since the patient himself probably cannot yet accept this more favourable judgment about himself, he will feel that he is being accepted by the therapist only on the basis of a quite false impression. Hence he will feel fundamentally insecure in the relationship, saying to himself in effect, 'There you see, I knew all the time he wouldn't be able to accept me if he knew what I'm really like. He *wants* to accept me, so he has to pretend to himself that I'm better than what I am. He has to whitewash me to make me acceptable to him. But it won't work; sooner or later the whitewash will rub off, and then when he faces the facts, he'll have to reject me.'

Privately, the therapist may think that the patient's self-judgment is too severe, or on the other hand, he may sometimes feel that it is not severe enough — that there are probably elements of realistic failure and guilt in his life which the patient is not yet facing up too. Or, more often, he may be inclined to feel that he (the therapist) is not in a position to form an opinion, since the facts are still largely unknown to him. However, neither of these judgments nor the withholding of judgment need do any harm, so long as they do not affect the therapist's firm determination to *accept* the patient at all costs, or his ability to communicate this to the patient himself. The important thing is that by his whole attitude the therapist can convey quite sincerely to the patient: 'Even if you *are* as bad as you think you are—or even worse—I will not reject you on that account, or on any other account either. I will go on accepting you no matter what'. In other words, the acceptance which the patient is given by the therapist, while not necessarily indifferent to moral issues, is in the final analysis quite independent of any moral judgment. Insofar as the relationship between therapist and patient is in any sense a 'saving' relationship, the 'salvation' that is offered is a salvation by 'grace' (i.e. love offered freely, apart from any question of merit or desert) and not salvation by 'works'.

Here we have got to the heart of the 'non-judgmental' point of view in psychotherapy. The real concern of the psychotherapist is not with judgment *as such*, but with judgment which implies or conveys to the patient the feeling that he is being rejected—or at least, accepted only on certain conditions. It is usually taken for granted that adverse moral judgment inevitably conveys this sense of rejection. But as we have seen, there is in fact, just as much chance that a 'favourable' judgment will convey the same impression in a more subtle, but no less real way. Even the steadfast refusal to pass judgment of any kind is not immune from this danger, because it may sometimes leave the patient with the uneasy feeling that he is being accepted by the therapist only because the latter has not made the moral judgment which he 'ought' to make, and which he will one day have to make. As we have seen already, the kind of acceptance which is most likely to be experienced by the patient as unconditional, is the one that can take into account the most adverse moral judgment possible against him—and still go on accepting him.[23]

III

We are now in a position, after this somewhat lengthy digression, into the significance of judgment for the psychotherapist, to take up the objection that was raised against our interpretation of the psychological effectiveness of John Wesley's preaching. I think it should now be evident that Wesley's clear insistence on the divine judgment upon man the sinner, far from vitiating the parallel we have drawn between the unconditional love of God that he proclaimed, and the psychotherapist's unconditional acceptance of his patient, actually makes it more impressive than ever.

The fears which psychotherapists have about moral judgment, implying rejection of the person judged, are by no means without foundation. This is the sort of thing that Christians have done—not always, but often; so often, in fact, that those outside the Church usually interpret our moral pronouncements as an attack on them, and react accordingly. It is easy enough for us to talk about 'hating the sin but loving the sinner' but it is not at all easy to do. After all, the sin is part of the sinner, and once hate enters into our attitude at all, it has a way of spilling over these subtle distinctions. Many a Christian has finished up hating the sinner, sometimes in self defence, because he unconsciously loves the sin.[24] From there it is a very short step indeed, to project similar attitudes onto God, and very often the divine judgment against sin has been proclaimed in such a way that God appears vindictive, vengeful and hating, a monster indeed, who will nevertheless turn all sweetness towards the sinner if only he will fulfil certain conditions. (Even this does not imply any radical change of character in God, but is possible only because in some way or other he agrees to divert all this punitive vengeance onto his own son.) The love of God is used in such preaching as a huge bait or blackmail, and the implication is fairly plain, that if the sinner will only 'repent and believe' God will stop hating him and start loving him. It is little wonder that some bold spirits would rather go to hell than be 'saved' by such a God. Christians may protest that this is a ghastly caricature of their faith, and so it is—but it is a caricature that has often been proclaimed and accepted as the genuine thing. If there is a widespread feeling that moral judgment inevitably involves rejection of the person judged, and in particular that divine judgment implies divine hostility, the Church must bear the major responsibility for this tragic misunderstanding of the Christian faith.

But there was very little of this, in the way in which John Wesley proclaimed the judgment of God. For him, judgment and mercy were not opposed; they belonged together. The love of God did not begin when his justice was satisfied, or man had fulfilled certain conditions, such as repentance and faith. God loved him long before that—before he could do anything but be a sinner. It was a love that could accept the very worst that was in man, that could take into account the most adverse moral judgment possible against him—and still go on loving him. God loves man *as a sinner*. In this, Wesley was of course only reiterating one of the major themes of the New Testament: 'But God commendeth his love toward us, in that, while we were yet sinners, Christ died for us'.[25]

To be sure, the sinner can be lost, but if he *is* lost it is never because God has ceased to love him. We have used the word 'accept' because it expresses most simply the essential quality of love, but we must not confuse this usage with the way in which the word is sometimes used to cover the whole transaction of justification or 'reconciliation with God', for there *are* conditions that attach to these transactions — inescapable conditions of man's response in repentance and faith. But these conditions, it will be noted, arise inevitably out of man's status as a responsible person—and not at all out of any conditional quality in the love of God. The parallel with the psychotherapeutic situation still holds. The therapist may go on giving his patient unconditional acceptance, but he cannot possibly give him unconditional recovery from his illness. This will depend on the patient's willingness to make a continuing response in terms of the relationship—i.e. genuinely to accept the acceptance he is offered, and in this growing confidence to talk out more and more of what is in him. But he does not have to make this response. Even if the therapist continues faithfully accepting towards him, the patient can, if he chooses, break the relationship and give up the treatment. But if he does this and does not recover, we would not of course attribute this to a failure or change of heart on the part of the therapist. Any 'cure' that could be given to him without his responsible co-operation would leave the patient less than a person, whereas the whole object of psychotherapy is to help him to grow towards true personhood. Likewise any salvation that could be given to man without his responsible co-operation would leave him a slave or a puppet, whereas the whole object of salvation is to lead him into 'the glorious liberty of the children of God'. To say that man's salvation is conditional upon his own response to God's grace, is the only thing that is consistent with the belief that God does love him unconditionally as a person.

It will be noted, however, that when the patient does freely respond in the psychotherapeutic situation, he is *able* to do this, only because of the unconditional love and acceptance that the therapist has given him, and in fact his own *ability* to respond grows in proportion to his growing confidence in his continuing love. This will serve to illustrate for us another major emphasis which John Wesley made—the doctrine of 'prevenient grace'— that God loves man and seeks his salvation long before man knows about this or makes any response, and that when man does respond, he does so freely and on his own initiative, but he is *able* to do this only because he has been and is loved in this way. As Dr Harald Lindstrom points out, this emphasis on prevenient grace was a necessary corollary to Wesley's Arminian theology.[26] The Calvinists insisted that man's salvation or damnation depended solely on the arbitrary choice of God. The grace which saves man must therefore be irresistible, and in the case of the elect, man's response of repentance and faith follows as an inevitable consequence. In rejecting all these propositions and maintaining God's willingness to save *all* men, and the genuine freedom of man's response, Wesley had still to acknowledge the fact that ultimately man was entirely dependent for his salvation on the grace of God. His answer to irresistible grace was 'prevenient grace'—the love which enables man's response (and without which it would not be possible at all), but does not coerce it. Man's response in repentance and faith is thus genuinely free and therefore responsible, but enabled by and therefore ultimately dependent on this unconditional love of God, which he can neither earn nor deserve. In this teaching, Wesley sincerely believed (and I think, correctly) that he was faithfully interpreting the New Testament, but again, the parallels to the modern psychotherapeutic situation are unmistakable.

I have already suggested that John Wesley never adequately worked out the full implications of these views for his doctrine of God.[27] It is, therefore, not difficult to discover other things in his various writings which, if they were pressed to their logical conclusion, would be somewhat inconsistent with this thoroughgoing Arminianism, his central emphasis. However, these other things never were pressed to their logical conclusion, and Wesley was therefore able to maintain with absolute clarity and conviction what men had to know if they were ever to be free of their spiritual chains—the all-inclusive and thoroughly dependable love of God. His emphasis on divine judgment, far from jeopardizing this proclamation, must have strengthened and deepened immensely his hearers' confidence in the unconditional quality of that love, while his long standing controversy with the Calvinists, and his positive affirmations which it called forth, established the belief that whatever happens to him, in spite of sin and in spite of judgment, man is *never rejected by God.*

IV

The full depth of the Christian proclamation of divine love is of course never reached till it includes the Cross. Indeed this is its real source and focus. Theories of the Atonement—attempts to explain the saving death of Christ—are notoriously inadequate, some more so than others, yet it remains a simple fact both of history and of contemporary experience that the preaching of the Cross has been and still is 'the power of God unto salvation'. Whatever the explanation, men have found in the death of Christ the greatest proof and evidence of the love of God that sets them free. Wesley's ministry was an outstanding example of this. He had no original theory of the atonement, and the ones he borrowed were neither very adequate in themselves, nor did they harmonize particularly with his general theological position. Nevertheless, the preaching of 'Christ crucified' was central in his message; it was from this that he drew all his most characteristic doctrine about the love of God, and it was to the dying and risen Christ that his converts felt indebted for the saving reality of that love in their lives. We have used the psychotherapeutic situation, first, to help us understand how love that at least tries to be unconditional works even on a human level to 'heal the broken-hearted . . . and set at liberty them that are bruised', and then to give us some understanding of the greater working of the love of God in the soul of man. I would suggest then, that we may without either irreverence or irrelevance, ask whether this line of thought has any light to throw for us on the Cross.

One of the most characteristic features of the psycho-therapeutic relationship is the process of emotional transference. Here, the patient begins to give expression to all the tangle of repressed emotions within him, by directing them towards the person of the therapist himself. Thus in the course of treatment the patient works through with him and on him the inter-personal conflicts which originally gave rise to feelings of such violence or intensity, that as a safety measure they had to undergo repression. Only in this more secure relationship, where the expression of such feelings will no longer be a threat to his safety (i.e. his love security) can the patient bear to acknowledge them. Naturally, the negative aspects of this process are very important and Suttie, rather significantly, likened the role of the therapist to that of a 'sacrificial victim upon whom all hates, anxieties and distrust is worked out, so that he is the mediator, the catalyst—whereby the separated psyche is re-integrated in its society'.[28] There is no doubt that one of the important functions of the negative transference is, as Guntrip says, 'to enable the patient to discover that after each emotional crisis, however difficult it has been, the relationship is still there as the enduring foundation of his hope for a "cure" '.[29] Paul Tournier brings this out in the following passage:

'See what happens with our patients. Often they are urged by a strong inner impulse to increase their aggressiveness towards us, or the insistence of their doubts and their negativism, as if to put us to the test. They have found in us a kind, understanding attitude, full of the love they so vitally need. But how far does it reach? It is natural we should love them, in so far as they show themselves confiding, frank and pleasant. But will it change if they become insolent, uncommunicative, sceptical; if they are rude, if they overstep the line, if they prolong the interview after it should have ended?

'It is like a defiance which they hurl at us, and they push it further and further as though to see whether ultimately they do not indeed run into a barrier, whether we shall not lose our temper, grumble at them, pass judgment on them, and lose patience. It must be realized that the stakes are enormously high. They have to know if the bridge over which they venture their life is firm.'[30]

The negative transference is part of the important process of having 'the very worst' that is in the patient accepted; he can only be absolutely sure that he is accepted when he can not only bring this out as something which he has felt toward someone else, but when he can turn it directly *against* the one who accepts him. The only love that man can finally trust as unconditional, unchangeable, indestructible, is the love that he can crucify, and find that it still goes on loving him.[31] Surely this was a most significant part of what Wesley's hearers understood in his preaching of Christ crucified, or when Charles taught them to sing

> See all your sins on Jesus laid:
> The Lamb of God was slain.[32]

It was only because these people felt that in some way all the hurts they had ever suffered, all the hate they had ever hated, all the foul things that were hidden from the light of day, need be hidden no longer, but could be brought to light and laid on this Christ who had proved on the Cross that his love could stand it all without breaking, that they were able to find ultimate security; only then could they let go for ever all the crippling defences that fear of losing love had built within their souls. Strip it free of all the dreary logic-chopping of forensic theology, and the immoral nonsense of penal substitution and the Cross of Christ still stands, as it has stood through twenty centuries of Christian experience, for the deathless love of the dying God.

To be sure, their language of redemption must often seem crude to our modern sensibilities, just as their emotional reactions were crude. We may drop all this talk of 'redeeming blood' and our gospel will sound much nicer, but let us beware of being too 'nice'—beware that we are not quietly omitting the underlying reality of God's love impaled by human sin. Whichever way you look at it the Cross was not 'nice', just as many of the things that men still struggle with in the dark caverns of their minds are not at all 'nice'. Neither in psychotherapy nor in religion will an attitude of dispassionate detachment and good taste carry us very far, for as Tillich reminds us, 'the knowledge of that which concerns us infinitely is possible only in an attitude of infinite concern.'[33]

But we must not imagine that the response of Wesley's converts was a mere outpouring of crude emotion, or that the positive side of their 'transference' issued in a sentimental attachment to the memory of the human Jesus. For at its heart there was a solid core of theological conviction. They took very seriously the claim of Jesus that 'He that hath seen me hath seen the Father'[34] and Paul's statement that 'God was in Christ reconciling the world unto himself'.[35] The hymn quoted above is in praise of Christ the Redeemer but it refers to him as 'God and King' and addresses him as 'My gracious Master and my God'.[32] For the early Methodist people the drama of the Cross was the drama of the Living God, and like hosts of their fellow Christians before and since, they laid the burden of their hurts and their hates on the heart of God, and knew themselves accepted and reconciled with the very 'Ground of their being'. For the message of the Evangelical Revival was to point to the Cross, and to say, in the words of James Denny, 'God loves like that'.

'Fear of losing the love of God', writes Paul Tournier, '—this is the essence of our human problem and of psychology',[36] and after describing some aspects of the negative transference in the passage quoted above, he goes on to say:

'But this behaviour of patients shows the vital need we all have of finding something absolute upon which we can count absolutely, something unfailing which gives the lie to all the relativities life teaches us through its many sufferings, wherein every trust has its limits, every hope its disappointments, every friendship its eclipse. This absolute is God; and what our patients are looking for when they put us to the test in this way, is at least some reflection of God, of a love which goes beyond mere convention; and it is a proof that they all seek God, even without knowing it.'[37]

The healing potentialities of deep psychotherapy arise from the fact that it is a genuine human analogue of divine grace, for unconditional love and acceptance are of the very essence of grace. Christians may hesitate to use the word like this, as though it applied more to corerct theology than to Chist-like attitudes. I do not think theology is unimportant, but at least it seems fairly certain that those who offer grace under any name whatsoever must be nearer to the kingdom of God than those who withhold it in the name of religion.

Paul Tillich reminds us that

'. . . in the fight against the anxiety of guilt by psychotherapy the idea of acceptance has received the attention and gained the significance which in the Reformation period was to be seen in phrases like "forgiveness of sins" or "justification through faith".'[38]

But just as Tournier suggests that the patient's need for acceptance points beyond the therapeutic situation, so Tillich suggests that the acceptance that is actually offered by the therapist *comes* from beyond:

'In the communion of healing, for example, the psychoanalytic situation, the patient participates in the healing power of the helper by whom he is accepted although he feels himself unacceptable. The healer, in this relationship, does not stand for himself as an individual but represents the objective power of acceptance and self-affirmation. This objective power works through the healer in the patient.'[39]

He adds, significantly: 'Of course it must be embodied in a person who can realize guilt, who can judge, and who can accept in spite of the judgment'.[39] Justification through faith, says Tillich, 'is in the experience of the Reformers the acceptance of the unacceptable sinner into judging and transforming communion with God'.[40]

V

The Reformers' doctrine of Justification through Faith was, of course, central to John Wesley's preaching, but as we have seen already he went much further than the Reformers themselves. Firstly because he saw it at work as prevenient grace, long before the actual transaction of justification; and secondly, because he freed it from the strange inscrutable decrees of God's election and offered it to all men. There is one important respect in which the love that was proclaimed by Wesley, and indeed by any active evangelist, is also more unconditional than anything encountered in psychotherapy: it is love that is offered to men *before* they have begun to repent, whereas the very nature of the psychotherapeutic situation implies that in some sense 'repentance' has already begun.

I am using 'repentance' here in the basic sense of the New Testament 'metanoia', i.e. a radical change of mind, a meaning of the word which has, I believe, been too much neglected in Christian thinking ever since Jerome mistranslated 'metanoiein' by the Latin *poenitentiam agere* in the Vulgate—and probably even before that. This narrowing down of the reference of metanoia so that it applies almost entirely to feelings of sorrow and guilt, has obscured the more fundamental meaning of the word, and our English term 'repentance' and its cognates, coming from the Latin rather than the Greek, simply perpetuate this obscurity. To be sure there are specific forms of metanoia that are mostly concerned with guilt, but even with reference to these we have to point out from time to time that a mere sense of guilt and sorrow do not constitute repentance but only remorse. What differentiates repentance from remorse is the desire for amendment of life—in other words the desire to undergo a radical change of mind. There are other forms of metanoia that may not be so obviously connected with conscious guilt feelings, or sorrow for deliberate wrongdoing, but are just as truly a desire to undergo a radical change of mind, and with many of these the psychotherapist is concerned. We need to retreat beyond both the English and the Latin then, to the language of the New Testament itself to discover the common ground between Christian and psychotherapist — a common concern with a radical change of mind.

In this sense then, we can say that the psychotherapeutic situation is normally one in which repentance can be taken for granted. The mere fact that the patient has come for psychotherapy indicates that he is dissatisfied with his life and personality as they are, and that he is seeking help to undergo some more or less radical change. It is in response to this that the therapist offers him an unconditional acceptance as the secure setting in which he may undergo that change—whatever it may prove to be. To be sure, the patient's desire for change may at first be rather superficial, although most people who want help at that level can get it by way of tranquilizers nowadays, without bothering a psychotherapist. The patient's repentance or desire for change will continue, and reach down to deeper levels of his personality as the course of therapy proceeds; but if this desire ever ceases to operate, as frequently happens, therapy will either be relatively complete or else stagnate at that point, and in either case the patient will normally cease coming for treatment. Thus, so long as a patient is undergoing psychotherapy, it can be safely assumed that he has an underlying attitude of 'repentance', as we have defined it.

The recognition of this fact would save a lot of misunderstanding between Christians and those who seek to share with them the insights of psychotherapy. We are so very often told that we must accept people as they are and not try to change them. Now we have seen the wisdom of this, and nowadays the enlightened Christian will recognize the evil of trying to impose any kind of change on another person, even if we believe it would be the 'right' kind of change. Nevertheless, he is usually a bit perplexed about this adage, because the New Testament seems to imply pretty clearly that we all need to undergo radical change, and if Christianity has nothing to do with this, then what is our Gospel all about? He would be saved this perplexity if he realized that when the therapist accepts his patient as he is, it is because both he and the patient have agreed from the beginning, that for his own good, the patient shouldn't *stay* as he is, but should undergo some sort of a change; however genuinely 'permissive' their joint venture in therapy is, both parties know that this is what it is all about. Because he can take for granted this attitude of repentance on the part of the patient, the psychotherapist works in an entirely different and easier situation than the Christian evangelist, who must so very often go out to meet men before they have acknowledged any radical desire for change at all, and must call them to repentance. To be sure he should listen to the psychotherapist's warning that we must not try to impose change on people, but he will still have to do something which is beyond the psychotherapist's concern —to present the Word of God in such a way that men shall become genuinely and freely aware of their need of 'metanoia'— a radical 'change of mind'.

Here we meet again the question of judgment. We have already seen how there is a sense in which the psychotherapist must accept the judgment which the patient has made against himself. Every person who has undergone repression has passed judgment against himself—of the most severe kind. Part of his own personality he has condemned, and rejected in the most decisive way. But this judgment in itself has become unconscious. He is no longer aware of it as such. Yet he may be aware of other things, of anxiety, psychosomatic illness, compulsive behaviour, or a rather persistent and pervasive sense of the frustration of life. These symptoms may be interpreted to him by his doctor, or he may add them up himself, and at length after much hesitation and many efforts to avoid the conclusion, he will arrive at the point when he says in effect, 'things are not what they ought to be with me. It is not merely a matter of outward circumstances; something's wrong with *me*, that I can't change by any effort of will power, yet change I must, and I will look for help'. At this point then, he has passed judgment on himself again, but this time quite consciously and deliberately, and it will be noted that this *acceptance* of judgment (i.e. this conscious judging of himself) is the beginning of his 'metanoia' or 'repentance'. From this point he is open to the accepting love which will enable him to come to grips with his deeper need. It will be noted, however, that this second judgment, unlike the first (repressive) one is in a rudimentary sense diagnostic rather than threatening or rejecting.

To be sure it may still have been a very hard judgment to accept. Few patients come to psychotherapy without an inner struggle to avoid such an admission of inadequacy. In trying to bring his patient to seek psychiatric help, the doctor may have to point out very sternly and clearly the probable consequences in curtailment of health, happiness and life energy if he refuses treatment, and he may have to head the patient off as he attempts all sorts of rationalizations and evasions. Thus the patient may come to feel at this stage that he is being badgered, or even threatened, or worse still he may experience a strong sense of rejection, jumping to the conclusion that the doctor is writing him off as 'loony'. However, if he can get through all this and accept the doctor's diagnosis as a realistic judgment of his need, there will probably come a time when he will look back and realize that during the course of his struggle to avoid this judgment, he was actually being met by a concern for his welfare, which was just as genuinely accepting and loving as that which he subsequently received during psychotherapy.

At any rate, judgment in this positive sense is inseparable from 'metanoia'. In attempting to meet human need on a much wider front than psychotherapy—not simply waiting for those who know they are in need, to come to her, but going out to seek and save those that are unwittingly lost—the Church, out of her love for men must preach both judgment and repentance. The peril of the Christian evangelist is, that being commissioned to proclaim this healing judgment of God, he may, unless his heart is filled with the love of God, slip over into our sinful rejecting kind of judgment. Moreover, projecting this onto God, he may so distort the gospel that far from proclaiming the unconditional love that sets men free, he may use the threat of *withholding* love to produce a change that may be mistaken for conversion, but is in reality a crippling and repressive maiming of the personality.

Q

I believe that our whole investigation of the work of John Wesley shows us how thoroughly he avoided this error. It is a measure of his own profound experience of the divine grace and genuine recovery of New Testament Christianity that when he proclaimed the judgment of God and called sinners to repentance, these only served to give greater depth and meaning to the theme that was the master passion of his life—the love of God for man, 'immense, unfathomed, unconfined'. The response of men and women to this proclamation of unconditional love, whether heralded by the more violent abreactions, or by the less spectacular forms of the lowering of repressions, was essentially one of joy and liberation of personality; a breaking down of inner checks and barriers to life's energies, a recovery from hopelessness, lethargy and vice, and the appearance of a spontaneous love with the most far reaching social consequences. . . . Anything further away from 'brainwashing' and the like, would be hard to imagine.

Paul Tournier goes to the heart of the matter thus:

'Then suddenly there dawns upon us the vast, entire endowment of God's free love and forgiveness and of the reconciliation he offers us in Jesus Christ. It is this which bowls us over, frees us from the burden of guilt, tranforms us, provokes "metanoia". This is the discovery which has always, in spite of the preaching of the Churches, to be made anew. It is this discovery which periodically in history gives rise to an outburst of infectious faith, mass conversions and irrepressible joy.'[41]

If some of Wesley's converts came to their joy through an agony of body and mind, this was their 'light affliction which is but for a moment', a creative travail which they found the courage to endure because they were held by a love that would not let them go, and had begun already to work for them 'an eternal weight of glory'.[42]

FOOTNOTES AND REFERENCES

1. Suttie, Ian D., M.D., The Origins of Love and Hate, Kegan, Paul, Trench, Trubner & Co., London 1935.
2. Op. cit., p. 200.

3. *Ibid.*, p. 213.

4. *Ibid.*, p. 202.

5. *Ibid.*, p. 200.

6. *Ibid.*, p. 23.

7. *Ibid.*, pp. 23-4.

8. *Ibid.*, p. 203.

9. *Ibid.*, pp. 53 and 201.

10. *Ibid.*, pp. 75 and 212.

11. *Ibid.*, Ch. XIV.

12. See the editorial introduction to the Pelican and Peregrine editions of *The Origins of Love and Hate* (Penguin Books).

13. Outler, Albert C., *Psychotherapy and the Christian Message*, Harper & Brothers, New York 1954, p. 37.

14. Foulkes, S. H. and Anthony E. J., *Group Psychotherapy—the Psycho-Analytic Approach*, Penguin Books 1957, p. 60.

15. Rogers, Carl, *Client-Centered Therapy*, Houghton Mifflin Company, Boston 1951, p. 159.

16. Suttie, *op. cit.*, p. 208.

17. *Ibid.*, p. 217.

18. *Ibid.*, p. 26.

19. 'Regulative Devices of the Ego under Major Stress' in the selected papers of Karl Menninger, edited by Bernard H. Hall under the title of *A Psychiatrist's World*, The Viking Press, New York 1959, p. 508.

20. *Clinical Studies in Psychopathology*, Arnold, London 1939, p. 234. Quoted by Dr Dicks in his Introduction to Guntrip's *Healing the Sick Mind*, p. 8.

21. Tournier, Paul, *Guilt and Grace*, English translation by A. W. Heathcote, J. J. Henry and P. J. Allcock. Hodder & Stoughton, London 1962, pp. 189-90.

22. Quoted by Gilbert Russell in his essay 'Individual Treatment in Psychiatry' in *Christian Essays in Psychiatry* edited by Philip Mairet, S.C.M. Press, London 1956, p. 137.

23. Cf. Tournier, *op. cit.*, pp. 105-7. After discussion with his friends the author admits the value of 'thoughtful and kindly judgment' but he does not develop the idea.

24. The Missionary in Somerset Maugham's famous story *Rain* is a classic portrayal of this kind of reaction in an extreme form.

25. Romans 5.8.

26. Lindstrom, op. cit., p. 45.
27. See above, pp. 131-2.
28. Suttie, op. cit., p. 248.
29. *Healing the Sick Mind*, p. 131.
30. Tournier, op. cit., pp. 192-3.
31. Cf. an extremely interesting article in the May 1962 issue of *Pastoral Psychology* (p. 12) by Herman Eichorn, 'Some Therapeutic Implications of the Crucifixion and Resurrection', in which the writer shows the pastoral outworking of this idea.
32. The Methodist Hymn Book, Hymn No. 1, v. 4.
33. *The Courage to Be*, p. 119.
34. John 14.9.
35. II Cor. 5.19.
36. Tournier, op. cit., p. 190.
37. Ibid., p. 193.
38. Tillich, op. cit., p. 156.
39. Ibid., p. 157.
40. Ibid., p. 156.
41. Tournier, op. cit., p. 193.
42. II Cor. 4.17.

CHAPTER 10

CHARISMA AND COMMUNITY

I

Before we leave our discussion of Dr Sargant's book there are two other matters that must be looked at: his estimate of the nature and functions of the Methodist Class Meetings, and the social repercussions of the revival.

If, in the face of sound psychology and historical evidence to the contrary, one could believe with Dr Sargant that Wesley's preaching made people break down under intolerable stress, then the somewhat melodramatic picture he suggests of the Methodist Class meeting as a sort of close-knit pressure-group, designed for the efficient indoctrination of the now collapsed and highly suggestible 'convert', would have some initial plausibility. If, however, we conclude, as I think the evidence obliges us to, that Dr Sargant's version of Wesley the hellfire preacher is without foundation, and that the personality changes undergone by his converts were in the direction of liberation and enlargement of personality rather than breakdown under stress, then his estimate of the Class meetings also becomes quite unconvincing.

It is this unsupported and insupportable estimate of Wesley's preaching as a form of brainwashing technique which is casually and confidently reiterated throughout Chapter 10 of *Battle for the Mind*.[1] It assumes the logical preamble to Dr Sargant's interpretation of the Class meetings as groups that carried on and consolidated the intellectual and moral coercion of their members. Already, he has assumed this position in a previous chapter by pointing out a comparison between the Class meetings and Communist indoctrination groups used by the Chinese 'in training active Communist workers to serve as a "transmission belt" between the party and the masses'. The passing reference to the Class meetings in this connection[2] may leave the reader uncertain as to how far the comparison is meant to be taken, but

245

he has at least been softened up to the idea, further insinuated in this chapter on 'Consolidation and Prevention', as much by means of innuendo and deft suggestion, as by explicit statement.

Thus, describing the origins of the Class meetings, Dr Sargant says:

'The Class Leader was originally required to visit all members of his class at least once a week, ostensibly to collect a small weekly contribution of money. This means of access to their home soon allowed him to decide whether a conversion was genuine or not; and he later tested his conclusion at the weekly class meetings.'[3]

Here we have the suggestion of something rather unpleasant, or even sinister, in view of the comparisons that have already been hinted at and are further developed in this chapter, between the Class meetings and Communist indoctrination groups, relying on 'informers' and all manner of group pressure and manipulation in order to reduce members to complete conformity and compliance with the 'party line'. Thus, describing the function of the Communist 'cell' meetings at which 'members are encouraged to air their doubts; and the confession of personal "deviation" is encouraged', Dr Sargant goes on to say:

'Thus it is easy for cell leaders as it was for Wesley's Class leaders, to know whether or not they have obtained a devoted and industrious worker for the cause. All successful authoritarian systems, whether political or religious, now use follow-up conditioning and extend it from the top to the very bottom of the movement.'[4]

And lest we should miss the implication of emotional pressure and coercion being brought to bear by both these movements in a similar way, Dr Sargant draws on his own imaginative reconstruction again, to remind us that 'The Class meetings were intended for those already sensitized by their sudden and overwhelming conversion experience'.[5]

Now, when we descend to the realm of sober fact we find that the Methodist Class meetings first arose between February and April 1742 (not till three years after the more violent conversion experiences began to occur), thus well over half way through the five-year period (1739-43) in which they were most common.[6] The Classes were not only for converts but also for people who had been awakened to a sense of need, but had not yet passed through a conversion experience of any kind.[7] Furthermore, our writer completely overlooks the fact that, comparatively speaking, only a few of Wesley's converts (probably less than two per cent) had these 'overwhelming' experiences[8] with which *Battle for the Mind* is concerned, and the records lead us to believe that the great majority of converts who attended the Class meetings had experienced the 'New Birth' in much less spectacular ways. Finally, as we have already seen, the conversion of these people, whether violent or otherwise, was so far away from anything akin to brainwashing that they were certainly not merely passive or plastic material 'sensitized' for indoctrination.

It is true that the original function of the Class leader was to call on the members of his Class and collect one penny per week from each one who could afford it, towards reducing the building debt at Bristol, and later towards philanthropic work undertaken by the Methodist Societies. This task, by the way, was undertaken quite genuinely—not 'ostentibly', as Dr Sargant says, as a sort of cover up for spying activities. Yet it was inevitable that in this weekly visitation the leaders would come to know the members of their Class more intimately, and to discover some who were members only in name, and whose attitude and manner of life showed plainly that they had fallen away from their original intention and were no longer in sympathy with the movement. Wesley saw in this fact, an opportunity to cope with the problems of pastoral oversight and discipline; problems which, in large cities like London and Bristol, had gone far beyond what he could cope with, and were threatening the well-being of the whole movement. Thus he trained his Class leaders to be pastors, and to enquire about the spiritual well-being of their members on their weekly visit, and if need be, to offer pastoral help, advice or rebuke, as well as collecting the Class money. But in the nature of the case, this pastoral enquiry was done quite openly, and not under cover of any other 'ostensible' activity. The house-to-house calling soon proved to be too inconvenient for all concerned, and it was arranged instead that each Class should meet weekly, with its leader, with the same two purposes in mind. Thus the Class meeting was born.[9]

The need for discipline within the Methodist movement at this time was very real. It had to be undertaken not in order to regiment the converts into conformity of belief, or to impose on them a pattern of conduct that was alien to their own desires, but rather, in order to protect them from a resurgence of the compulsive and destructive forces of evil from which they had so recently broken free. So many of these people were as yet only one step away from lives of viciousness and immorality, and although they had begun a new life, they so often had to live it in the same old brutalizing environment with all its temptations, and were often torn by doubts within and threatened by persecution and ridicule without. They sometimes desperately needed the spiritual comfort and support, as well as the restraining discipline of their fellow pilgrims, and the Godly counsel of more experienced Christians. They needed somewhere where they could sometimes unburden their souls with the story of their betrayals and stumbling, along the way instead of burying or being buried by the weight of guilt and failure that would destroy their fellowship with God; and of course they had to do this in a company where they would run no risk of being written off as hopeless failures, but would always be accepted as long as they *wanted* to be accepted, because the forgiveness of sins and the renewing grace of God were realities of their common need and their common experience.[10]

Inevitably, there were those who failed and lapsed back into the old life, but they were not harshly treated. They were sought out and every means of exhortation and pastoral help was used to try and restore them, and many were brought back into the way by this means—but not all. Yet no one was cast off because he had failed—how could he be, in a group that was really a society for *sinners* seeking full salvation? He was only lost to the fellowship when he no longer *wanted* to succeed—when he had shown with absolute clarity that he no longer shared the aims of the movement, i.e. he was no longer seeking full salvation at all. Even then his expulsion from the Society and Class meeting was not really an effort to coerce him into conformity, but a step taken with much regret for the sake of those who remained and had still their warfare to accomplish; nor did he cease to be an object of the seeking and prayerful concern of the Class members after he had gone from their midst. Disciplinary expulsion from the Class meeting was thus very largely the official recognition of what had already become a de facto situation,[11] but the break had to be made clear for the sake of all concerned.

'All sin', said Wesley, 'is of an infectious nature', and furthermore anything which laid the movement open to legitimate scorn from its many critics would inevitably have its effect on the morale of those who were taking their first faltering steps along the way of salvation. As was the case with the whole of his ministry, it was the care of people, not the coercion of people, that led Wesley to adopt disciplinary measures.

II

Obsessed as he is with his ideas of indoctrination, Dr Sargant seems to think that Wesley was a stickler for conformity of belief, and that he insisted on every one of his follows accepting his own particular orthodoxy. Nothing could be further from the truth. Those whose preconceived image of Wesley includes the traits of bigotry and intolerance should read his famous sermon on 'The Catholic Spirit',[12] which he set as a doctrinal standard for himself and his people. As a document combining the utmost clarity of conviction with the broadest sympathies and most Christian tolerance, this could well serve as the charter for much that is best in the modern ecumenical movement—and it was written two centuries ago! The two preceding sermons on 'The Nature of Enthusiasm' and 'A Caution Against Bigotry' would also make enlightening reading for the author of Battle for the Mind. Writing to Vincent Perronet, his 'Plain Account of the People Called Methodist', Wesley recounts the small beginnings of the movement when he and his brother began to preach in London ten years before, and says: 'The points we chiefly insisted on were four: first, that orthodoxy, or right opinions, is, at best, but a very slender part of religion, if it can be allowed to be any part at all'.[13] And later, in the same document, describing the development of the Societies he writes:

'The thing which I was greatly afraid of all this time, and which I resolved to use every possible method of preventing, was, a narrowness of spirit; a party zeal, a being straitened in our own bowels; that miserable bigotry which makes many so unready to believe that there is any work of God but among themselves.'[14]

Wesley himself subscribed to the doctrinal standards of the Church of England. He could not with justice be accused of regarding matters of doctrine as unimportant, but on the other hand he could never see them as all-important. The Methodist Societies were not originally intended to constitute a Church, and Wesley deliberately designed them for a broad tolerance and openness in matters of doctrine, in order that no doctrinal tests would limit their membership, and no mere orthodoxy ever become a substitute for their own constitutive purpose — the common pursuit of salvation in all its fullness. Thus, preaching in Glasgow in 1788, after the inner life of the Methodist Societies and Classes had become known to thousands of people over a period of more than forty years, Wesley could say, and later publish, without fear of contradiction:

'There is no other religious society under heaven which requires nothing of men in order to their admission into it, but a desire to save their souls. Look all around you, you cannot be admitted into the Church, or society of the Presbyterians, Anabaptists, Quakers, or any others, unless you hold the same opinions with them, and adhere to the same mode of worship.

'The Methodists alone do not insist on your holding this or that opinion; but they think and let think. Neither do they impose any particular mode of worship; but you may continue to worship in your former manner, be it what it may. Now, I do not know any other religious society, either ancient or modern, wherein such liberty of conscience is now allowed, or has been allowed, since the age of the Apostles. Here is our glorying; and a glorying peculiar to us. What society shares it with us?'[15]

Yet Dr Sargant obviously thinks that one of the functions of the Class meeting was to enforce a rigid Wesleyan orthodoxy, and he says by way of illustrating this point:

'The importance of these class meetings in maintaining the power of Methodism during the eighteenth and nineteenth centuries can hardly be overestimated. Wesley wanted to be rid of all who doubted his particular views on the correct way to salvation—he had broken, among others, with Peter Bohler who had helped to convert him, and for a time even with George Whitfield . . .'[6]

Now, we have already seen something of Wesley's theological controversies, and the issues over which he felt obliged to differ strongly with others. Yet in none of these did he ever consider that he was defending his own 'particular views on the correct way to salvation', but maintained that he was simply contending for what was set out in the New Testament and the formularies of the Church of England; and on all the major issues, I think, the subsequent history of the Church will bear him out.

He parted company with the Moravians (not Peter Bohler particularly, by the way, but Molther) over the doctrine of Stillness—the teaching that those seeking salvation should completely neglect all the means of grace and simply remain still and wait for the divine miracle. As we have seen already, he found it necessary to dispute on the one hand with those who taught that good works were a *condition* of, or necessary to earn or deserve, our salvation, and on the other with those who denied or neglected the fact that good works of Christian morality were a necessary *expression* of salvation. But his greatest controversy of all was, of course, his difference with Whitfield and the Calvinists over their teaching of a limited atonement which applied only to the 'elect'. Now in all these controversies, I think it will be seen that Wesley was on the side of spiritual liberty, and every one of the views he was repudiating—had they been allowed to flourish unchallenged—would have narrowed down and restricted the range of Christian life and experience. But when we think today, of the doctrine of justification by faith alone, or the teaching that Christ died for all men, or that those seeking salvation should go to Church and use the means of grace, or that Christian faith should find expression in Christian morality—does anyone imagine that these are peculiarly Wesleyan or Methodist teachings? Of course not. We recognize that they are simply New Testament Christianity, and that is all they were in Wesley's day too.

To be sure, his doctrines of 'Assurance' and 'Perfect Love' could with more justice be termed 'particular' emphases of Wesley's teaching, and I think we must also admit that the psychological subtleties of the doctrine of 'Perfect Love' partly eluded his struggle to fit them into a scriptural framework. Nevertheless, a survey of the history of Christian doctrine shows that neither of these teachings was an innovation of John Wesley. And while he had good reasons to defend them, both because they were scriptural and because they safeguarded some very important elements in the Christian experience and pursuit of salvation, he certainly never used them as a rigid test of orthodoxy, or as an occasion for expelling people from the Methodist Societies.

The fact is, that Wesley was not very interested in uniformity of belief for its own sake, and I am sure that he never saw the Class meetings as a means of securing it. He was much more concerned to maintain the fellowship of Christian life and experience, which he knew could survive along with many differences of theological opinion. But does tolerance for another's freedom of belief mean allowing him the right to propagate teaching which will destroy the spiritual freedom of others? Wesley, the practical pastor, said 'No', and there were, therefore, times when he felt obliged to part company on this account.

Certainly, the Class meetings had their growing pains, but they survived these and became the richest source of Christian fellowship and family freedom in the Methodist movement. There is ample evidence to support Wesley's own description of this:

'Advice or reproof was given as need required, quarrels made up, misunderstandings removed: and after an hour or two spent in this labour of love, they concluded with prayer and thanksgiving. . . . Many now happily experienced that Christian fellowship, of which they had not so much as an idea before. They began to "bear one another's burdens", and naturally to "care for each other". As they had daily a more intimate acquaintance with, so they had a more endeared affection for, each other. And "speaking the truth in love, they grew up into Him in all things, who is the Head, even Christ".'[17]

If we want to find anything like a modern parallel with this, I should think that we shall need to look in the direction, not of the Communist 'cell' or indoctrination group, but of one of the more creative and effective group meetings of a movement like Alcoholics Anonymous. The sort of 'Big Brother is watching you' image which Dr Sargant seems to have of the Class leaders is quite mistaken, and as for either brainwashing or indoctrination, here is Wesley's advice to his people, which I believe both he and his leaders took very much to heart:

'Beware you are not a fiery persecuting enthusiast. Do not imagine that God has called you (just contrary to the spirit of Him you style your Master) to destroy men's lives, and not to save them. Never dream of forcing men into the ways of God. Think yourself, and let think. Use no constraint in matters of religion. Even those who are farthest out of the way never compel to come in by any other means than reason, truth and love.'[18]

The misleading picture of the Class meetings which we have in *Battle for the Mind*, as a means of 'follow-up conditioning', goes right back to the underlying philosophy of the book. The word 'conditioning' we first encountered in the descriptions of Pavlov's experiments, where it bore a specific and clearly defined meaning. But by now it has, without explanation, become stretched in all directions, but still with the same coercive suggestion of reducing human behaviour to the level of an engineered and automatic response. All training has now become conditioning, and it is not without significance that at the beginning of this chapter, the animal trainer and the school teacher are linked together as facing essentially the same problems.[19] All education then presumably becomes indoctrination, a thought which will not disturb the author so long as children are being indoctrinated with the 'right' beliefs. All significant changes of personality or behaviour are brought about by some process which is in principle akin to brainwashing and the effect of all human group life is simply to restrict the spontaneity of the individual and condition him towards conformity.[20] Here in a nutshell—and a very narrow nutshell indeed—is Dr Sargant's version of 'the nature and destiny of man'.

Battle for the Mind is a study in slave mentality and its whole psychology is too thin altogether to take in anything as creative and liberating as the early Methodist Class meetings, or the Evangelical Revival in which they played such an important part.

Of course the most significant argument against any coercive or repressive interpretation of the Evangelical Revival, is the kind of people it produced—and this is undoubtedly the way in which Wesley would have answered Dr Sargant. Fortunately we have plenty of vivid contemporary accounts and biographical material concerning the rank and file of the early Methodist people. Their morals were strict, but infused with a genuine love of their fellows, rather than with legalism. In this respect they recaptured what was best in the Puritan tradition, redeemed from most of its moralism. After acknowledging their Puritanism, Rupert Davies adds

'But those who had really caught the meaning of Wesley's message had something else about them also: an inward, serene gaiety which comes out over and over again in Charles Wesley's hymns, springing from the joyous assurance of salvation which Calvinism fails to give. And, as a result, the Methodists knew not only how to face hardship and scorn without being much troubled, but also how to die.'[21]

Dr Leslie Church's two valuable books to which we have already referred are the best source of information about these people, and they are very human documents. Their world seems so different from ours, and sometimes they strike us as rather quaint folk. Yet as we come to know these people in all the vicissitudes of their Christian pilgrimage, in their amazing good will, generosity and courage, their cheerfulness and resilience in difficult circumstances, their heroic and compassionate ventures in philanthropy and social service—and then we remember what they were—we are lost in wonder and gratitude to God. These people were not 'good' in any mere conventional way—they were above all, real and their goodness had that quality of reality that only arises out of inward freedom and makes any suggestion of regimented minds or imposed behaviour patterns simply ridiculous. Compared with us, their opportunities for life were in many ways very limited, yet by and large they had undoubtedly discovered what so many of our own generation are still searching for—authentic existence.

III

It hardly needs to be added that Dr Sargant's remark that 'Wesley had taught the masses to be less concerned with their miserable life on earth, as victims of the Industrial Revolution, than with the life to come; they could now put up with almost anything',[22] is a misconstruing of the facts which fits in all too well with his general misconception of the early Methodists as a body of people well drilled and indoctrinated into a docile and submissive otherworldliness. As we have seen already their new-found spiritual experience did give these people the ability to 'face hardship and scorn without being much troubled'; but it is quite mistaken to suggest that they were so caught up in roseate visions of the hereafter that they became quite indifferent to social conditions or the needs of their fellows. The complete opposite was the case. It was not Wesley, but the politician Burke who said that the deserts of the poor would be adjusted in 'the final propositions of eternal justice'.[23] 'The Methodists were not only interested . . . in preparing men and women for another world, but also were impassioned in their determination to alleviate their physical and economic distress in this.'[24] And their rediscovery of practical Christianity 'was not only a channel for divine mercy, but also for human kindness'[25] that was expressed in an amazing variety of philanthropy and social service including visitation and provision for the prisoner, the poor and the aged, practical employment schemes, a lending society to held the unemployed set up their own modest business, free dispensaries for the poor, charity schools and orphanages, a Christian community for hospital visitation, a Strangers' Friends Society and many other enterprises. From the vantage point of vastly different times some have found it easy to sneer at all this 'mere benevolence', but it was carried out with a spontaneous kindness and humanity, long before such practices degenerated into self-conscious righteousness or a form of social condescension. It was so very often the poor helping the poor, and at times the whole movement had a co-operative character about it. Above all it was well organized, sustained and carried on, not at second hand or through some fund raising committee, but by the rank and file of the Society members who were well acquainted with the poor and needy of England.[26]

To be sure, all this was philanthropy, not social reform. Wesley did make public protests about the economic condition of the poor, and even some suggestions for rectifying it, but these didn't go far into the problem, and the social work into which he led his people was aimed at relieving immediate distress, rather than seeking out the causes and changing the structure of society. In this, the Methodists shared many of the limitations of their contemporaries, and we may, if we choose, criticize them for not trying to establish the welfare state. On the other hand, while their first ventures in social service left the rank injustices of the social order largely unchallenged, Wesley called his people to a new conception of stewardship in the use of money; and the moral and spiritual transformation wrought by the grace of God, and the co-operative enterprises they undertook enabled thousands of people to greatly improve their economic condition and their standards of living and literacy in a surprisingly short time.

Politically, Wesley was a conservative, and during his lifetime at least, the movement had little affinity with political radicalism. Its social work was motivated more by love of the oppressed than by hatred of the oppressor. While it used to be asserted that Methodism saved England from violent revolution, historians are now inclined to discount that view. The fact is that social reform and the enfranchisement of the common man took a different course in England from what it did in countries like France and Russia, and the reasons for this are probably quite complex, and some of them go back a long way before the eighteenth century. Nevertheless, there can be no doubt that the Evangelical Revival was one very powerful influence in determining the course that social reform did take, and to the charge that it delayed social progress by making men content with the status quo Dr Henry Bett remarks that 'it would be difficult to find any evidence of this in the lives of the early Methodists or in the history of the times'.[27]

On the contrary, it created a new social conscience in England and provided the moral and spiritual dynamic of most of the major social reforms of the next century. As Dr Bett says, it produced a 'new philanthropy which reformed our prisons, infused leniency and wisdom into our penal laws, abolished the slave trade and gave the first impulse to popular education'.[28] The influence of the Class meetings, far from inculcating a docile other-worldliness was so often the original ferment of social reform. For, as Dr Leslie Church points out, in these Classes 'men learned to talk, to read and to discover one another. Through them the masses became articulate, and in their fellowship began to plan a new world.'[29] As Dr Wearmouth has shown, they eventually produced many of the men who forced the passing of the Factory Acts.[29] Large numbers of the common people redeemed from hopelessness and moral degradation, found a new dignity and self respect as well as a new concern for the welfare of others. Many of them learned through the group life of the Evangelical Revival, the value of co-operative movement and the arts of organization and leadership, and it was from amongst their ranks that there eventually emerged many of the pioneers of Trade Unionism,[30] and later, of the political Labour movement[30] in Britain.

There is no doubt that all this went far beyond anything Wesley had foreseen or intended; had he lived to see the rise of the Trade Unions, for example, it is perhaps doubtful whether Wesley the political conservative would have been as responsive to the contrary winds of the Spirit as Wesley the ecclesiastical conservative had been a century before. It is probably true also that, during some periods of the nineteenth century, anyway, the main stream of Wesleyan Methodism followed rather too faithfully the political conservatism of its founder; a step which he himself would scarcely have approved, and it was left for Methodists of the breakaway Primitive Connexion, in co-operation with others, to work out the implications of his spiritual radicalism in active social reform. But if the Church of the Evangelical Revival did nothing, for example, to help the Tolpuddle Martyrs, we should not forget that it undoubtedly did *produce* them. The turn which events eventually took, is another indication that a movement may have an inner logic of its own, which will, in the long run, entail consequences that were not necessarily part of the original intention. We may, nevertheless, believe in the long-range purposes of God which men may serve even when they do not *fully* perceive them.

R

The immediate results of the Evangelical Revival in practical good will and philanthropy show that the miracle of grace certainly produced no opiate resignation or indifference to social conditions, and if its more important long-range effects owe very little to the political foresight of John Wesley and, sometimes, it must be admitted, reflect little credit on many of his followers, they do at least bear witness to something of the spiritual dynamic and the revolutionary possibilities for man and society, that are hidden in the unconditional love of God accepted as salvation by his children.

*   *   *   *   *

In the course of our discussion it has become important for a number of reasons to draw the clearest possible contrast between two quite different kinds of personality change that are possible for man, each of which may occur in a variety of circumstances. The first kind of change, seen most simply in brainwashing, but also employed in advertising, propaganda and many other fields, and typical of certain kinds of religious technique, is essentially coercive and repressive, undermining personal integrity and restricting spiritual freedom in order to redirect a person's thought or conduct in ways that he has not freely chosen for himself. The second kind of personality change which we have sought to illustrate from modern psychotherapy and the genuine experience of Christian conversion, is essentially liberating and 'open', breaking down emotional repression and freeing a person from both inhibition and compulsion so that he may enjoy more fully the autonomous control of his own life.

While Dr Sargant's book displays no awareness of this issue at all, it is interesting to notice another psychiatrist who deals with the subject of brainwashing, making essentially the same distinction that we have made. At the end of his long study of brainwashing in China, Dr Robert J. Lifton has a very interesting chapter on what he calls ' "Open" Personal Change' which he describes as 'an experience of individual change very different from that promoted by thought reform—one characterized by "openness to the world" rather than by personal closure'.[31]

This 'open' and creative kind of change in human personality, and the ethical possibilities that flow from it, are directly relevant to our contemporary interest in modern man's 'coming of age', but we have also claimed that they belong to the very essence of New Testament Christianity. They represent the true inward work of religion in which the love of God, utterly gracious and without condition, sets us free from all manner of spiritual bondage, and calls us to our full human stature and responsibility, so that a genuine 'worldly holiness' can be at work in the affairs of men. Both the inwardness of religion and the free love of God have been seriously obscured for the modern Church by certain prevailing movements in contemporary thought, but it would seem to be urgently necessary for the very survival of the race, that the kind of liberation of personality which they effect, should again become a possibility for large numbers of people.

But that must be the subject of another study. In the meantime we must affirm that to be a Christian means to take Jesus Christ as the one who reveals the ultimate truth about God, to open our lives to the utterly simple and inexorable love of this man, to watch by the Cross and feel the absoluteness of this sacrifice, the unconditional quality of this mercy, and in the very depths of our being to believe—both for ourselves and for our fellows—that 'God loves like that'. This, and this alone, is to enter into the joy of our Lord, to be God's freemen, to begin by the sheer miracle of grace to be like Jesus himself, 'the man who was free for others'.[32]

'If the Son therefore shall make you free, ye shall be free indeed.'[33]

FOOTNOTES AND REFERENCES

1. Sargant, *op. cit.*, pp. 214 ff. (197 ff.).
2. *Ibid.*, pp. 156-8 (147-8).
3. *Ibid.*, p. 215 (197).
4. *Ibid.*, pp. 218-19 (200-1).
5. *Ibid.*, p. 216 (199).
6. See above, pp. 140-1.
7. Davies, Rupert, *op. cit.* (Pelican edition), pp. 73-4.

8. At the time of Wesley's death there were 72,000 members in good standing in the Methodist societies, and of course there must have been many who had died in the past half century, and others who had lapsed. If, for good measure, we multiply by four, the figure of 234 cases of violent conversions recorded during the period of their greatest frequency, it would appear that two per cent would be a fairly liberal figure for the proportion of folk who had had such experiences among the total Methodist constituency.

Dr Sargant's need to heighten and exaggerate the dramatic character of the movement is also shown by his description of Wesley's own conversion. We learn that at that rather quiet and unemotional meeting in Aldersgate Street, Wesley's heart was not only 'strangely warmed' as he tells us himself, but also 'finally and suddenly warmed' (op. cit., p. 222 (203)).

9. See Wesley's 'A Plain Account of the People Called Methodist' Works, Vol. 8, pp. 243-4.

10. It is reasonable to suppose that in any close-knit group there would sometimes be the temptation to bring emotional pressure to bear on the individual, and we would be rash to assert dogmatically that this *never* occurred in the Class meetings, even in the early days. In later times the Class meetings waned in effectiveness, but the nature of the movement as a whole, the contemporary descriptions and the character of the people would all seem to indicate that during the full vigour of the revival, emotional coercion, when it occurred at all, was exceptional.

11. Cf. McConnell, F. J., in *John Wesley*, Epworth Press, London 1939, pp. 138-40.

12. Forty Four Standard Sermons No. XXXIV.

13. Wesley, op. cit., *Works*, Vol. 8, p. 240.

14. *Ibid.*, p. 248.

15. *Journal*, May 18, 1788.

16. Sargant, op. cit., p. 215 (198).

17. *Works*, Vol. 8, p. 244.

18. Sermon on 'The Nature of Enthusiasm' — Standard Sermons No. XXXII.

19. Sargant, op. cit., p. 214 (197).

20. Cf. the reference to group psychotherapy, Sargant, op. cit., p. 225 (206).

21. Davies, op. cit. (Pelican edition), p. 93.
22. Sargant, op. cit., p. 219-20 (201).
23. Bett, op. cit., pp. 200-1.
24. Wearmouth, op. cit., p. 216.
25. Ibid., p. 202.
26. See Leslie Church, More About the Early Methodist People, Ch. V.
27. Bett, op. cit., pp. 200-1.
28. Ibid., p. 200.
29. Church, op. cit., p. 182.
30. Church, op. cit., p. 184, and Bready, op. cit., pp. 389 ff.
31. Thought Reform and the Psychology of Totalism by Robert J. Lifton, M.D., Victor Gollancz, London 1961, pp. 462 ff.
32. See Paul van Buren, The Secular Meaning of the Gospel, S.C.M. Press, London 1963, Chapter V.
33. John 8.36.

INDEX

264 BATTLE FOR THE FREE MIND

268   BATTLE FOR THE FREE MIND

Reformation, the 131f, 152, 182f, 202, 237f
Regulative Devices of the Ego under Major Stress 221, 243
Reisman 79
Relevance of Christianity, The 212f
religious beliefs 68f, 72ff
Religious Ideas of the Old Testament 35
religion, social function of 190
repentance 238ff (see also 'metanoia')
repression 55f, 62f, 65, 70, 126, 153f, 188f, 194, 209, 216, 220f, 227f
responsibility 70, 112
Richardson, Dr Alan 35, 114, 137
Robinson, Dr H. Wheeler 35
Robinson, Dr J. A. T. 35, 92, 109, 115, 136f
Robinson, the Rev Wm. 18, 20, 91
rocket scientists 78
Rogers, Dr Carl 78, 82ff, 86, 91f 219, 243
Romans, Paul's epistle to the, 70, 91 160, 231, 243
Routley, Dr Erik 70, 91
Russell, Bertrand 35
Russell, Dr Gilbert 56, 67, 243
Rutherforth, Rev Dr 168f, 174, 178
Ryle, Prof Gilbert 30, 35

salesmanship 76
salvation 19f, 101, 120, 128, 169, 172, 192, 201f, 209, 231, 251
sanctification 176f
Sargant, Dr William 14-24, 31f, 37f, 41-5, 47f, 50, 54ff, 58-75, 84f, 87, 91, 97-105, 120, 126-9, 132-6, 138-40, 145-56, 160, 171, 175ff, 181, 209, 245, 249f, 253f, 258f
science 11, 24, 27, 33f, 76, 78, 88ff, 93, 165
scientific method 24, 41, 49
Sechenov 88
Secker, Bishop 186
Secular Meaning of the Gospel, The 259, 261
Sermon Register (Wesley's) 123, 138
Sermons, John Wesley's 105, 108f, 118f, 121-4, 126f, 130, 135f, 138, 151f, 176, 249, 253, 259
sense of sin 199ff
Sherrington, Sir Charles 34
Short History of Psychotherapy, A 57f, 67

Skinner, Prof B. F. 82ff, 85, 91f
Slater, Dr E. 19f
social conditions 185f, 188f, 192, 221
social organisation 11f
Some Issues Concerning the Control of Human Behaviour 82ff, 85, 91f
Some Therapeutic Implications of the Crucifixion and Resurrection 244
Sons to Samuel 196ff, 211f
Son to Susannah 134, 208, 214
soul 33
Southey, Robert 97, 103, 134f, 167, 171f, 178
sovereignty 117f, 123, 196
Soviet policy 88
Spiegel, Dr J. P. 150, 181, 209
Spirit and Forms of Protestantism, The 211
Spirit of Methodism, The 212, 255, 259
sports 187
Stafford-Clark, Dr D. 35, 50, 53, 56, 66f
Stapledon, Olaf 34
Stephen, Sir Leslie 133f, 210
Strawson, the Rev Wm. 109, 114f, 136f
Studies in the Soul 34
Sugden, Dr E. H. 130, 136, 139
suggestibility 15, 75, 98, 101, 154f
suggestion 49f, 52, 62ff, 76, 153f, 156, 183
Super-ego 129
supernatural, the 166, 170-4
Surprised by Joy 35
Suttie, Dr Ian D. 46, 216ff, 220f, 234f, 242ff
symptomatic relief 52
Synoptic Gospels 109, 114, 121

Tavistock Clinic 218
Techniques of Persuasion 79f, 92, 133, 139
Telford, J. 134
temperamental types 39
Temperley, H. W. V. 97, 134, 210
Tennesse Snake Handlers 14
terminal exhaustion 99
Tertullian 116, 137
Thought Reform and the Psychology of Totalism 258, 261
Thouless, Dr R. H. 177f
Tillich, Paul 92, 236ff, 244
Tillotson, Archbishop 192
Times, The 198
Todd, John 134, 136
Tolpuddle Martyrs 257

GEORGE ALLEN & UNWIN LTD
London: 40 Museum Street, W.C.1

Auckland: P.O. Box 36013, Northcote Central N.4
Bombay: 15 Graham Road, Ballard Estate, Bombay 1
Barbados: P.O. Box 222, Bridgetown
Beirut: Deeb Building, Jeanne d'Arc Street
Buenos Aires: Escritorio 454-459, Florida 165
Calcutta: 17 Chittaranjan Avenue, Calcutta 13
Cape Town: 68 Shortmarket Street
Hong Kong: 105 Wing On Mansion, 26 Hancow Road, Kowloon
Ibadan: P.O. Box 62
Karachi: Karachi Chambers, McLeod Road
Madras: Mohan Mansions, 38c Mount Road, Madras 6
Mexico: Villalongin 32-10, Piso, Mexico 5, D.F.
Nairobi: P.O. Box 4536
New Delhi: 13-14 Asaf Ali Road, New Delhi 1
Ontario: 81 Curlew Drive, Don Mills
Philippines: Manila P.O. Box 4322
Rio de Janeiro: Caixa Postal 2537-Zc-00
Singapore: 36c Prinsep Street, Singapore 7
Sydney, N.S.W.: Bradbury House, 55 York Street
Tokyo: P.O. Box 26, Kamata

THE REVEREND A. D. GALLOWAY

FAITH IN A CHANGING CULTURE

Christendom is our heritage. What is to become of it? Everyone knows that the church must change with the times. But where should we set the limits of change? When is a Christian not a Christian? How can we be both faithful to the past and honest with the present?

This calls for a penetrating analysis of the whole relationship between religious faith and secular culture. In conflict they destroy each other. In union they devour each other. But in situations of true social growth they exist for each other. The Judao-Christian tradition is pre-eminent as an expression of this creative tension between religious faith and secular culture.

How can the Church be Catholic—open towards every age and every culture? How can the same church be also Apostolic—founded upon a definite ecclesiastical and cultural tradition? These two questions lie at the heart of the matter. Suddenly, with a new urgency, they have become crucial for every denomination.

Dr Galloway's approach to these problems is perceptive, honest and refreshing. The many churchmen who today feel some estrangement from tradition yet are also perplexed by modernity will find him particularly helpful. But this is not a piece of ecclesiastical trouble-shooting. It is a fundamental theological investigation.

Demy 8vo

ERNEST W. BACON

SPURGEON: HEIR OF THE PURITANS

No biography of the great preacher Charles Haddon Spurgeon has been published for over thirty years, and the time is ripe for a new study of his life and his extraordinary influence.

Some new facts and stories concerning the great preacher's ministry and philanthropic works are included in this book, together with a charitable reappraisal of the famous 'Down Grade' controversy which caused such a storm in his later years.

It is the author's hope that this book will strengthen Christian witness, encourage Biblical preaching and be a blessing and source of inspiration to Christian believers of all denominations.

Demy 8vo

JEAN CHARON

MAN IN SEARCH OF HIMSELF

Taking George Breuil's grim jest that, as the twentieth century pro-gresses, man is reverting to the cave, the author strives to show how the intellectual caveman can break free from his den.

He develops the theory that in the study of his psychic make-up we shall find a better understanding of man's true vocation in the cosmos, that by modelling ourselves upon Einstein's methods of General Relativity, we can produce a field language for the study of 'the mechanisms of life'.

Like Alexis Carrel the biologist thirty years ago, he is a specialist broken out of his cell; and as he bursts into this new world, he declares, 'I have seen landscapes often new to me, that filled me with wonder'.

M. Charon is well known in the scientific world for his Eléments d'une Théorie Unitaire d'Universe published in Paris and Geneva in 1962. He has also written La Connaissance de l'Univers, which won the Prix Nautilus, and Du Temps, De l'Espace et des Hommes.

Demy 8vo

MARTIN BUBER

KINGSHIP OF GOD

First published in 1932, this classic work has now passed into a third edition from which this translation has been made. The book com-bines the results of years of Bible studies in a theological commentary which treats of many old testament problems including the Gideon Passage in the Book of Judges, to be explained, in the author's words, 'in terms of the situation of an absolute divine rulership'. Dr Buber also deals with the Kingship of God in the Ancient Orient, the West-Semitic Tribal God, and the Faith of Israel on which he comments, 'This is what it comes to: the realization of the all embracing Rulership of God is the Proton and Eschaton of Israel'. This transla-tion of a theological work of cardinal importance will be welcomed throughout the English speaking world.

Demy 8vo

LONDON · GEORGE ALLEN & UNWIN LTD